The ONLINE
Genealogy
HANDBOOK

The ONLINE Genealogy HANDBOOK

Brad & Debra Schepp

STERLING

New York / London
www.sterlingpublishing.com

STERLING and the distinctive Sterling logo are registered trademarks of Sterling Publishing Co., Inc.

Library of Congress Cataloging-in-Publication Data

Schepp, Brad.

The online genealogy handbook / Brad and Debra Schepp.

 p. cm.

Includes index.

ISBN 978-1-4027-5255-1

1. Genealogy—Computer network resources—Handbooks, manuals, etc. 2. Genealogy—Computer network resources—Directories. 3. Internet research—Handbooks, manuals, etc. 4. Web sites — Directories. I. Schepp, Debra. II. Title.

CS14.S34 2008

929.10285—dc22

　　　　　2008013756

10 9 8 7 6 5 4 3 2 1

Published by Sterling Publishing Co., Inc.

387 Park Avenue South, New York, NY 10016

© 2008 by Brad Schepp and Debra Schepp

Distributed in Canada by Sterling Publishing

c/o Canadian Manda Group, 165 Dufferin Street

Toronto, Ontario, Canada M6K 3H6

Distributed in the United Kingdom by GMC Distribution Services

Castle Place, 166 High Street, Lewes, East Sussex, England BN7 1XU

Distributed in Australia by Capricorn Link (Australia) Pty. Ltd.

P.O. Box 704, Windsor, NSW 2756, Australia

Sterling ISBN 978-1-4027-5255-1

For information about custom editions, special sales, premium and corporate purchases, please contact Sterling Special Sales Department at 800-805-5489 or specialsales@sterlingpublishing.com.

To Dan: Friends? Friends. Buddies? Buddies. Pals? Pals. Better than that; we're brother and sister.

—DS

To Brother Dan and his faithful companion, Fred.

—BS

Contents

Acknowledgments

So many people helped us as we worked to explore online genealogy. First at the top of that list is Stephanie Korney. She is a tireless worker and a researcher beyond compare. We simply don't know what we would have done without her through every step of this journey. Special thanks go out to those who shared their stories with us: Jan Jero; Debbie Warila; Ken Dorris and Louisa Ryan of the Church of Jesus Christ of the Latter Day Saints in Camptonville, California; Alta Flynt; John Myrick Cherry III; Eldred W. Melton; Mary Stickney; Nadine Snider; and Rex Bavousett. In addition to these wonderful storytellers, many experts made special contributions to our project: Maureen Taylor of The Photo Detective (www.photodetective.com); Nan Card, Curator of Manuscripts, Rutherford B. Hayes Presidential Center (Fremont, Ohio); Pamela Dunning, Director, Wiscasset (Maine) Public Library; Paul McWhorter of www.old-picture.com; Kelly Schrum, Director of Educational Projects, Center for History and New Media, George Mason University; Rebecca Skloot, contributing editor at *Popular Science* magazine; and Christopher Dunham of The Genealogue (www.genealogue.com).

We would also like to thank the members of the Roots-L mailing list for their unfailingly interesting discussions and generosity—and to the many unsung volunteers worldwide who are doing look-ups for strangers and copying genealogy records of all kinds to make them available to other researchers online.

Our agent, Marilyn Allen, of Allen and O'Shea, has always been a steadfast and true advocate of our work—thanks again, Marilyn. Meredith Hale of Sterling Publishing is a wonderful editor. Even when our inner children emerge, and we really don't want to make those last few changes, the book is always better for having made them. We'd also like to thank Hannah Reich, our production editor, for all her hard work behind the scenes and her attention to detail; our copy editor, Molly Morrison, for bringing such a careful eye to this project; and our proof-readers, Patricia Nicolescu and Penelope Haynes, for catching those last details that we never would have seen.

Last of all, we would like to thank our family for making us laugh, keeping us going, and always reminding us what's most important.

Introduction

Digging into your family's roots has become wildly popular. The reasons for setting out on the search for family history may be wide and varied, but one constant factor is that to find out who came before and where they came from can help you understand who you are right now. We all want to belong. In a world that seems to spin faster every year, it's kind of nice to know how your own particular crowd came to be. Admit it: You're curious. That's why you're reading this. But consider yourself forewarned: This curiosity can very quickly become an obsession. You may just be starting a journey that you'll never finish. You may spend the rest of your life surrounded by tidbits and facts. But don't worry; you'll love the trip. After all, you are the hero of your own life story, and now you'll get the chance to fill in a lot of details.

Along the way, you may find out exactly why everyone called your great-uncle "Pug." You may never have thought to ask before, but the truth behind this moniker will probably tickle you. Or, you may come across an ancient photograph that proves you are not the first one to have struggled with that goofy cowlick! You'll find that the more you learn, the more you'll want to know; and each time you add another piece to the puzzle, you'll encounter another mystery that will lead you even deeper into your search. The day will come when you'll have a gift for your future family; a gift that only you can give. We'll help you every step of the way.

You couldn't have asked for a better time to begin this journey. Easy access to the Internet lets you do a lot of your searching from the comfort of your own home. However, the sheer number of genealogy Web sites and products—surname sites, ethnic sites, geographic location sites, maps, scanned original documents, government archives, software, magazines, advice columns, blogs—can be overwhelming. You can easily go astray in your search and end up swinging from the wrong family tree. Or, you could get stuck a couple of generations back with no way to look beyond for the next branch. This is also a trip that could cost you much more than just your spare time. Some genealogy sites cost money, and some are worth every penny, but we'll point out the many sites that will get you started and even move you along the genealogy road toll-free. We've evaluated hundreds of resources and personally visited hundreds of Web sites to find the ones that are worth a visit (and a few off-the-wall sites just for fun). Because of our extensive experience as Internet experts and researchers, we understand the most efficient way to verify and evaluate information found online.

We also like stories, and lots of them. We've included stories and anecdotes from professional and amateur genealogists whose experiences show the victories and frustrations that are consistently present in the research game. We've also included some tips for the research that you'll need to do the old-fashioned way—in person or over the phone. Computers are wonderful, but nothing can replace a one-on-one conversation with a relative who has actually known some of the people you are researching. You may also want to visit historical societies or other repositories of genealogical information that have not yet put information online.

Best of all, you'll see that you are not alone in trying to piece together an ancestral puzzle. From the first chapter, which provides an overview of the terms, documents, and resources you'll find along the way, to the last, where you'll get some fun ideas about what to do with all your research once you've gathered it, we share our insight and introduce you to some fascinating people. Whether you've been poking around your family history for some time or you've just begun your search, you're bound to find something new, fun, and interesting here. So settle back and get ready for a fabulous journey. You're sure to make friends along the way and, who knows, you may even discover family you never knew you had!

Brad and Deb Schepp
Bradanddeb.com

Chapter 1

An Educated Traveler

I s there a pirate in your past? Do you descend from the crowned heads of Europe? Who are you? We all want to know where we came from and how we got here. Modern astronomers look to the dust in outer space for answers to these age-old questions, while genealogists have always relied on the dusty records and documents found in courthouses and libraries. Now that we have the Internet, however, we can forgo the dust altogether and look for answers in the online universe known as the World Wide Web.

This chapter shows you how to begin your genealogical travels using the information that is available online—and there's a lot of it! In fact, there is so much information that you could become overwhelmed without a trip guide to see you through. That's where we come in. In the following pages we cover the wonders and perils of the Internet. You'll learn some genealogy terms that will help you get started, and you'll see the difference between primary and secondary evidence. We'll offer you an overview of the genealogy records that you can expect to find online. We'll address your need to keep things organized, and we'll provide examples of charts that display information in a graphic format. Finally, we'll take you on a detailed tour of two excellent Web sites that can jumpstart your search for ancestors.

It's easy to get excited about finding information on your long-lost ancestors, especially if you find a piece of evidence that suggests you are related to royalty, a favorite movie star, or an important historical figure.

However, we would like to caution you against drawing conclusions too quickly from what you find online. Only through careful research can you be confident about tracing your origins on the map of human experience. So, with that said, get ready for an interesting ride!

Your Education Begins

When you start out on a journey, you usually make an itinerary and consult a map. While it's possible, and even fun, to just go, we think you'll agree that trips are more enjoyable and less stressful when you have a plan. The same is true when you begin your genealogy journey.

With genealogy, you'll become something of a time traveler. You start in the present with what you know, and through perseverance and a few "magic beans" discovered on the Internet you soon find yourself immersed in another place and time.

Because you need as much information as possible about this other place we call the past, you'll need to be a historian, too. As you discover the names and dates associated with your ancestors, you'll find that this information is not enough in order to really know about them. You'll want to know more about the times in which they lived.

What were their houses like? What kinds of clothing did they wear? What work did they do? Was there a war . . . a hurricane . . . an epidemic? Did they leave home to live in another place? And if so, why?

Spelling: Make It Easy on Yourself

If you want to be taken seriously in your genealogy research, you first must learn how to spell genealogy correctly! Mark Howells of the genealogy megasite Cyndi's List (fig. 1-1), has created a useful memory aid to help you remember the right spelling. When you need to spell genealogy, just recall the following sentence: Genealogists examine needed evidence at lots of grave yards. The first letters of each word in the sentence spell *genealogy*!

The lives of humans are impacted by forces and events beyond our control, and so it is important to get a sense of the eras your ancestors lived in, as well as their geographic locations, in order to get your bearings.

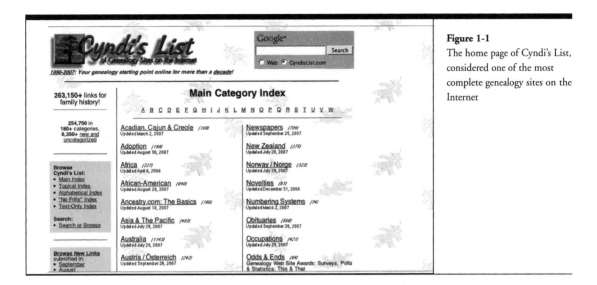

Plus, knowing as much as possible about the period in which a person lived often opens up new lines of research and helps with tracking down elusive bits of family history.

So let's start your journey as a time-traveling scholar!

A Little History

Human beings have a natural interest in what came before them. The earliest myths and legends are early attempts to describe how the world began. In ancient cultures, records of family ancestry were important as a way to determine lines of royal or priestly succession or property inheritance. The ancient Assyrians, Egyptians, and Chinese cultures kept detailed records of ancestry. The Chinese encouraged ancestor worship, which required people to know the names of their forebears. The Greeks traced their family lines to prove they were descended from gods and goddesses, while the ancient Romans were interested in recording differences in ancestry between the noble classes and the plebeians, or commoners. The Romans were the first to give their male children both personal and family names as an aid in following family lines. The Maori of New Zealand can recite their ancestral line back to A.D. 1200.

While some researchers claim that they can trace their ancestry back to Adam, there are many difficulties associated with making the leap from the early

Middle Ages (approximately A.D. 450 to A.D. 750) to biblical times. It is difficult to separate fact from mythology in the sources that survive from those years, and there is often considerable confusion between tribal and individual names.

Fortunately, research into relatively modern times is generally more successful. The English, for example, can create reliable pedigrees dating from the 1500s via church records. If you are researching British ancestors, you can thank Henry VIII for making things a little easier for you. In 1538, he required churchmen to begin keeping a record of christenings, baptisms, marriages, and burials.

Settlers in the American colonies wanted to save their traditional customs, so they continued the practice of recording these events. In the early colonial years, churches kept records, but later on towns took over the responsibility. In 1632, the Virginia general assembly enacted the first civil law requiring that these vital records be kept.

After the American Revolution, people were eager to trace their ancestry to the heroes of the war and to the signers of the Declaration of Independence. The Daughters of the American Revolution (DAR) was established in 1890 to preserve the history of these individuals and to encourage patriotism. The New England Historic Genealogical Society, the oldest genealogical society in the United States, was founded in 1845. More recently, interest in genealogy got a huge boost in the United States from Alex Haley and his book *Roots: The Saga of an American Family* published in 1976. The book, and the television series that followed, inspired many Americans to explore their own family histories. Genealogy fulfills a basic human need to understand where we came from. Even the U.S. Senate has gotten into the act. In 2001, a resolution was passed that declared October as Family History month. The resolution specifically cited the Internet for the growing numbers of people researching their genealogy and looking for contact with distant family members. Genealogy is frequently listed among the most popular hobbies in the United States.

The Biggest Library in the World

Always remember that you don't have to take your genealogy journey alone. Many travelers have gone before you, and they've left signposts, warnings, and markers to smooth your path. Plus, you have at your disposal the best vehicle ever created for such a trip—the Internet.

You can find information about almost anything online, including your own family. The ready availability of online resources for genealogy research has helped the current interest in family history to blossom.

It is no longer necessary to spend time and money traveling to distant libraries, courthouses, and other document repositories in different states, or even countries, to obtain documentation of a family's history. Many documents required for solid genealogy research are now accessible on the World Wide Web. These documents include census and land records, birth and death records, published family histories, directories, newspaper archives, and other local and federal government documents. In addition, individuals working on their family lines often create Web sites that document their research, so family members working on different paths of the same family line can communicate quickly and easily, asking questions and sharing information through e-mail and instant messaging (IM).

Warning! Internet Ahead!

Just as there are dangers on any trip into unknown territory, however, you must be aware of the pitfalls of genealogy research in general and of online research in particular. Not all information on the Internet is legitimate. Anyone can post information online, regardless of whether it's true or not. Family Web sites claiming to have original and complete research about a family line often include information that has not been thoroughly investigated. In their enthusiasm, amateur genealogists rush to post their newest "finds" online, sometimes simply copying and pasting information from other sites. This means that an error made on one Web site can proliferate throughout the online genealogy universe, as mistakes are compounded by well-meaning researchers. To make matters worse, there are even some unscrupulous people who purposely try to lead searchers astray.

So whenever you find information online, be sure to consider the source and double-check it with what you already know. Try to find several sources to confirm each "fact," and if you can't, set that piece of information aside until you can. Researching a family line is a long-term activity. You don't need to find everything at once, so don't expect to. The more thorough and patient you are in your fact finding, the better your genealogical records will be. Remember, once you start researching your family history, you take on the responsibility of passing accurate information on to your descendants.

Words You Need to Know Right Now

Ancestor: An individual from whom a person is descended.

Ancestral file: From the family history department of the Church of Jesus Christ of Latter-day Saints (LDS), this system uses several chart formats to link individuals to their ancestors.

Ancestry: All of an individual's ancestors as far back as they can be traced.

Collateral line: A line of descent that links individuals who share a common ancestor, but who are related through an uncle, aunt, cousin, or nephew, for example, rather than through a parent.

Common Ancestor: A person through whom several people can claim descent.

Descendant: Your descendants are your children, grandchildren, great-grandchildren, and so on; anyone to whom you are an ancestor.

Direct line: The line of descent traced through persons who are related to one another as child and parent.

Family group sheet: A form that displays the genealogical information of a nuclear family, typically including dates and locations of births, deaths, and marriages.

Family pedigrees: Family group sheets that are linked in a computer system so that database records associated with the individuals listed on the sheet can be accessed easily.

FamilySearch: This Web site, created by the Church of Jesus Christ of Latter-day Saints (LDS), is a collection of computer files and programs that include: the Family History Library catalog (the Family History Library, located in Salt Lake City, Utah, was founded in 1894 to gather genealogical records and assist members of the Church with their family history and genealogical research), International Genealogical Index, Social Security Death Index, and the United States Military Index. The resource can be accessed on computers located at Family History centers or on the Web at FamilySearch.org.

GEDCOM: Acronym for genealogy data communications, a standardized way of formatting family-tree information in a text file so that it can be used by any genealogy software program. The standard was developed in 1985 and is currently owned and managed by the LDS family history department.

Index: In genealogy, this refers to a list of names, arranged alphabetically, taken from a specific set of records. For example, an index of a census record lists the names of people found in a particular set of census records.

Maternal line: A line of descent traced through the mother's family.

Paternal line: A line of descent traced through the father's family.

Pedigree chart: A chart that displays an individual's ancestry, which is also known as a family tree, and shows birth/death dates, marital status, names of parents, grandparents, great-grandparents, and so on, through several generations.

Soundex: A phonetic indexing system that puts names with similar pronunciations but different spellings into the same group. This allows a search for ancestors who may have used different spellings of their names over time. For example, a relative by the name of White may have been a Wyatt.

Source citation: A note that indicates exactly where a piece of information was found, which is included on a genealogy chart or in a genealogy software program's database.

Transcript: A document that is an exact copy, word for word, of another document's text, including any mistakes made in the original and using the original punctuation.

Vital records: Documents that are used by civil authorities to record births, deaths, and marriages of individuals.

Witness: A person who is physically present at an event, for example, a wedding, or at the signing of a document, such as a will, who can say that the event or signing actually occurred.

Analyze This!

As you keep a skeptical eye on the information you find online, you'll also need to be aware that not all "facts," even those from seemingly reputable sources, are equal. The best genealogists analyze, verify, and document every piece of information they find. You must distinguish between direct and indirect evidence, and between primary and secondary sources. Direct evidence relates to a specific issue and offers a clear conclusion that needs no other supporting information. For example, a birth certificate is direct evidence of a date of birth. Indirect evidence can also be called circumstantial information. It requires you to seek additional information to reach a reliable conclusion. For example, information about the location in which an individual's will was probated might lead one to believe that that person died there as well.

Primary sources are records that were created at the actual time an event occurred. They include documents such as birth and death certificates and handwritten sources such as diaries and letters. Primary sources can include written accounts of events, if these accounts are recorded soon after an event and if the event was witnessed by the person who wrote the account. Photographs and other materials created at the time a specific event happened are also primary sources. Primary evidence is best, and should be used before relying on secondary evidence.

Secondary sources are typically created a significant length of time after events occurred. You might find a birth date on a document other than a birth certificate, but if the document was created after the date of the actual birth, it is considered a secondary source. Accounts of events written by people who were not actually present are also considered secondary sources. Even an account by someone present at an event that happened a long time ago may be considered a secondary source, because human memory is often unreliable.

It is important to have a standard for evaluating all of your discoveries. One standard, which is used in court cases, is known as a preponderance of the evidence. This standard assigns weight to evidence based on the quantity collected. One letter may be slight evidence; twenty letters are a preponderance. Once you have a preponderance you can assign different weights to the individual items.

Many primary sources can be found online. For example, the original Constitution of the United States is available on the U.S. National Archives and Records Administration Web site (http://www.archives.gov/ exhibits/charters/constitution_zoom_1.html), and original letters written by George Washington during his first years as president can be downloaded for free at Footnote.com. State and county Web sites make many primary sources available online, and international documents can be found on official Web sites maintained by other countries.

But don't get too tied up in knots trying to figure out whether something is a primary or secondary source. Overemphasizing documentation and citation can bog down your search. Always remember that information is subject to interpretation and that human beings can make mistakes. Although secondary sources may seem like the poor stepchildren of genealogy, they very often provide correct information. They can also give clues about where primary source materials can be found.

Don't Jump to Conclusions

Family stories are sometimes more than a little exaggerated. Legends can evolve, and memories fade over time. Just because you've always heard about your great-uncle's career in professional baseball doesn't mean that he really played in a major league. It may turn out that he really only played sandlot ball.

Here's a little story about how a family legend was debunked by an astute genealogy researcher. The grandmother of a friend of ours was born in Texas at the turn of the twentieth century. Grandma's family had come from the South, and she was very proud of her Confederate heritage. She always said she was descended from a proud Confederate officer. When our friend got started in genealogy, she approached the family line with Grandma's stories in mind. Imagine her surprise when she found out that, far from being an honored Confederate officer, the ancestor in question had actually fought on the side of the Union and was "hung for a Yankee" by Confederate sympathizers!

Documented Proof

You'll probably begin your online search with so-called vital records. These are documents that record date of birth, marriage, divorce, and death. In the pre-Internet days, genealogists had to visit municipal and state recorders' offices in person or pay substantial fees to receive copies of documents by mail. Many of these records are now available online at the Ancestry Web site (www.ancestry.com), the Social Security Death Index (ssdi.rootsweb.com), or World Vital Records (www.worldvitalrecords.com). The availability of records depends on the laws of particular states and countries. If the records themselves are not available, you should be able to find on the Web the procedures for requesting copies of the records and the contact information for doing so.

Birth Records

Birth records usually include the mother's full maiden name, the father's full name, the baby's name and date of birth, and the name of the county in which the baby was born. Other information may include where the baby's parents were born, the parents' addresses, the number of children the parents have, and the parents' race and occupation.

Cemetery Records

Cemeteries typically record the names and death dates of people who are buried on their grounds. They also have maps showing the locations of specific graves. Some cemeteries may also record names of relatives of the deceased. The grave markers themselves frequently provide birth and death dates, and some even include the names of other family members. At the Web site Ancestors at Rest (ancestorsatrest.com), you can perform free searches of databases that cover coffin plates, death cards, funeral cards, and tombstone inscriptions.

Census Records

A census is an official count of people who live in a specific location. A census provides information such as the names, ages, and ethnicity of individuals. Some also record citizenship status. The government of the United States started collecting census information in 1790, and a federal census has been conducted every ten years since. Some states have also conducted their own counts. A portion of the federal census provides information about people who died during the census year.

Church Records

Churches keep official documents about their congregations. The information usually covers dates of christenings, baptisms, marriages, and burials. The records of these events generally include names, dates, locations, parents' names, names of witnesses, and participants' addresses. Churches also keep records on their cemeteries and burials.

Land Records

Land deeds represent a record of the ownership of a specific piece of land by an individual, and they provide a variety of related information. Most include the name of the landowner, the location of the property involved, and the dates that the person purchased and sold the land.

Marriage Records

Marriage records include the full names of both the bride and the groom, the date of the wedding, and the name of the county where the wedding took place. They may also include the names of the couple's parents, the couple's addresses, information about previous marriages, and the names of individuals who served as witnesses to the marriage.

Military Records

In the United States, state, local, and federal governments have always kept records of military and civilian workers. Most of these records include an individual's name, birth date, address, spouse's name, branch of the military he or she served, beginning and ending dates of the service period, death date, and burial site.

Naturalization Records

To become a naturalized U.S. citizen, an immigrant must be able to prove that he or she has been a legal, permanent resident in the country for a specific amount of time. The period of time varies according to whether or not the individual is married to an American citizen. The documentation required in the naturalization process represents a treasure trove of information, and while even The National Archives (www.archives.gov/genealogy/naturalization/naturalization.html) admits there is no standardization in the content or existence of naturalization records, there are several resources that you, the budding genealogist, can check. These include county and federal court records.

Immigrants must file several forms in court before the naturalization process can proceed. These documents must include an individual's birth date and place, the date he or she arrived in the United States, where he or she lived at the time of naturalization, and a personal description. In some cases, the records give the occupation of the immigrant and the name of the ship on which he or she arrived.

Passenger Lists

Names and information about passengers who arrived in the United States via ship were included on passenger lists, which were given to customs officials at each port by the ship's master. Passenger information varied significantly before 1820, the year after which the lists were officially required by the U.S. government.

Probate Records

Probate records provide information about the disposal of a deceased person's property. The records may include a will, if one exists. Probate records usually provide the name of the deceased individual, that individual's birth date or the age at death, property, names of family members, and the location of the last residence.

Social Security Death Index

This index of death records generated by the U.S. Social Security Administration typically includes the names of deceased recipients of benefits, whose family members applied for Social Security death benefits after the death. There are millions of these records, which also include about 400,000 railroad retirement records dating from the 1900s to the 1950s. You can access the Social Security Death Index for free via Roots Web (ssdi.rootsweb.com). Information about railroad retirement records is available at the U.S. Railroad Retirement Board Web site (www.rrb.gov/mep/genealogy.asp).

A Question of Form

You'll be using a variety of forms to record and organize the information that you find on your genealogy journey. The first forms you will need—

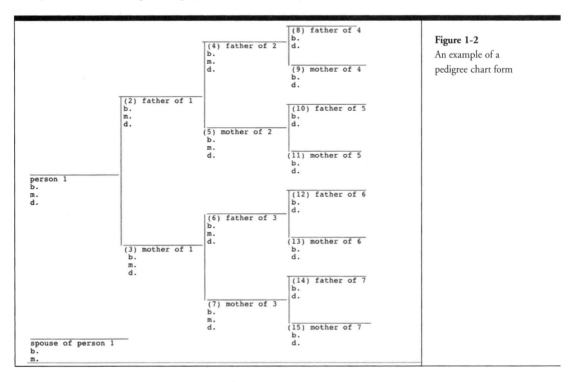

Figure 1-2

An example of a pedigree chart form

a pedigree chart and the family group sheet—can be downloaded from Web sites such as FamilySearch.org and Ancestry.com.

The Pedigree Chart

A pedigree chart (fig. 1-2) provides spaces where you can enter your name (person 1). So you begin with yourself and work backward in time to your parents, grandparents, and great-grandparents. For each person on the chart, there are spaces for their birth, marriage, and death dates. Filling in this chart helps you see what basic information you already have about your nearest relatives. Include the maiden names of your female ancestors, if possible. Female ancestors tend to be very elusive, so the more information you have in the beginning, the better.

The Family Group Sheet

A family group sheet (fig. 1-3) covers more information than a pedigree chart and provides a different way to look at a family line. A family group sheet includes spaces for the full name of the husband and wife, including the latter's maiden name, and the full names of their parents. There are also spaces to record the birthplace and birth date for each individual, as well as the death date and location and the place of burial.

A family group sheet allows you to record the names of other spouses that a husband and wife may have had, and the names of all the children resulting from their marriage. All of the children's birthplaces and dates can be recorded on this form, as well as death dates and locations, the dates and locations of the children's marriages, and the names of their spouses.

That's a lot of information to have on one little form! Filling out the pedigree chart and the family group sheet provides a good foundation for beginning your ancestor hunt.

Some Other Helpful Forms

For further help in getting started, you'll find that Web sites like FamilySearch.org, CyndisList.com, and Ancestry.com, along with many others, also provide useful forms. These tools can help you plan your research, record what you've done, and list the sources you've consulted. You can also find forms to create a sort of table of contents for the information you collect, so you can keep track of your information more easily.

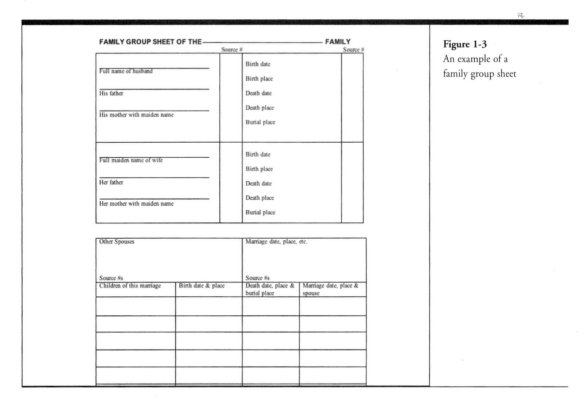

Figure 1-3

An example of a family group sheet

Visit These Web Sites First!

Now that you've come this far, you've probably noticed the interesting problem with online research—there is just so much information! While we'll cover the best of the best genealogy sites on the Web in a later chapter, there are two Web sites you should take a look at as you start out. We've mentioned them already, so you can probably guess what they are: Cyndi's List and Ancestry. Many other excellent Web sites offer genealogy advice, online databases, and relevant records, but eventually any genealogy research will bring you to these two sites, so you may as well begin there and become familiar with what they provide.

Cyndi's List

Cyndi Howells "went live" with her Web site of genealogy-related Internet links, Cyndi's List, (fig. 1-1) in March 1996. At that time, the list proudly announced 1,000 categorized genealogy links. Within two months the number of links had doubled, and a year later there were

17,300 links in over sixty categories. The site had grown to incorporate more than 195 separate Web pages.

Cyndi continued to improve her site, consistently adding links and features, and on its tenth anniversary in March 2006, Cyndi's List offered 251,235 total links, 242,672 categorized links, and 8,563 links submitted by visitors in the What's New section. The site had grown to 684 Web pages and has an average of 2 million page hits every month. That's a lot of genealogy research going on!

It is easy to see why Howells's site has become the premier source for both beginning and experienced genealogists. The list is categorized and cross-referenced and functions as a free starting point for online genealogical research. Howells characterizes her site as a "card catalog" to the genealogy resources in the Internet "library" and as a "research portal." National media outlets such as *Newsweek* magazine and The History Channel have acclaimed Howells's site as the most comprehensive list of genealogy resources available on the Internet. The amount of information on the list is nothing short of amazing, and it is difficult to know where to start. Cyndi makes it easy, however, by providing long lists of topics useful for beginners and many links to sites that will allow you to download relevant forms and charts for free.

Ancestry.com

All genealogy roads eventually lead to Ancestry.com (fig. 1-4). The folks in charge of this site are making it their business to collect all records, documents, and manuscripts of interest to genealogists. You can still find some of this information for free at smaller sites, but if you really want to dig deep into your family history and connections, you'll need access to Ancestry. Many libraries and universities have subscriptions to the site, so you can browse its offerings that way, or the site's fourteen-day free trial offer can help you decide whether you want to commit to a paid subscription. Prices for subscriptions range from $12.95 per month to $29.95 per month, depending on the information you want to access.

Ancestry also has numerous databases, chief among them the collection of U.S. census forms. It also provides online versions of numerous obscure local and family histories, published and unpublished, and you can start to build your own family tree online. You can search the literally

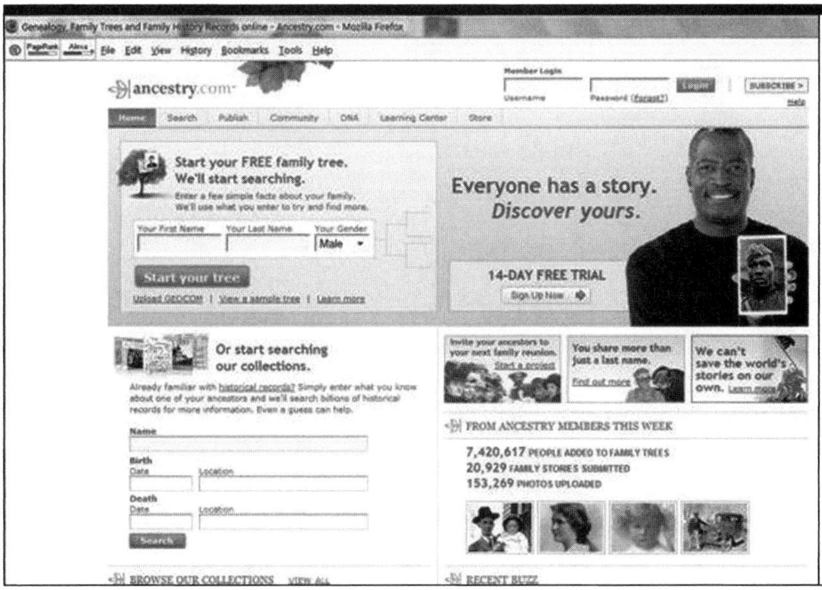

Figure 1-4
The home page of
Ancestry.com, a site
you'll refer to repeatedly

billions of records online at Ancestry, and then organize the results using the resources on the site. Ancestry has made it easy to share information and even photographs with whomever you choose.

The newest feature available at Ancestry is its DNA Ancestry option. It is now possible to get your DNA tested for genealogical purposes through the Ancestry Web site. The procedure involves selecting the appropriate type of DNA test, getting a test kit, swabbing your mouth to get a DNA sample, and returning the test kit for testing in a laboratory. The results you receive could lead you to distant cousins and an expanded family tree! You can share the results of your test by entering the information onto the site. According to the experts at Ancestry, the new DNA feature will provide a validation of your research, help you overcome obstacles to your search, find and collaborate with relatives you didn't know you had, and learn about the ancient origins of your family line.

Ancestry.com also provides several Learning Centers to help you with your research. These centers provide census records, vital records, family trees, immigration records, military records, directories, family and local histories, newspapers and periodicals, court, land, and probate records. This site should be kept in mind during your genealogy explorations. Remember, however, that you won't find everything about your ancestors on Ancestry—nor should you want to. One of the most rewarding things about doing a family history is actually connecting with relatives to share stories and memories. Ancestry.com won't have all the details about Grandpa's cross-country motor trip in his Ford Model T, for example. You'll have to talk to Grandpa to get the real story!

The Research Process

The genealogy research process is similar to any kind of research. First, you collect your information. Then you organize it into meaningful groupings. Finally, you create reports that communicate the information in a useful way.

Begin with What You Know

All genealogy experts agree that the best way to start your research is to begin with what you already know. Start with facts you already have about your family members. Do you know the last names and maiden names of individuals? Do you know where they were born? Do you know where they lived and the years they lived there? Do you know if they traveled, where they went, and with whom they journeyed? Collecting all of this information at the start will save you time in the long run.

Start with your copies of the pedigree chart and family group record forms, which you can either pick up at a local LDS Family History Center or download from sites such as FamilySearch.org and Ancestry.com. Cyndi's List also provides a number of sources for useful forms. On the pedigree chart (fig. 1-2), fill in your name and birth date. Add the names of your parents and their birth and/or death dates. Continue with the same information for your grandparents and great-grandparents. Fill in as much information as you have. The pedigree chart acts like table of contents for your family line and gives an organized view of the basic information you have and what you still need to find. Once the pedigree chart is done, move on to the family group record (fig. 1-3). Be sure to include information about brothers and sisters, cousins, aunts, and uncles. All of these collateral relatives are important to your family line. You never know where you'll find a clue to elusive information! When you've filled out these two basic forms to the best of your ability, it's time for the real fun! You're now ready to talk with relatives and friends of the family, looking for whatever information they may have. Of course, remember the previous warning that not all information gathered through talks with individuals is reliable, so you'll have to verify what they say. Otherwise, you may spend a lot of time researching people who don't belong on your family tree!

Asking Questions

Most of the time, you'll want to talk with immediate family members and your oldest relatives first. Later on, you may want to contact more-distant relatives through regular mail or e-mail. As mentioned earlier, many families have built Web sites devoted to their genealogical research, and you can contact people of interest through them. (E-mail lists and Internet newsgroups also provide ways to contact distant family members, but more on these later.)

Probably the most powerful benefit of the Internet for genealogy is that it makes it easy to contact people who are working on the same family lines as you are. Once you've contacted another researcher, you'll find that he or she has additional contacts who are also working the same ground. You won't be traveling the genealogical roadways alone! Halvor Moorshead, genealogist and publisher of *Family Chronicle Magazine,* said in his article "First Things First" that 90 percent of his personal family tree resulted from contributions from other people. He also noted, however, that mistakes show up in many of these contributions and that they should be verified, especially if the information is the result of someone's recollections years after the fact.

Regardless of how you get your interview, the kinds of questions to ask are basically the same. The list of topics that can be covered in these interviews is limitless, but be sure to include questions about childhood, family traditions, growing up, historical events, and memories of previous generations. Other possible topics are politics, religion, military service, an era's popular culture, pets, travel, family recipes, medical history, marriage, and clothing styles.

🔍 Five Good Questions to Ask the Old Folks

Here are some questions you can ask your older relatives to get your interview started. Once they begin to talk, be flexible enough to follow their lead. You never know where or what you might discover in someone else's memory bank!

1. What is your earliest childhood memory?
2. What was your favorite thing to do for fun?
3. What world event(s) had the biggest impact on you while growing up?
4. How is the world different now, as compared to when you were a child?
5. Was your name ever in a newspaper?

Let's Get Organized

By now, you've probably realized that you can collect enormous amounts of information about your family via the Internet. What do you do with all that information? How will you ever be able to find a particular story or fact or person in your genealogical haystack? Fear not. The trailblazers of genealogy have developed time-tested ways to stay organized. Chapter 3 is devoted to the topic of organization, but here are a few pointers.

Before computers, researchers kept their information in a series of paper files. For some, this is still the best way to proceed. As a beginner, you may feel more comfortable keeping paper records. However, computer programs designed specifically to handle genealogical information have made the organization process much easier. Web sites such as Ancestry.com make it possible to keep all of your genealogy research stored online. These sites offer many options that let you research your family tree, type your information into their ready-made formats, and store that information in their central repositories. With advances in computer database technology, these sites also make it possible for all of your information to be linked. This simply means that you can easily search through many types of data about a single person. You can also link your information to the research of other people who are working on collateral branches of your family. In this way, you can become part of a community of searchers that celebrates each other's discoveries.

Looking Ahead

In Chapter 2, we look at some of the tools of the online genealogy trade. This means software, folks! We'll give an overview of some of the most popular genealogy software products available for PCs as well as Macs, list and compare their functions and prices, and discuss their suitability for your particular genealogical needs and desires. So sit down at that keyboard, grab that mouse, and get ready for some software talk.

Chapter 2

Tools
You'll Use

Once you start relying on the Internet for your genealogy research, it's just a matter of time before you'll want a software program that is designed to handle the specifics of that research. There are more than forty genealogy software programs on the market, most designed for the Windows operating system. But Mac users also have some good options available to them. Programs range in price from $29.95 to $99, and some are free. All of the programs have features designed to make entering, saving, and retrieving your genealogy information as simple as possible. There are many Web sites that offer reviews and comparisons of genealogy software to help you make the best choice for your particular needs. Cyndi's List alone offers more than 500 links to sites that discuss genealogy software.

In this chapter, we discuss what you'll get—and what you won't get—in some of the most popular genealogy software programs. And yes, we know, the mere idea of talking about software can make our eyes glaze over, too. But once you realize how genealogy programs can simplify your recordkeeping, you'll be glad you took the time to investigate your options. And think about how you'll feel when you display your first ancestor chart, beautifully designed and printed via your chosen software, to your family and friends. There's sure to be applause all around! Please note that the software products that are available change frequently (as does the information about them), so it's best if you check out manufacturers' Web sites for current information.

What's Your Pleasure?

Choosing software is essentially based on personal taste and the limits of your budget. Some people swear by Family Tree Maker, while others praise The Master Genealogist to the skies. Your choice will also depend on what you want to do with your software program.

Some software programs let you make wall-sized charts of your family tree, while others let you include photographs, audio, and even video elements. Some people want to use their genealogy software to build a family Web page, while others just want a basic way to store names, dates, and events on the computer. There are programs that fit any and all of those requirements.

Are you thinking about sharing the information you find with other people online? If so, the top genealogy programs give you the means to upload your data to an online site such as RootsWeb (www.rootsweb.com). The main purpose of RootsWeb is to connect you with other people who may be working on the same family line so that you can share genealogical research. Family Tree Maker, for example, lets you save your family tree in the standard GEDCOM format to the RootsWeb site. Some software even allows you to create a Web page from within the program without the need to add any extra utilities.

Maybe you're planning to write a book using the information you find and store using your genealogy software program. Some programs have more and better features for printing family histories in book format than others. Before you decide, think about how you prefer to navigate around the computer screen. Some people would rather click the mouse to move between options, while others feel more comfortable using the computer keyboard. You should also consider the kinds of charts and reports that can be printed with the software you choose, since there are many options available, and if you have information that has been created in programs other than your genealogy software, you'll want to be able to bring that information into the program without losing any data.

Some researchers want to be able to submit their family research to the FamilySearch site at some time. The site offers its resources to anyone, regardless of culture, ethnicity, or religion, who wants to research family roots. If you want to submit your information, you must choose a software program that supports the special fields required to note the rights held by the LDS Church.

Finally, think about whether you enjoy learning about the features of a software program, or if you just want to use it straight out-of-the-box, without a learning curve. Some modern genealogy software offers such a large number of features that you may find it too time-consuming to learn how to use them all. You may even find that a particular program has too many features, which overwhelm you with tools that you'll never need. Always balance what you need with the price of the product. Don't pay for features and capabilities you'll never use.

If you're a beginner, it may be even more difficult for you to know what you need, but there is a simple way to find out. Most of the top genealogy software makers offer trial versions of their products, or demos. These allow you to try either a complete version of the program or a version that offers limited capabilities and features but is still functional enough to give you an idea of how the full version will work for you. Demos are generally available at the software developer's Web site, where you can also find information about the particular product, including a list of features, price, sample screenshots, and the kind of support and help you can expect to receive from the company after you've purchased the product.

A word to the wise is appropriate here. When you're doing your research, be sure to note what kind of support the company offers after you buy their software. Good support means you won't get stuck in the middle of a project without help. Companies usually offer support via e-mail free of charge for a period of time, and some provide telephone support for limited periods as well. Some companies will even promise lifetime support with the purchase of their software. Don't underestimate the value of having someone to contact when your software seems to be fighting you!

Start with the Basics

Your genealogy software program should allow you to access, record, and review your information easily. It should be simple enough for you to use as a beginner while providing sufficient capabilities as you gain more experience. The software should be simple to set up and install, be user friendly, well organized, and easy to navigate. It should provide all the features you need for researching and organizing your family information: reports, charts, Web access, and search capabilities. A comprehensive genealogy program will have useful Help features and good user documentation to support you. There should be relevant Frequently Asked Questions (FAQs), e-mail and telephone support, and online tutorials available to teach you how to use the program effectively.

In the early days of genealogy software, you had to think about all kinds of technical issues when you were choosing software, such as what kind of video card your computer had and whether you had enough RAM or hard disk space. Today, about the only thing you need to consider is whether you are using a PC or a Mac. If your computer is less than ten years old, you'll probably have more than enough memory and processor speed to run the most popular genealogy programs.

Speed Is Good!

Since you're planning to use the Internet for genealogy research, it will pay, over time, to install a high-speed Internet connection. For example, many programs interact directly with the features of the Ancestry site, but you could grow old trying to take advantage of these options over a dial-up connection! Most people have broadband access to the Internet through DSL or cable, but if you haven't switched over yet, you will likely consider doing so after spending a few hours trying to download census forms!

What to Look For

At its simplest, genealogy software automates some of the more mundane tasks associated with recording information. Most programs also allow you to generate charts in the proper format or publish your family tree on the Web with the click of a mouse. All genealogy programs will aid you in organizing your research, creating reports, or searching the Internet, but some programs are better than others in particular areas. This is why you should have a good idea of what you want to do with the information you find before you go shopping. Let's look at the basic features you should expect from any software you consider.

Easy Data Entry

Your program should make it easy to record the birth dates and birthplaces of individuals, along with the dates of their marriages, deaths, and other events in their lives. You also want to be able to record the sources where information was found, so that everything will be appropriately documented. Most programs also allow you to add biographical information and pictures, and to link individuals to families.

Easy Navigation

You should expect easy navigation from one screen to another. Most popular programs allow you to view information in individual, family, or pedigree formats. You should be able to move through different generations to edit information easily, and you should expect to have a simple way to print out reports. Almost all genealogy programs create family group sheets and pedigree charts from the data you enter so you don't need to fill them out by hand.

All the popular genealogy software programs work with the standard GEDCOM file format. This lets you share your data with people who may use a different genealogy program. As mentioned in Chapter 1, GEDCOMs are computer files that hold the genealogy information you've created in a format that can be used by any other genealogy program. (This also allows you to transfer your family information to other programs without having to retype it.) When you're evaluating software, you'll want to pay particular to attention to how easily you are able to export the data to a GEDCOM file.

Easy Report Creation

A genealogy program will let you create narrative family histories and other reports using information you've entered about your family. Reports can display all of an individual's ancestors and descendants for a specific number of generations. Citations for your sources may be displayed as footnotes or endnotes on the report, and the software will automatically generate an index of the names included in the report. Reports are often provided in a book format.

Graphic charts represent another type of report. Most programs have the ability to create family trees that incorporate diverse graphic elements. The software will let you choose from a set of format templates for the design of your chart and allow you to customize your charts by adding photographs or changing colors and fonts. You can print out these graphic representations on standard-sized printer paper, but many programs now give you the option to send your charts to a service bureau that can print them in large sizes suitable for wall display.

Most of the popular genealogy software programs will also allow you to create multimedia presentations. You can add and edit photographs, create slide shows, or create a multimedia scrapbook that includes still pictures, video, and sound.

Direct Access to the Internet

And, of course, you want to be able to use the Internet directly through your genealogy program. Most programs will now let you access online databases, such as those found at Ancestry.com, and automatically search them for names in your family line. Most will also let you create your own Web pages by creating reports using hypertext markup language (HTML), the language of the Web. With just a few clicks, your software should create pages automatically.

So what are the most popular genealogy software programs? Now that we have you thinking about your basic needs, let's look at the top genealogy programs for PCs and Macs. The overall subject of genealogy software could fill the pages of an entire book. For our purposes, we'll compare common features of just a few programs.

Top Programs for PCs

Luckily for the rest of us, software reviewers plow the fields of genealogy software. They've done us a great service by providing an overview of the software, which lets us make the best choice for our particular needs.

We've taken it a step further and scoured the Internet for the best genealogy software review sites, including Eastman's Online Genealogy Newsletter, the genealogy section of About.com, and Louis Kessler's genealogy software review site, to come up with the following selection of top programs. We've chosen these programs on the basis of their popularity with users, array of features, and rankings at the review sites.

Table 2-1 (page 32) provides a comparison of popular Windows-based genealogy programs.

Legacy Family Tree, Deluxe Edition—$29.95
(www.legacyfamilytree.com)

Legacy Family Tree 6.0 (fig. 2-1) is highly recommended for beginners and experienced researchers alike. It combines easy navigation with many useful features. Its interface is intuitive and easy to use, and its flexible data-merge capabilities make it simple to add files without causing any problems in what you've already entered. Additionally, you can directly import data that was created in the software programs Personal Ancestry File (page 34) and Ancestral Quest (page 36). Of course, you can also use the GEDCOM format to import data. The Source Clipboard feature allows you to note sources for the information you find.

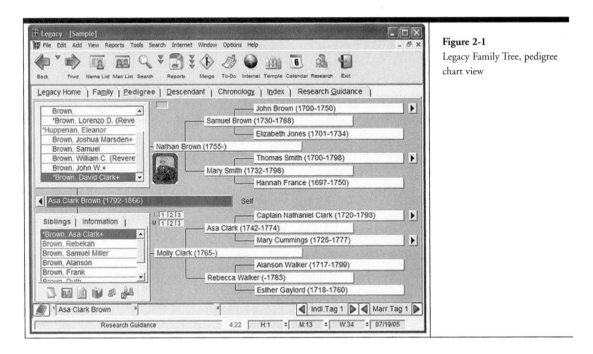

Figure 2-1
Legacy Family Tree, pedigree chart view

The program provides a wide variety of report options, along with all of the standard charts you'd expect. The IntelliShare feature allows groups to coordinate their work and receive updates on any changes made, so it's perfect if you are collaborating with other family members on research.

Pictures, sound, and video can be added to events, master sources, and citations. The software also provides easy-to-use Web page creation tools, so you can publish your family tree on the Internet. If you want to have fancy wall charts, however, you'll need to use an add-on piece of software called Legacy Charting Companion.

The program features global search-and-replace, auto-complete so you don't have to retype information, and an alarm clock that keeps you on track. There are several different options for how you view your data: Family View, Pedigree View, Descendant View, and Index View. The deluxe version also has a Chronology View. Legacy also includes publishing capabilities that allow you to create a family history book.

Some of the new features in version 6.0 include Research Guidance and Publishing Center. Research Guidance helps you locate records that are relevant to your ancestors. It reviews an ancestor's timeline and suggests preliminary sources so you can check whether someone else is doing similar research. It also helps you to prioritize goals into a to-do list. Publishing Center allows you to choose one or more reports and put them together into a single large book report. The program then indexes and cites all the information from the reports and generates a table of contents. Finally, this feature lets you add a title page, preface, dedication, copyright notice, and introduction to your book.

You might want to start with the free standard version of Legacy to try out the program. If you like it, you can upgrade to the paid version later. The standard version is fully functional, but provides fewer features than the deluxe edition and limits the number of entries you can make in some areas. The software is available for purchase by download only.

RootsMagic—$29.95 *(www.rootsmagic.com)*

RootsMagic (fig. 2-2) is a user-friendly program with enough features to keep you occupied for quite a while. It offers three ways to view your data: Pedigree View, Family View, and Descendants View.

The edit screen allows you to enter as many facts as you want for each individual that you include. Types of facts are listed, but you can add a fact that doesn't fit into any of the categories. You can also add an

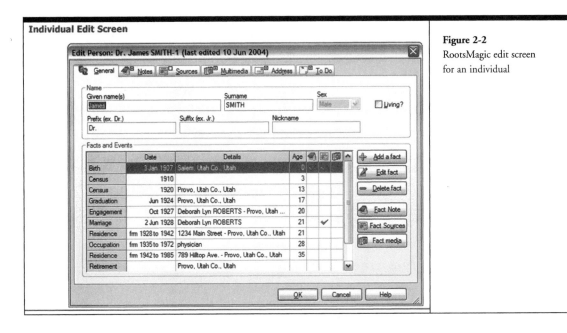

unlimited number of source citations for each fact. The Explorer search system allows you to find any person in your file very easily, so you can quickly add, edit, or remove information.

There are a number of printer-friendly documents available, including pedigree charts, family group sheets, six different styles for narrative reports, several lists, mailing labels, calendars, relationship charts, blank charts, and a custom-report generator. With RootsMagic you can also create enormous wall charts and order printed versions up to 100 feet long. So if you're looking to make a really big impression at the family reunion, this may be the way to go! Finally, the program can generate Web sites automatically from the information you enter.

One of the least expensive genealogy programs available, RootsMagic is also one of the easiest to use. There is an adequate Help section, and you can either use the FAQs feature for support or send a question to the online forum.

Family Tree Maker 2008—$39.95

(www.familytreemaker.com)
This is the latest version of the very popular genealogy program from the folks at Ancestry.com. Because the program is tightly integrated with the

Web site, when you choose Family Tree Maker (fig. 2-3), you'll gain access to the features and capabilities of the site.

Figure 2-3
Family Tree Maker, family screen view

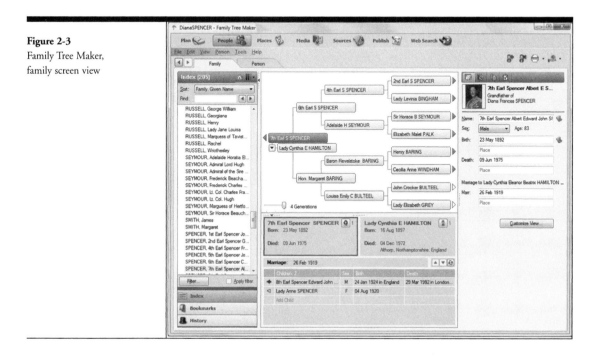

Family Tree Maker helps you create a family tree, beginning simply with individual names, dates, and events. The 2008 version is a complete update of the program. Its new features include a new user interface that mixes the elements of a pedigree chart and a family group sheet, so it's even easier to enter, look at, and edit your information. The Web Clipper feature lets you merge information that you find anywhere on the Web into your own family tree. The program has been upgraded to allow for easier management of photographs, video, and sound files so you can use them in your charts and reports. A timeline feature allows you to high-light personal, family, and world events that occurred during your ances-tors' lifetimes. It also provides a dynamic listing of all the people and events that are associated with a particular geographic location. You can import data created in other genealogy programs, including Personal Ancestral File (page 34), The Master Genealogist (page 35), and Legacy Family Tree (page 28).

Table 2-1

Comparison of Popular Genealogy Programs for Windows

	Legacy Family Tree Deluxe	Roots Magic	Family Tree Maker	Personal Ancestry File (PAF)	The Master Genealogist	Ancestral Quest
Web site	legacyfamilytree.com	rootsmagic.com	familytreemaker.com	familysearch.org	whollygenes.com	ancquest.com
Price	$59.95 download w/CD and User Guide and upgrade to Version 7 plus training videos; $39.95 download w/CD and User Guide; Standard Edition is free	$29.95 full; $19.95 upgrade	$39.95	Free	$59	$29.95
Free demo	•	•		•	•	•
Download	Standard Edition	•		•	•	•
Available on disk	•	•	•	•	•	additional S&H fee
Report and chart options	Ancestor; descendant; pedigree; multiple lines of descent; book format	Ancestor; descendant; pedigree; Family Group Sheets; wall charts; book format; create shareable CDs	Ancestor; descendant; narrative; to-do lists; book format; wall charts; many add-ons	Ancestor; descendant; narrative; to-do lists	Narratives; forms; charts; to-do lists; plan DNA log; box charts	Pedigree; Family Group Sheets; ancestry charts; descendant charts; genealogy book reports; fan charts; calendar report; wall charts
Report formatting options	Colors; fonts; size; many others	Colors; fonts; size; many others	Flexible formatting; many add-ons		25 "fancy frames"; many others	
Custom reports	•	•	•		•	•
Import / export GEDCOMs	•	•	•	•	•	•

	Legacy Family Tree Deluxe	Roots Magic	Family Tree Maker	Personal Ancestry File (PAF)	The Master Genealogist	Ancestral Quest
Multimedia support	•	•	•	•	•	•
Multiple search options	•	•	•	•	•	•
Relationship calculator	•		•	•	•	•
Date calculator	•		•	•	•	•
Supports source documenting	•	•	•	•	•	•
Web pages	•	•	•	•	•	•
Additional features	DNA log; calendar creator; many add-ons available to extend functionality	Back up directly to CDs; video tutorial included with RootsMagic CD	Back up data by automatically creating a member tree on Ancestry.com; strong integration with Ancestry.com		With purchase of CD, you receive The Universal British Directory of Great Britain 1791; most extensive features, but steep learning curve	"Tip of the Day" feature helps you learn the program quickly; includes special features for Jewish researchers
System requirements	Vista, XP, ME, 2000, NT, 98, 95	Vista, XP, 95, 98, ME, NT, 2000, and 2003	Windows XP / Vista	Windows 98, NT, 2000, ME, or XP	Windows 98, NT, 2000, ME, or XP	Windows 95 or newer
Technical support	Online user's guide; online training videos; online FAQs	Online FAQs; web-based e-mail form; online message board; online mailing list; update notification	Training video; Online documentation and help files; e-mail; phone support (some fee-based); online forums	Excellent support online; e-mail; local LDS Family History Centers and PAF user groups	E-mail; phone; fax; online guided tour; online FAQs; online forums; user groups; online chat	E-mail; phone; Yahoo group forum online

By using the software along with Ancestry.com, you can compare information you find on the Web site with information in your family tree, then use a "merge wizard" to import just the new facts and records you select. You can also utilize the "contextual search" feature, which suggests other records relevant to individuals in your family line. Particularly important is that all of your Family Tree Maker information can be backed up automatically to the Ancestry site via the "member tree" option. This option lets you upload your family tree and have it displayed, either publicly or to a select group of viewers, online. Saving your data online ensures that the information is protected and won't be lost if your home computer crashes. The new Ancestry Press self-publishing tool makes it possible to create quality books using the information you find out about your family.

Note that long-time users of Family Tree Maker have had some complaints about the revamped version, and many recommend using earlier versions of the software (version 16 seems particularly popular) until more of the kinks have been worked out. There are also plans to reinstitute some of the popular features that had either been dramatically changed or eliminated altogether. For more information about this, visit Eastman's Online Genealogy Newsletter (blog.eogn.com).

Personal Ancestry File—Free *(www.familysearch.org)*

Personal Ancestry File, or PAF among those who are "in-the-know," is offered free of charge by FamilySearch.org, a nonprofit service sponsored by the LDS Church.

PAF is the oldest genealogy program available. Most other genealogy programs follow PAF's lead in the way they import and export GEDCOM files. Its intuitive design makes it simple for beginners to use, and it is easy to install. The program supports your research tasks in an organized and efficient way, but other programs provide more report options. On the other hand, there are excellent Help and user documentation with PAF, which make it very good for beginning genealogists— plus, it's free! You can consult the Getting Started Guide, take lessons in the provided tutorial, and consult the FAQs for information. The Feedback option allows you to submit your questions to experts.

The software offers all the necessary features you'd expect in a genealogy program and is quite powerful. It has limited multimedia capabilities, so if that is an important feature for you, you should probably try one of the other programs.

PAF has the best support network of all available genealogy programs. Free support is available through any LDS Family History Center, PAF user group, or online (www.familysearch.org). The support of the LDS Church makes it likely that the program will continue to be available in the future.

PAF is a very good choice if you are looking for a user-friendly program and if you are not particularly interested in publishing your family tree information in a book or online. And . . . did we happen to mention that it's free?

The Master Genealogist—$59 *(www.whollygenes.com)*

At the other end of the complexity scale is The Master Genealogist (TMG). Users applaud the program's many features, and it is generally considered the best when it comes to sourcing information. However, it has a steep learning curve and is one of the more expensive programs.

This is a program for serious genealogy researchers. It offers more depth and flexibility than other products and has major organizational strengths. It comes with every feature you might need for managing large amounts of data, sources, and photographs. It includes to-do lists, reference materials, charts, and forms. You can keep track of any correspondence you have and any expenses you incur from your genealogy efforts. The program allows you to create a Web page of your data or publish a book with a table of contents, footnotes, and a bibliography! It doesn't get more professional than that.

TMG was created by experienced genealogists who knew exactly what they wanted from their software. These experts also understood the common research problems you can run into as you investigate your family tree, such as conflicts in the data, uncertainty about dates, unwed parents, adoption, changes in spelling, old-style spelling, multiple lines of descent, contradictions in source materials, and missing and/or sensitive data. The creators of TMG took steps to give the program enough flexibility to handle these challenges.

You'll need some computer savvy to use TMG, but its installation is relatively easy to perform. The program offers a number of Help options, including Tips and Hints windows, an online guided tour, FAQs, and a way to check for program updates. E-mail and telephone support are available.

However, some users find TMG difficult to navigate, and if you don't like to read instructions, don't even think about getting this program. You'll have to read the user manual and the Help text if you want to use TMG's wide range of features.

It has been said that the only thing TMG doesn't come with is a person to enter your data for you and that this would be a great help for beginning users. The program can do everything you could possibly think of, but it can be confusing and difficult to use. This, coupled with the relatively high price tag, makes TMG appropriate for researchers who already know a lot about computers and genealogy. But it probably is not the best choice for beginners, who may be overwhelmed and intimidated by it. Unless, of course, you love a challenge.

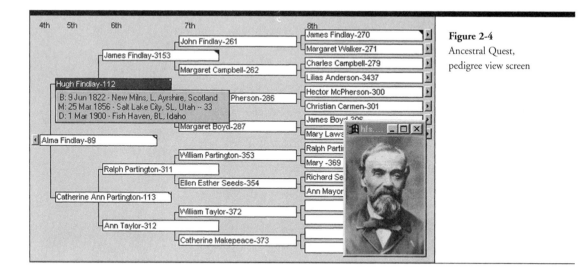

Figure 2-4
Ancestral Quest, pedigree view screen

Ancestral Quest—$29.95 (*www.ancquest.com*)

This program is a major contender for first place among genealogy software for PCs. Ancestral Quest (fig. 2-4) has many of the same features as Family Tree Maker and Legacy Family Tree. It offers multiple options for outputting data and includes multimedia and Web page construction capabilities. You can easily create pedigree charts, family group sheets, ancestry charts, descendant charts, genealogy book reports, fan charts, and other documents.

With this program, entering and documenting your information is easy and intuitive. The program has a data-entry field for just about any kind of data you might want to include. It even has a page that allows for documenting your sources in a very detailed way. Plenty of help is available right on the screen.

The extensive Help features are a major bonus. The program offers a Tip of the Day window every time you start up, so you'll learn about its features quickly and effortlessly. You can contact support via e-mail or telephone, and there is a discussion group available at Yahoo! Groups, so you can share your experiences with the program with other users (groups.yahoo.com/group/AncestralQuest). The software is also easy to install.

Links to online genealogy databases, including Ancestry.com and FamilySearch.org, are included. Ancestral Quest is simply one of the best genealogy programs for beginners and experienced researchers alike, and should definitely be considered.

Top Programs for Macs

Mac users have fewer choices for genealogy software than PC users, but that doesn't mean that the programs available for the Mac are any less appealing or less full-featured. Following are descriptions of some of the genealogy programs ranked among the most popular at online software review sites, such as Eastman's Online Genealogy Newsletter (www.eogn.com) and Lou Kessler's Genealogy Software Links (www.lkessler.com/gplinks.shtml). A point-by-point comparison of features for the Mac programs included in this section is presented in Table 2-2 (page 40).

Reunion—$99 *(www.leisterpro.com)*

Reunion (fig. 2-5) is the best-selling genealogy program available for Mac users. It is easy to use but quite expensive (no surprise to Mac users). Entering your information is easy, and the program allows you to create very large charts with customizable colors, fonts, and more. You can chart up to 99 generations! With the Zoom feature, you can examine various parts of a large chart on your computer screen.

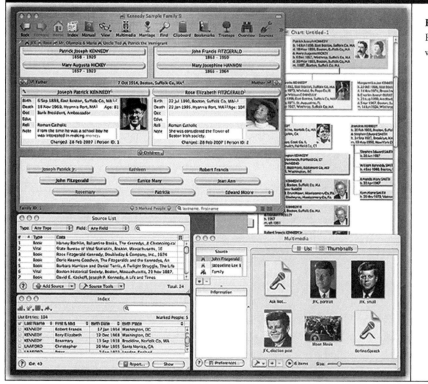

Figure 2-5
Reunion screen with several windows open

The special strengths of the program are found in the way it handles multimedia files. You can digitize anything—sound files, old movies, photographs, maps, wills—and link them to people and families. You can link several multimedia elements to a single record, or one such element to many records. How's that for flexibility? And since we're talking Mac, the program lets you take your information with you via an iPod card, so you can share it on the go. It will automatically build Web pages for you with all the required HTML, images, and graphics files. You can choose from a number of ready-made styles that feature so-called cascading style sheets, which is a standard way to format pages for display on the Web. Reunion supplies many options for creating really attractive family group sheets, person sheets, questionnaires, and blank forms. These can be used to collect information from your relatives. Printable forms are available for any group of people in your file, so you can, for example, easily create a customized questionnaire for all of your cousins. You can also create cascading pedigree charts, a series of graphic charts with four or five generations on each page. Telephone and e-mail support are available, and through an online community called ReunionTalk you will find help and inspiration. There is also an electronic manual linked to the Help button. You can click the button from anywhere in the program and it will take you to the appropriate place in the manual where you'll find the answer you need.

Heredis, Full Version—$69 *(www.myheredis.com)*

The main benefit of Heredis is that it takes advantage of a Mac's integration capabilities to allow you to carry the list of people you are researching on your Palm handheld. You can also keep your events organized via iCal so that on a particular day your calendar will show you what was going on in an ancestor's life on that date. There is also a direct link to iPhoto for photographs stored in Heredis. The family tree charts are wonderful works of art that allow you to include pictures on the tree.

The program offers many charting features and capabilities, and you can even create a multimedia CD-ROM with your family information. It will also publish your information as a Web site, using intelligent media management that associates any kind of media with any type of data. The software can create a descendant family wheel and an innovative 3D tree as well. However, Heredis is relatively difficult to use and may be overwhelming to a beginning genealogist. Help features include e-mail support and a user guide, context-sensitive aids, and online documentation. Overall, the program is priced right and has powerful features, but it may be too much of a hassle for most users. There is also a standard version that can be downloaded for free.

iFAMILY for Tiger—$30 *(www.ifamilyfortiger.com)*

The format of this genealogy program is a two-paned window. The top part of the window displays a family chart that holds data for up to six generations (fig. 2-6). In the bottom part of the window you can highlight and edit information about any individual that you select from the family chart. There are twelve viewing and editing options available.

Table 2-2

Comparison of Popular Genealogy Programs for the Mac

	Reunion	Heredis	iFAMILY for Tiger	Family	Personal Ancestry File
Web site	leisterpro.com	myheredis.com	ifamilyfortiger.com	saltatory.com/ familyabout.html/	familysearch.org
Price	$99 full; $59 upgrade	$69 full; $49 upgrade	$29.95	$29.95	Free
Free demo	•	•		•	•
Download	•	•	•	•	•
Available on disk	•				•
Report and chart options	Descendant; pedigree; fan-style; timeline; up to 99 generations; graphic forms; book-style; cascading pedigree charts	Ascendant, descendant; no limit on generations; hour-glass; fan-style	Descendant; ancestor; pedigree; family group sheets		Ancestor; descendant; family histories; pedigree charts; family group records
Report formatting options	Color; font; font size; border; shadow; on-screen editing via drag-and-drop	Opens reports in Rich Text Format (RTF) in your word processor	Uses your word processor to print files		
Custom reports	•	•			
Import/ export GEDCOMs	•		•		•
Multimedia support	•	•		•	•

	Reunion	Heredis	iFAMILY for Tiger	Family	Personal Ancestry File
Multiple search options	•	•	•		•
Relationship calculator	•				•
Date calculator/ conversion	•	•			•
Supports source documenting	•	•	•		•
Web pages	•	•			•
Additional features	Mailing lists; birthday/ anniversary lists and reminders; Pod cards make information portable via an iPod; photo slideshows	Display of all information in a single screen; 3-D display of family tree; database merging; export files to Palm handhelds; create interactive CD-ROMs	Excellent handling of images in 50 different formats; Transcribe Function for transcribing old certificates and photos of tombstones	Storyteilling feature allows addition of "stories" to each individual; tight linking with iSight and iPhoto	
System requirements	OS X 10.3.9 or newer	OS X 10.1.3 or newer	OS X.10.4 and newer	OS X 10.3 or newer; iPhoto integration requires 10.4 or newer	OS X
Technical support	Phone; e-mail; online forums	E-mail; online FAQs; online updates and patches	Online forums and FAQs	Online documentation	Excellent support options; online guides and documents; e-mail; local support via LDS Family History Centers and user groups

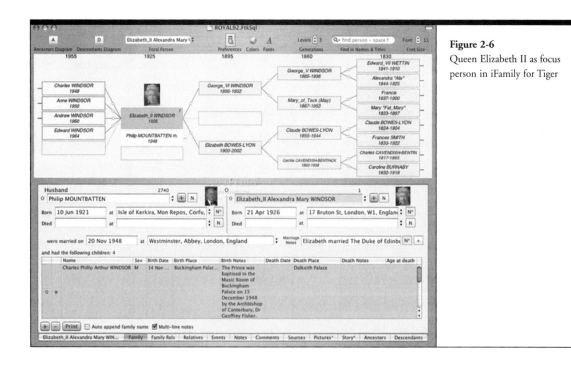

Figure 2-6

Queen Elizabeth II as focus person in iFamily for Tiger

New entries are created by clicking on one of the empty boxes in the family chart. If there are additional details you want to add, you can use the bottom part of the window to input information, photos from the iPhoto library, or data sources. Any information you enter is automatically saved, but if you use the family chart to enter your data, you have to hit the Return key to save it. iFamily has an excellent search tool that helps you to find anything in your database very easily, and results are generated from single letters to help you find individuals quickly. The simple interface makes the program appealing for beginning genealogists, but its data-entry quirks may be too troublesome for some users. On the other hand, many users have given the program glowing reviews because entering data via the two-paned window is so very simple. The program will not run on Mac OS versions before OS X 10.4 (Tiger).

Family—$29.95 *(saltatory.com/familyabout.html)*

Family is designed for OS X 10.3 and was created with a specific philosophy in mind: simplicity in genealogy. Family associations (fig. 2-7) are created by clicking and dragging, and you can easily add and rearrange people in the database. It is very easy to associate pictures and stories with individual people. There is tight integration with the built-in cameras in most newer Macs and PC laptops. Another option is to buy a camera that you add to your computer as you would any peripheral (such as those made by Logitech).

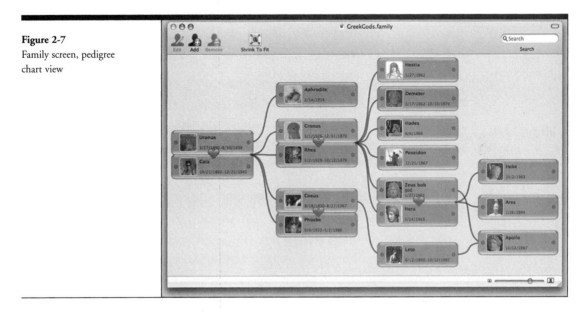

Figure 2-7
Family screen, pedigree chart view

A particularly innovative feature of Family is Story Telling. The program allows you to include an individual's story as well as any other information about them, complete with links and images. When organizing documents, you can associate them with the appropriate person in the Family Album file, which makes it easier to keep track of where they are.

Personal Ancestry File

The Personal Ancestry File for the Mac comes from FamilySearch.org. It has the same features as the PC version and is also available at no cost.

Genealogy Software Utilities

What's the difference between a program, an application, and a utility? According to the wizards at Webopedia (www.webopedia.com), an online encyclopedia dedicated to computer technology, computer software can be divided into two general categories: systems software, which includes operating systems like Windows Vista or Mac OS X, and applications software, also known as end-user programs, which include word processing software, spreadsheets, and genealogy software. Applications software cannot work without an operating system.

A program is an organized set of instructions that makes a computer do certain predetermined things; without programs, computers are useless. A software utility is a program that performs just a single or a very few specific tasks; for example, an operating system like Windows Vista or Mac OS X includes utilities that manage your printer or your Internet connection. Genealogy utilities offer supplements to your genealogy program by letting you perform unique and useful tasks, such as additional ways to organize your notes or letting you map areas mentioned in deeds.

Clooz for Windows XP—$39.95 *(www.clooz.com)*

Clooz is an electronic filing system that helps to search for and retrieve critical facts found along the road of a genealogy journey. It offers over a hundred templates for specific genealogy records, including U.S. federal census population schedules, birth, marriage, death, naturalization records, correspondence, passenger lists, and farm and city directories. Clooz can also import GEDCOM files and can be used, either by itself or together with a genealogy program, to help keep track of all paper and electronic documents that have been collected in your research. Information and sources added to Clooz can be saved directly into Legacy Family Tree 6.0.

DeedMapper for Windows XP and Vista—$99
(www.directlinesoftware.com/fact2.htm)

This is an impressive utility that can be used to analyze old grants, land patents, deeds, and claims. With this tool, you can print pictures of individual plots that are scaled to the United States Geological Survey topographic map scale (or any other scale), find genealogical relationships through records of land sales, end the confusion associated with people who have the same name by looking at their landholdings and transfers, or create a map of all the landholders in a region. You can purchase optional computer maps, which are available at various prices. These maps plot streams, roads, railroads, and public land sections, among other features, and let you plot your deeds and place them accurately on modern maps. You can also use your own scanned images in place of the optional maps, and deeds can be exported to Google Earth.

GEDclean for Windows 95 or higher—$9.95 download, $14.95 on CD with manual *(www.raynorshyn.com/gedclean)*

This useful piece of software might save you a lot of trouble! If you plan to share your genealogy information with other people via the GEDCOM format, this program will let you "clean" the personal information associated with any living relatives out of the GEDCOM, so it is not shared with strangers. The utility was the first of its kind and has been in use since 1996.

GenScribe for Mac—$12
(users.rcn.com/psherman/genscribe.html)

Here's a tool to help you plan and manage your genealogy research. It lets you create to-do lists, record data found via its standard text-entry fields and templates for U.S. censuses, manage linked subprojects, review research you've already done, keep track of page-by-page searches in materials that are not indexed, and assign file numbers to research items and print cover sheets that help you find hard copies of the research at a later time.

Bygones for PC or Mac—Free
(www.macgenealogy.org/bygones)

This is a genealogical note-keeping system in the form of a computer database. It lets you record notes on your computer as you perform your research. It also has databases that can create an index of information in the notes, keep track of correspondence, create timelines for your family lines, and create to-do lists for research tasks. You can also use it to enter information on important source materials, the locations where you've done research, spelling variations and Soundex codes for surnames, or scanned materials such as maps, photos, and other documents.

Looking Ahead

Now that you've considered a variety of tools to help you with your research, it's time to move on to the subject of organization. How will you impose some order on the notes you've taken and documents you've discovered? Even before a single fact is uncovered, you should have a plan in mind to organize what you learn. It will be much easier to start this task as you begin than it will be to go back and try to make order of scattered and varied tidbits as you begin to see that stack grow. We'll revisit the topic of genealogy forms too, since putting the right information into the right form will help you store your information and, more important, let you find it when you want it! We'll be doing a little more computer talk too, particularly about the need to back up your computer files so you don't lose the information you've put into your genealogy program. Without backups, you could lose all those incredible stories and clues you've collected about your ancestors. We also offer hints about how to develop a backup system that won't be too tedious to use.

Chapter 3

Keep Your Records Straight or Lose Your Way

A funny thing happened on the way to writing this chapter—we got disorganized! The Internet makes it easy to gather information, but it won't help you keep it in order. Part of the problem is the pack-rat syndrome, which is the curse of all researchers. We need to collect and keep every snippet of information, because, after all, we may need it someday! With all you can find online, before you know it, you can easily be buried in your own treasure.

Expert genealogists agree that organization is key, right from the start. We simply cannot overstate the value of a workable filing system. That said, even the experts acknowledge that no single system is right for everyone. Categorizing, it seems, is an individual sport. Philosophically, it's no less than making order out of chaos, and you need to do this in a way that makes sense to you. While we can suggest specific procedures and methods, such as using folders or notebooks, ultimately the decisions about how to proceed lie with you and with the information you find for your particular family. What is a budding genealogist to do?

We have explored the abundance of available recommendations and advice, and have come up with a two-part approach. One part involves getting your information into your genealogy software program and saving it. The other, and arguably the more critical part, addresses what to do with all the paper you'll accumulate as you research your family line.

In the Computer Lane

Computers are supposed to cut down on the need for paper documents. Right? That's the theory, but anyone who has used computers for any length of time knows that they tend to generate piles of paper and make existing piles grow even bigger! This happens for several reasons, including the fear that a computer crash will wipe out hours or, in the case of genealogy, years of work. And the media (CD or hard drive) used for storing digital information does not last forever.

How Long Will CDs and DVDs Last?

According to the Optical Storage Technology Association (www.osta.org/technology/cdqa13.htm), CDs will last 50 to 200 years. Other estimates suggest they will last only two to five years. Quite a range! The debate involves the materials and methods used to make a compact disk. It seems that factory-pressed CDs differ from recordable CDs (the ones that can be burned on a computer) in that data in a factory-pressed CD is actually pressed into the media and won't disappear unless the CD is physically damaged. Recordable CDs use dyes with properties that change when heated, and the different types of dye do not all have the same stability or life expectancy.

As you can see, there is no easy answer to the question of how long digital media will last. It depends on the type of dye used, the physical construction of the media, the conditions in which the media is stored (air quality, temperature, humidity, etc.), and the conditions at the time the media was manufactured. Quality can vary from batch to batch in the same media and brand. However, there is a consensus that recordable CDs (CD-Rs) can last several decades.

Other relevant factors to consider are the quality of the CD burner, the recording speed (fast burns are less stable than slower ones), and the methods used to label and store the media. The data on a CD is held in the dye layer that is on the side with the label, which can be scratched, destroying the data.

DVDs are another story. With DVDs, the data is held in a layer that is inside the media, which is made of a laminate of several layers. These layers can delaminate, or come apart, and destroy the data. Recordable DVDs generally fail from the outside in, however, so you can enhance their readability and discourage failure by recording on only 80 to 90 percent of the DVD's capacity. This leaves the outside edge, which is more prone to failure, blank. If it fails, you don't lose anything. While there are some differences in the construction of DVDs and CDs, the life expectancy of a recordable DVD is about the same as a recordable CD.

Labeling practices have a major impact on the life of optical media. Adhesive labels and the solvents in pen-type markers can penetrate the layers of the media and eventually destroy your data. You should follow archival guidelines NOT to label the CD or DVD. (If you must write on the media, put your labeling on the inner hub, which doesn't store any data, and use a pen that won't rub off.)

Also, CD+RW or DVD+RW erasable media are much less stable than media that can be recorded on only once (CD-R and DVD-R). Erasable media should not be used for any permanent recordings.

Paper or Plastic—What's the Difference?

It is important to remember that paper documents and digital materials are very different, and that often digital media are more fragile. The longevity of computer files is uncertain. For example, the machines and software used today to read your digital files may not be available in the future. Remember the floppy disk? When was the last time you used one of those? Computers today don't even have a drive to accommodate them!

According to the Library of Congress, the average life of a Web site is between forty-four and a hundred days! The Internet has made it possible for almost anyone to publish information, but much of what has been published in the past no longer exists. The Library of Congress cites the example of the national elections of 1994, which were the first in which the Web played a major part. Today, the Web sites involved are no longer available.

It is possible to put a paper document or a photograph into a box and trust that, barring fire, flood, or other disaster, the document or photograph may be read or seen in fifty or a hundred years. Digital materials, on the other hand, are iffy. If you don't take active steps to preserve your family records or digital photographs, it is likely that they will be lost.

The Library of Congress is committed to saving digital information that could be lost. With the help of a network of preservation partners—Web sites, digital images, digital television, and other digital materials—the Library of Congress has preserved over 66 terabytes of digital files as of July 2007. This is the text equivalent of about 66 million books. For more information about the sustainability of digital materials, visit the Sustainability of Digital Formats section of the Library of Congress Web site (www.digitalpreservation.gov/formats/intro/intro.shtml).

Checking That Rearview Mirror, or Backing Up

Now that you're totally panicked about the idea of losing all the information you've collected and put on CDs, DVDs, and your computer hard drive, we'd like to let you know that there's hope. It comes in the form of what is commonly known as backup.

The most important thing you can do for yourself and your descendants is to BACK UP all of your digital genealogy data. You've probably heard this advice many times from computer experts and nonexperts alike, but it bears repeating because it is so important! Isn't it better to spend a little time, boring and tedious as it may be, to make several copies of your information and store them in separate places so you'll always have your data, regardless of whatever disaster may strike? Just ask the folks who've experienced hurricanes in Florida or New Orleans. Most of us may never see that kind of disaster, but we are all likely, at one time or another, to experience a computer crash. It's not a question of *whether* your computer will crash, but *when*.

There are essentially two approaches you can take to backing up your data. One involves the program backup function within your genealogy software program. (Be sure to read the part of the manual or user's guide that tells you how to back up the information you've entered into the program.) The other is a complete system backup, which refers to copying everything on your computer onto a CD, DVD, or another disk drive (a second internal hard drive, an external, portable hard drive, or onto an Internet Web site shared-backup location).

Generally, your genealogy program will offer you an opportunity to back up a file on your computer when you shut it down. This kind of backup only takes a few minutes, and if the data is somehow damaged at a future time, the backup file will let you return to exactly where you were when you last backed up the data. If you don't see a command or button that lets you backup your files, look for a backup option in the File menu. It may be called Backup, Export, or Export GEDCOM file, depending on your program. Again, read the manual!

A complete system backup lets you make a physical copy of everything that is on your computer—all those old e-mails, Grandma's recipes, stuff you've downloaded from the Internet, along with all your operating system files and whatever else the computer needs to operate correctly. You can also choose to back up only the parts of your system that you specify at one particular time. For example, you could decide to back up all the data added since a certain date. Once you've told the system what you want to back up, it will record all the data onto a CD, DVD, or other disk drive.

You can buy relatively inexpensive external hard drives in several sizes to use for this purpose. The drives usually come with their own software. You just install the software according to the manufacturer's instructions and choose whether to have a complete system backup or an incremental backup, which will copy only the files that have been created or changed since the last backup. It's simple to set up an automatic full-system backup, and you must do it. You can lose data as a result of something as simple as a power failure or even an inadvertent mouse click. Having your backups on a portable hard drive means you can just take the drive with you if you have to leave your home or office in a hurry during an emergency. On a happier note, it also allows you to easily share your progress the next time you visit far-flung family!

Another backup option is to use a Web site that enables you to securely store your data online. Ancestry.com offers a backup option for your GEDCOMs, and sites like Mozy (www.mozy.com) will automatically perform backups for you. Mozy (fig. 3-1) lets you simply check boxes next to the files you want backed up and schedule the times you want the backups performed. The service does everything else, even encrypting your files on your computer for security before sending them to Mozy's storage data center. You have the option of restoring your files from multiple file versions. For example, you can choose to restore files you made up to thirty days in the past. The free version of Mozy gives you 2 GB of storage; a subscription version is available for a monthly fee of $4.95, for which the service backs up your entire computer system and imposes no limits on the size of data.

Figure 3-1
Mozy is a program that easily enables you to back up important files.

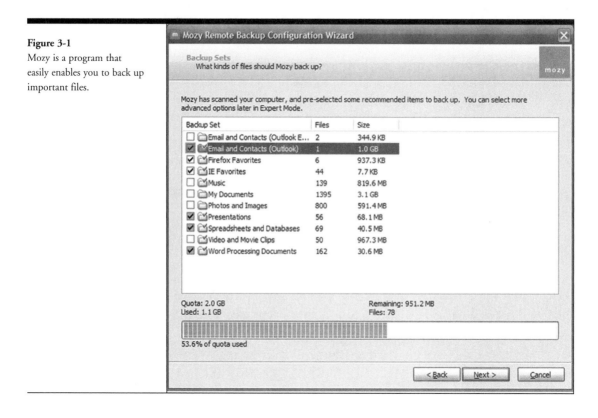

Another way to back up your genealogy information is to create a GEDCOM file of your program's databases and a ZIP file of photographs and scans you've made of documents. A ZIP file is in a compressed format so the data takes up less storage space. Attach these files to an e-mail message and send it to yourself. You can also burn these files to CDs and store them somewhere safe outside your home. Whatever system you choose, *back up your data now!* You'll thank yourself later.

There is no way to ensure that materials will be around forever, but the Internet has made it easier for information to be shared and stored in many different locations. Once you put stories of Uncle Charlie's life online—on a Web site, in a shared GEDCOM, or in an e-mail or forum post—you are no longer the only person who has that information. If your disk of Uncle Charlie's life story gets destroyed or lost, chances are you can find the information somewhere.

More and more public records are put online all the time, and millions of these records are also microfilmed and stored in multiple locations. You don't want to have to collect information again if you can help it, though, and that's where your paper records and computer backups come in.

You should also make an effort to keep your computer equipment updated. Technology changes quickly, and you don't want to be stuck with the 8-track cassette of computer storage! Try to keep up with equipment trends so you don't end up with data in a format that can no longer be accessed. Make sure all your software programs are also updated, so you can take advantage of any new features and improvements.

Along the Paper Trail

As you research your family, you'll collect an ever-increasing number of pedigree charts, family group sheets, census forms, birth and death certificates, and various other documents. There can sometimes be a large number of forms documenting a single individual, so when many people in a family line are being investigated, the number of forms can be overwhelming. This is when you need a filing system. Experienced genealogists generally use either a folder-based system or a notebook-based system.

The main advantage of a notebook system is that the pages are held in place. If you should drop a bunch of folders, you would face the tedious and upsetting task of refiling everything. Also, the information in a notebook is in the same place every time you consult it. It doesn't need to be removed and then carefully replaced.

The following systems are only some of those being used by actual researchers, and they are meant only as suggestions. Often, a combination of methods is helpful. Remember, any system you use needs to make sense to *you*.

The Four Files

One system devised by genealogy researchers over time combines proof files, surname files, portable files, and computer files. Proof files are the originals of all the documents you gather, such as birth and death certificates, photographs, copies of secondary sources, letters, marriage licenses, and so on. These papers should be kept in a safe place. Surname files are the working copies of the proof files, along with notes about clues to follow. Portable files hold copies of the master information on all of your ancestors, including copies of family group sheets and pedigree charts. Computer files are stored digitally and include detailed information and source citations about everyone you are researching.

You should start with a pedigree chart that shows all of your known ancestors. It is also recommended that you use the so-called Ahnentafel system of numbering.

Ah, Ahnentafel!

Ahnentafel is a combination of two German words: *ahnen*, "ancestor," and *tafel*, "table." So an Ahnentafel chart is an "ancestor table." This numbering system makes it easy to organize a pedigree chart and communicate the chart's information to others.

A standard pedigree chart assigns each person a number. The Ahnentafel numbers are exactly the same as those in a pedigree chart, but they are presented in a more condensed way, as a list. They are especially useful when sharing information with another researcher, since they show gaps in information clearly, as numbers that have not been assigned. This leaves blank lines in the list. Below is an example of an Ahnentafel chart:

1. first individual (you or your children as a group)
2. father
3. mother
4. father's father
5. father's mother
6. mother's father
7. mother's mother

8. father's father's father

9. father's father's mother

10. father's mother's father

11. father's mother's mother

12. mother's father's father

13. mother's father's mother

14. mother's mother's father

15. mother's mother's mother

16–31. great-great-grandparents

32–63. great-great-great-grandparents

(For an example using President George W. Bush, see www.wargs.com/political/bush.html)

This system allows you to see the relationship of any person on the chart to you. You (or your children, if you choose that method) are always Number 1. Each new generation entered has twice the number of ancestors as the previous generation, so by the tenth generation you have information on over 1,000 ancestors! Every father (male) on the chart has an even number and every mother (female) on the chart has an odd number (her husband's number plus one).

Traditionally, an Ahnentafel chart includes a person's full name and the dates and places of various events, such as birth, death, or marriage, if they are known. The chart lists only ancestors in your direct line. Most genealogy software programs will create Ahnentafel charts for you.

After you've filled out the pedigree chart and done your numbering, you can begin the work of organizing your information. In your proof files, it's important to have a system that will identify every family group, so you can keep the information separate, but still accessible. Files can be kept by surname, with two copies of the proof records for each wife. This is so one copy can be kept with the wife's father's family, and one with the husband. When files get too large, you can then separate them by generation, labeling each file with the identification numbers (Ahnentafel numbers) of the parents.

The surname files are the working files you'll use when researching a particular surname. These files should include as much of the following information as you have for each individual: an ancestral timeline so you can see if the generations overlap appropriately, pedigree charts for the surname, a correspondence log, and copies of any letters you've sent or received. Starting with the most recent generation in the front of the file, include a family group sheet with enough pages to comprise all the children, a research record on which you've recorded or checked off information that you've found so far, copies of the proof file information, and generation dividers.

The portable files allow you to take along some information when you visit a research site to ensure that the family you've found is really the one you are looking for. These files should include pedigree charts, a location directory so you can check whether you have ancestors in a particular geographical area, an alphabetical list of surnames you're interested in, family group sheets, and other notes you've made that may be of use. The family group sheets should include the basic information about birth, marriage, death, and burial with dates and places for each of these events. All of this should be cross-referenced with the surnames of both the husband and the wife.

Computer files are kept in your genealogy software program, of course, but they also include other bits and pieces you may have downloaded from Web sites, or documents that you've scanned for future reference. Computer files should not replace the paper files, but offer a way to share and organize the information you've collected.

It's important that you establish a sequence for handling any new information. For example, you can update the portable file first and then enter the data in your computer file. After that, you update the surname file, and finally, place the appropriate documents and records in the proof file. If you create such a sequence and follow it consistently, you'll have all of your records updated in a timely manner and prevent missing important steps along the way.

How Eventful!

An alternative to organizing your genealogy information by surname is to organize it by event. Proponents of this method say it allows an event to take priority over the people who are associated with it. This eliminates duplication and redundancy in the files. When using such a system, you'll need to number every one of your documents and create a cross-referenced index to the names of individuals contained in the documents.

If you want to try this system, you must first sort all your genealogy documents by type of event: all birth records in one stack, all marriage records in another, and so on. Then you give each document a unique number based on the event type. For example, your records might be labeled Birth 001, Marriage 001, and Death 001. Never write on the documents themselves, especially if they are originals. Instead, buy top-loading, plastic sheet protectors and place the labels on the outside top corner. The documents can then be stored in binders by type.

Follow the Yellow (and Blue and Red and Purple) Brick Road

A system shown to us by Kenny Dorris and Louisa Ryan at our local LDS Family History Center relies on color coding to help you follow a family line back through the generations. It is based on the (free) Personal Ancestral File (PAF) software program from FamilySearch, and uses four colors on a pedigree chart to show the relationships between people and to trace direct ancestral lines.

We talked with Kenny and Louisa about organizing our genealogy information because we knew they had lots of experience. They've both been working on their genealogies for over 30 years. When we asked what they would tell someone just starting out in genealogy research, Kenny said the first thing to do was to get "The Box." We were puzzled.

"The Box?"

"Yes, you know. The Box, where everyone puts all of his or her genealogy records."

Oh, THAT box. It was good to know that even experts have a collection of unorganized papers in a box somewhere! In addition to The Box, you'll need a two-inch three-ring binder notebook with a vinyl cover, a set of sheet protectors that have five index tabs (for five generations), a lot of plastic protector sheets, and four markers: blue, red, purple, and yellow.

Once you have the required materials, fill out a pedigree sheet with as much information as you know, starting with yourself in position Number 1. All the ancestors on your father's side are represented by the blue lines, while all those on your mother's side are red lines. The lineage of your father's mother is represented by purple, while that of your mother's mother is yellow. The color coding makes it easy to see how the family lines go back through time. This is a simple visual solution to a complicated information problem. All the information for five generations can be easily categorized using the Book One system described below.

Making Book One

According to the genealogy experts at FamilySearch, you should begin your family recordkeeping by creating what is known as Book One. In this book, you will place printed reports about yourself, your family, your descendants, and the first four generations of your ancestors and your spouse's ancestors. The book is an organized way to save pedigree charts and family group records for future generations. Book One should include only information about the ancestors named on a five-generation pedigree chart. Earlier generations can be put into however many separate books you'll need, starting with the sixth generation.

The essential materials to be included in Book One are two five-generation pedigree charts, one for you and one for your spouse; a family group sheet for your family that shows you and your spouse as parents, as well as the names of your children; a family group sheet for each one of your married children, if any; a family group sheet for each one of your married grandchildren, if any; and a family group sheet for any married great-grandchildren.

The tab categories provided in this system are: Our Family, Our Descendants, [the husband's] Ancestors, [the wife's] Ancestors, and Miscellaneous. Your pedigree chart should be put in a sheet protector and placed behind the tab that has your name on it. Your spouse's pedigree chart should be put in the first sheet protector behind the tab with his or her name on it.

The family group record for your family goes behind the Our Family tab and the family group records for married children go behind the Our Descendants tab. Records for married grandchildren should be placed behind their parent's family group record in order of their birth. Records for any married great-grandchildren should be behind the family group sheet of their parents.

A family group sheet should also be filled out for each of the ancestor couples shown on the five-generation pedigree sheet. These should be put into the binder in the order they are shown on the chart: parents, grand-parents, great-grandparents, and great-great-grandparents. Then, do the same for your spouse's ancestors.

To make these people come alive, you might also include life sketches, or short biographies. A life sketch should be only one page long, and lim-ited to no more than two people as the subject (for example the subject and one other person). Include pictures, if possible. You can write a life sketch for each of the couples on the pedigree chart. You can also include other genealogical charts in Book One as needed.

The FamilySearch experts suggest that you take Book One with you to family reunions and other family events, where it may spark the inter-est of other family members who may be able to fill in informational gaps in your genealogy. Creating Book One imposes some order on your family history records, and the finished book provides a reference point in your research. Combined with the color coding, this system will allow you to find your information more easily.

Picking Up Roadside "Litter"

A funny thing can happen with genealogy information. Documents that you've looked at a million times can suddenly provide new clues! One of the people interviewed for this book, Jan Jero of Family Tree Growers, is a self-described "saver." She writes inspirations for future research and promising clues to follow on little scraps of paper.

She says this pays off occasionally, such as the time she reviewed a random note left by her mother. The note read, "Daddy was born in Willa Cather's house N.W. of Red Cloud." This led Jan to research the life of author Willa Cather and to "read more of Willa's writing than I ever knew existed." She discovered that the Cathers did have a house (farm) located 14 miles northwest of Red Cloud, Nebraska. The family sold the farm, "stock and all," and moved into town in 1884. Jan knew her grandfather had been born in 1888, so she believes it is possible that his parents bought the Cather farm in 1884. But because she is a good researcher, she's still looking for land records or other evidence that will prove this actually happened. If she hadn't saved and reread that little scrap of paper, this promising lead would have been lost.

Jan is also lucky enough to have a considerable number of family heirlooms, including several albums of tintypes. When looking through an album that she had examined many times before, bemoaning the fact that none of the people pictured were identified, a calling card fell out of the book. On the card was a name Jan recognized as one that her mother had mentioned. While Jan didn't know the exact relationship of this person to her family, a few searches at Ancestry.com showed her that the woman named on the calling card was her mother's cousin, on Jan's grandmother's side.

Jan continued searching and found the woman had married a "Payne." She also found the record of the husband Payne's death in Nebraska and discovered the woman had moved to Washington, D.C., to join his family after he died. The next Payne connection Jan located concerned a man who had an "encounter" with a young George Washington before he became our first president, and some additional investigation turned up a screenplay that offered an account of Payne's argument—and subsequent physical altercation—with Washington over an upcoming election. (You can read the screenplay at Sanderson Beck's Web site: san.beck.org/WASH4-Virginia.html).

These random clues and the interesting finds that result, illustrate how you just never know what note, heirloom, or random scrap of paper will yield important information. But you need to be able to store information and find it again to make use of it!

Jan's personal filing system begins with a 1.5- to 2-inch, three-ring binder. She likes this size because "it doesn't weigh a ton when full." She places her family group sheets in front, and then follows them with a census backup and any miscellaneous records (obituaries, marriage records, burial records, draft cards, etc.) that provide evidence for the information that's on the family group sheet. When a binder is nearly full, Jan looks for a good place to split it off, starting a new binder for that branch of the family. She advises leaving some space in each binder so you can include future finds. Jan also has several miscellaneous binders. One holds information about possible family connections that haven't been proven yet, and another contains family narratives that she writes when she has enough information about a family branch to do so.

The main Web sites Jan uses are RootsWeb, FamilySearch, and Ancestry. She's also found that the Web site of the McMillan Memorial Library in Wisconsin Rapids, Wisconsin, and its Ask McMillan service (e-mail: askmcm@scls.lib.wi.us) can be of great use in getting information about burial sites, marriages, causes of death, and so on. Other Web sites she uses regularly include Civil War Soldiers and Sailors System (www.civilwar.nps.gov/cwss) and Genealogy Books (www.genealogy-books.com/index.html).

Chart Your Course

Now you have a general idea about how to handle your paper documents, but what documents are we talking about? We've mentioned the family group sheets and pedigree records, which are the mainstays of your genealogical adventure, but there are a number of other useful forms and charts that can also help you bring order to chaos. Many of these forms can be downloaded for free. Forms and charts are offered in several formats, including plain text (TXT), Microsoft Word (DOC), Adobe Acrobat (PDF), and Microsoft Excel spreadsheets (XLS). One interesting example, and an extremely useful chart, is the relationship chart shown in figure 3-2. This illustrates the "cousin" relationship between two people. How often have you heard "second cousin once removed" and wondered just how that worked? This chart will make it all clear!

Common Ancestor	Child	Grandchild	G-grandchild	G-g-grandchild
Child	Sister or Brother	Nephew or Niece	Grand-nephew or niece	G-grand-nephew or niece
Grandchild	Nephew or Niece	First cousin	First cousin once removed	First cousin twice removed
G-grandchild	Grand-nephew or niece	First cousin once removed	Second cousin	Second cousin once removed
G-g-grandchild	G-grand-nephew or niece	First cousin twice removed	Second cousin once removed	Third cousin

Figure 3-2
This is an example of the kind of useful relationship chart you can download from the Internet at no charge

Ancestral Chart

The names of individuals from whom you directly descended are recorded on an ancestral chart. These are likely the people you want to include when you're putting together a complete family unit in your records. The ancestor chart is a quick reference for monitoring the progress you're making with these family lines and the tasks that you've yet to complete to reach your goal.

Research Log

You may find it useful to keep a research log that lets you record every document source you've searched. It acts as a reminder of the records you've already looked at, as well as telling you where you've found specific information in case you want to revisit that source.

Research Extract Sheet

This is most often used to provide a summary of the information that you find at a repository but are unable to photocopy. You can also use the sheet when you don't have a hard copy of a document, but have pertinent information, and for items such as deeds in which it may be difficult to find certain information quickly.

Census Extraction Form

These forms provide an organized way to copy and file census information. They are available for every census year from 1790 to 1930 at Ancestry.com (www.ancestry.com/trees/charts/census.aspx). You'll also find forms for the 1890 Veteran's Schedule, the 1850 and 1860 Slave Schedules, and the Canadian and United Kingdom census records on the site.

Probate Record Checklist

Some researchers use this checklist to keep track of the microfilm, book, and page numbers of where they have found probate information, including the name of the person who died, where he or she lived, and the names of any people mentioned in the probate record. The checklist also notes the relationship between the deceased individual and the others mentioned in the record, and whether or not these people received any property (and the type of property) from the deceased.

Research Notes

It's a good idea to record all the information about a single family or sur-name on a separate piece of paper. Putting notes about two families on the same sheet will only be confusing later on. So how do you file the notes if they pertain to several different families? Take the information from the notes and put any new or different facts on the family group sheets and pedigree charts. Remember to record the source of the infor-mation on the family group sheet. Make photocopies of the notes and other documents instead of retyping them. Every time a piece of data is recopied by hand, the chance of mistakes multiplies, which is why you should always keep your original notes. Figure 3-3 shows an example of a research checklist that can help you keep track of what you're doing.

Research Checklist

Name:_____

Birth _____
Marriage _____
Death _____

Birth Record:

Baptism _____
Bible _____
Birth Certificate _____
Delayed Birth Certificate_____

Death Records:

Death Certificate _____
Mortuary_____
Cemetery_____
Gravestone _____
Obituary _____
Newspaper _____

Probate Record:

Will _____
Inventory list_____
Estate Sales _____
Guardianship _____

Military Records:

Branch of service _____
Dates of enlistment _____
Wars fought _____
Veterans pension _____
Widows pension _____

US Census Record:

1790 _____
1800 _____
1810 _____
1820 _____
1830 _____
1840 _____
1850 _____
1860 _____
1870 _____
1880 _____
1890 _____
1900 _____
1910 _____
1920 _____
1930 _____

State & County Census Record:

_____
_____
_____

Mortality Schedule::

_____
_____

Land Records:

Deeds & Abstracts _____
Tax lists _____
Land grants _____

Miscellaneous Records:

Occupations _____
Pension records _____
Organizations _____
Voting records _____
Passenger lists _____
Immigration _____

Figure 3-3

Here's an example of a research checklist for helping you stay on track.

Correspondence File

Another very useful file is a correspondence file. In this file, you keep copies of any letters you write regarding your genealogy research and any replies to this correspondence. When you receive a reply, attach it to the copy of your letter and file it in the relevant family folder or notebook. Correspondence should be filed by date, with the oldest letters at the front of the file, followed by subsequent letters in chronological order. Keeping the correspondence file in this order allows you to easily access your original, see whether you've received an answer, and make decisions about whether to follow up on the correspondence or not. You can also keep a log or record of all the letters you send.

Free at Last

Here are a few Web sites that provide a variety of useful and free genealogy forms. You should also check out Cyndi's List (www.cyndislist.com) and Ancestry.com for additional free forms.

Family Tree Magazine's Downloadable Forms
(www.familytreemagazine.com/freeforms/)

This site offers many kinds of forms in PDF and TXT formats.

Bailey's Free Genealogy Forms
(www.cs.williams.edu/~bailey/genealogy)

The forms here are available in PDF format and include a family record sheet, pedigree chart, two different types of timelines, research log sheet, correspondence log sheet, cemetery information sheet, and a rather interesting family relationship chart in the form of "family graph paper."

Free Genealogy Forms
(www.free-genealogy-forms.com)

This is an especially useful site because it offers forms relevant to countries outside the United States. It includes U.S. census forms, British census forms, Canadian census forms, Irish census forms, Scottish census forms, general research forms, special state censuses, and vital records request forms.

Rest Stop

Experienced genealogists have developed their own unique ways to handle data. You can either follow their lead or blaze your own trail. The task of gathering family information really has no end. If you're doing it right, you'll be doing it all your life.

Encourage your children and other family members to get interested in genealogy so that they will want to preserve and continue your hard work. Share your information with people who will respect it. Use high-quality paper for your records and always back up your computer files. Make copies of valuable original documents and photographs and store the originals using archival methods. Keep multiple copies of information in several different places, so your chances of losing important data are minimized. Most of all, don't wait! Get your family information recorded now before it's lost forever. Then, back up your systems before disaster strikes.

Looking Ahead

In Chapter 4, we take a closer look at the kinds of records you will find as you research your family. The most fundamental records for a genealogist are the census records. We examine some of the elements that make up a census search and note some of the quirkier features of census data. We also discuss other kinds of records that can help you track down those elusive ancestors, such as state and local land deeds, marriage certificates, and military records. We take a look at ship manifests, maps, gazetteers, and other geographic aids and even explore some of the more off-the-wall records that may offer surprising clues.

Chapter 4

Understanding the Records

O nce you've decided how to organize your documents, it's time to go get some good ones! But be forewarned, there are many, many records available on the Internet, and as interest in genealogy grows, the number of Web sites offering previously inaccessible information only increases. We'll start with Ancestry.com, because it boasts the most comprehensive collection of U.S. federal census records. When we made our first steps into the wilds of genealogy research, we thought it would be a simple matter of looking up a name in the census, writing down the birth and death dates, and entering that data into our fabulous genealogy software. However, once we looked at actual census forms online, we quickly realized that there is no such thing as a simple search. The early censuses each had their own format and included different questions. The information was subject to the foibles of the census takers, and the "truth" of the information depends on who provided it. We examine some of these issues in detail in this chapter.

In addition to the census records, there are many other records available online that can help you fill in gaps in your research. Land records, vital records (birth, death, and marriage documents), and ship manifests are among the sources available for finding ancestors who immigrated to the U.S. and melted into the pot. We go beyond those records to discuss more obscure sources, such as family deeds and online family Bibles. So let's go find some cool stuff!

Making Sense of the Census

The U.S. federal government has conducted a census, or enumeration of the population, every ten years since 1790. You can research the census records for 1790 through 1930. But not all the information gathered in the census is complete. The 1930 census is the most recent one that you can actually search, because, by law, there is a seventy-two-year hold on census information. Genealogists are eagerly awaiting the release of the 1940 census in 2012. Census records are the Mother of All Genealogy Records for the United States. But not all censuses provide the same information.

Censuses for 1790 Through 1840

The first census was performed because it had been mandated by the U.S. Constitution and made law by President George Washington. It was meant as a simple count of the inhabitants of the United States, but did not include slaves or "untaxed" Native Americans. Because the Revolutionary War was still so present in the minds of our leaders, one of the purposes of the count was to determine the number of men available for military service. Sadly, a large part of the 1790 census was destroyed during the War of 1812.

That first census documented about 3.9 million Americans. The first census-takers provided their own paper for recording the information. They turned over the information they collected to the government on pieces of paper ranging in size from four inches to three feet!

The census records from 1790 through 1840 don't have a lot of information that is of use to genealogists, since the only name included was for the head of the household. Other family members were represented in specific age groups by sex. Still, consulting these early censuses is helpful because they provide the number of children in a family and give an idea about their ages in that year. The records also provide information about where the family lived, so you can narrow your research to focus on a particular geographic area.

Census of 1850

The 1850 census was the first one to list the name of every person in a household, along with each person's sex, age, "color," occupation, and birthplace. Birthplace was denoted by state, territory, or foreign country.

It also gave the value of any owned real estate although usually just for the head of the household.

Census of 1860

The 1860 census was basically the same as that of 1850, but it included a new question about the value of personal property in addition to the question about real estate. There were special schedules for slave inhabitants that were recorded in the southern states. These named the slave owner only and indicated whether a slave was black or mulatto. The sex and age of the slave were also recorded. This census also had a mortality schedule that listed information about people who died during the previous twelve months. Farms and plantations that produced at least $100 per year were listed in an agricultural schedule.

Are Your Answers on a Slave Schedule?

The censuses taken in 1850 and 1860 include slave schedules. In the federal census, the term *schedule* refers to the type of questionnaire(s) used in that census year. Figure 4-1 shows a blank slave schedule form for 1860. In these years, each slave was counted individually, but full names were not often recorded. The slave schedules are organized according to the owner's name, and list the age, sex, and race of each person in the household. Figure 4-2 shows a portion of the 1860 slave schedule for Alachua, Florida. Even without names, you can find clues for identifying ancestors by comparing ages and races of people in the households listed in the slave schedule.

Census of 1870

The 1870 census recorded the month of birth for children born during the census year, with the age given as a fraction (1/12 for a one-month-old baby, for example). It also provided the month of marriage for all marriages occurring in 1870. The 1870 census listed the state or territory in which an individual was born, or the country for those who were foreign-born. For those born in Germany, the census lists the province as well. Additionally, there was a space to indicate whether an individual's

Figure 4-1

Blank 1860 slave schedule form

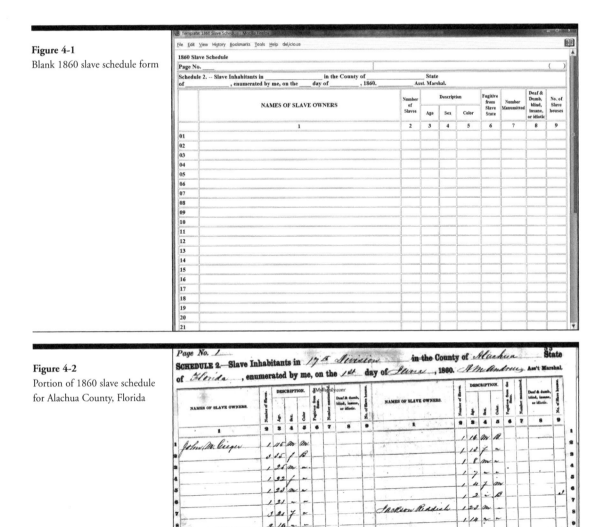

Figure 4-2

Portion of 1860 slave schedule for Alachua County, Florida

father or mother had been born in a foreign country, but the name of their birthplace was not recorded.

Census of 1880

The 1880 census was the first to add two pieces of information that are very important to genealogists. One was the relationship of each person in the household to the head of that household. The other was the state or country of birth for both the father and mother of every person listed in the census. Individuals who were born or who died after June 1, 1880, were not included in the count.

In this year, census takers were required to pass a written test and women were allowed to become census takers.

The "Lost" Census—1890

The 1890 census is the bane of all genealogy researchers because it was almost completely destroyed by fire in 1921. Often, 1890 is where you can begin to lose the threads of some of your family lines. Individuals listed in the 1880 census have frequently "disappeared" by the 1900 census, and it's a challenge to track them down. The 1890 census is probably one of the toughest obstacles, or brick walls, as they are called by genealogists, to overcome in a genealogy search. But some of the original information survives. The National Archives and Records Administration (NARA) and the Allen County Library in Fort Wayne, Indiana, have partnered to reconstruct the data from other sources. A bundle of Illinois census forms from 1890 was found in 1942, and in 1953 other portions of the census were discovered. These documents include some 6,000 names. (For further details on these discoveries, visit the National Archives 1890 census Web page at www.archives.gov/genealogy/census/1890/1890.html.)

Up in Smoke

According to various accounts from the time, a small fire started in a carpentry shop in the basement of the Commerce Building in Washington, D.C., on the afternoon of January 10, 1921. Before being noticed, the fire spread to a neighboring hallway and moved toward the opposite end of the building. Because of space limitations, the original documents from the 1890 federal census were stacked in an area outside of the building's fireproof vault. The documents were piled on rows of shelving made of pinewood. The census records, thirty years old by that time, were very dry, and they burned rapidly. The firefighters met with such heavy smoke when they arrived that it was difficult to determine the fire's origin. Hoses poured water into the entire basement area through broken windows and through holes chopped into the floor above. It took three hours to get the fire under control, and by then the basement was flooded to a depth of several feet. The 1890 federal census records were severely damaged from both the fire and the water used to extinguish it. The census included approximately 62 million entries, and less than 1 percent of these records survived.

The collection of replacement data created by NARA, and the Allen County Library includes fragments of the original census, special veterans' schedules, a number of Native American tribe censuses for years close to 1890, state censuses for 1885 or 1895, city and county directories, alumni directories, and voter registrations. You can find this information at Ancestry.com in a collection that has been characterized as the "first definitive online substitute for the missing census." It includes over 20 million records, and more will be added as they become available.

Census of 1900

The 1900 census includes each individual's month and year of birth and the number of years each couple had been married. It lists the number of children a woman had ever had residing with her in the home and the number still living in 1900. This census also stated whether a family owned or rented its residence, if that residence was a house or a farm, and whether there was a mortgage on the property. For individuals born in other countries, the 1900 census gave the year of immigration and whether the individual was naturalized.

Census of 1910

The 1910 census offers information similar to the 1900 census, with the addition of information about whether a marriage was a first marriage, and if not, what number it was. This census also listed the language an individual spoke, his or her employment status, and whether the men in the household had served in the Union or Confederate army or navy.

Census of 1920

The 1920 census was very similar to that of 1910, but it did not include questions about employment, service during the Civil War, number of children born, or the length of time a couple had been married. This census had several new questions, however. These covered the year of naturalization, the individual's original language, and the native language of the individual's mother and father. The 1920 census was also indexed for each state and territory.

Census of 1930

One of the most interesting things about the 1930 census is that it asked whether or not a household owned a radio. It also included new questions about the individual's age at the time of his or her first marriage, whether a man was a war veteran and which war he fought in, the value of a home owned by an individual or the amount of rent a family or individual paid each month. The 1930 census did not ask about the year of naturalization. To facilitate finding names in the census, Soundex indexes, which use a code to address the issue of different name spellings, were created in 1930 by the U.S. Works Progress Administration (WPA) for names in twelve southern states.

Tips for Census Researchers

There are several things you should keep in mind when searching federal censuses. First, decide which of the censuses apply to the birth and/or death dates you have for the individual you are researching. It is usually best to begin with the 1930 census and work backward. Get as much geographical information as you can, noting the city, county, and state associated with your family member. Counties are especially important because many of our ancestors lived in rural areas identified chiefly by county. Always consider different spellings of the name you are researching. It's amazing how many variations of a name you will find in the census records. Use the Soundex system to help you with this (page 75).

You should also review all the schedules included in a particular census. For example, the 1850 census has five different places where names are recorded: the schedule for the free population; the slave schedule, which lists the names of slave owners or those of overseers, if the owners were absent; and separate schedules for industry, agriculture, and mortality.

Another very important thing to remember is that you will often be working with indexes of information rather than the information itself. Data recorded in an index can be wrong. Always check the actual record.

For example, look at the actual census form that includes your ancestor's name. Copy the information you find in the census on an extraction form. These forms provide a clean slate on which to record the often hard-to-read information, making it easier to file the information later. Ancestry.com has extraction forms designed specifically for each census (www.ancestry.com/trees/charts/census.aspx).

Sometimes the Census Seems Senseless

There's no easy way to say this: Sometimes what you'll find in a census seems like nonsense. What's with the handwriting? And why does it say that your great-grandfather came from Germany when you know he came from Sweden? How can the birth date of your grandmother indicate that she was nine years old when she had your mother? Why has your great-uncle disappeared from the 1880 census when you know he lived his entire life in the same place? This is just the nature of census research. Let's examine some of these issues individually.

Census Takers

The people hired as census takers, or enumerators, were not always well educated or even suited to the task. They did have to know how to read and write, and they were frequently natives of the area they were assigned to cover. But often they didn't follow instructions about how to fill out the census form. Some used odd abbreviations, and they tended to write down names as they heard them, without asking for a correct spelling. Many were poor spellers and had terrible handwriting. Additionally, census takers weren't required to follow a particular route, but only to cover the whole territory assigned to them. This means that neighbors may be listed several pages apart in the census, and if an enumerator missed a page on the form for some reason, the numbers referring to a family member or dwelling can be out of order. Some even made up information that they didn't have!

Handwriting, Terrible and Stylish

Handwriting styles change over time. Just look at the Declaration of Independence and compare the handwriting to your own. Sometimes, the most difficult and frustrating part of dealing with the census forms is trying to read the handwriting. Census takers did not think that researchers would be consulting these forms years later; they were just counting the people in their districts and reporting their findings to the government.

There are some things you can look out for when reading census forms from the Colonial and Victorian periods. The first *s* in a pair frequently looks like a backward lowercase *f*. Sometimes double letters were written with a tilde (~) above them to indicate their doubling. Abbreviations of names typically used the first three or four letters of the name, plus the last letter in superscript (Marg^t). First letters of names were not always capitalized, and sometimes initials were recorded as given names. Census takers also used flourishes and swirls in their handwriting that changed the appearance of a letter or an entire word.

Sometimes the handwritten forms were posted in public places so people could review them to ensure their accuracy, but they might also be rewritten several times (to put names in alphabetical order, for example). Every time they were copied, there was the chance that mistakes could creep in.

The Treasure Maps Web site has a page devoted to the quirks of old handwriting (amberskyline.com/treasuremaps/oldhand.html). Here you'll find examples of abbreviations, that strange *f* letter that often appears in early documents, and common abbreviations used for names, locations, and occupations. Many of our ancestors didn't know how to write and would make a mark for their names. This mark was not always the *X* as depicted in old movies, but a distinctive sign that was unique to the individual. Treasure Maps has examples of some of these marks. Ancestry.com also provides examples of handwriting to help you decipher handwriting found on census forms.

Is That Right or Wright or Reit? Let's Check Soundex

Something else to consider when researching census records is the way in which names are spelled. The spelling of a surname can change significantly over time. And while it may seem like a simple thing for a census taker to write a person's name correctly in the appropriate space, this is not the case. Enumerators typically wrote names down phonetically. In many cases, particularly in areas where many immigrants settled, which resulted in mistakes. National and regional dialects also significantly impacted a name's phonetic spelling.

To help overcome this problem, researchers use the Soundex system. Soundex encodes surnames based on how they sound rather than how they are spelled. Names like Smith and Smyth have the same code and are indexed together. When names sound the same but have different spellings, there are different Soundex codes based on the variation of the name's first letter.

Soundex is a phonetic index, not an alphabetical one. With Soundex, a name is always described as a code consisting of a letter and three numbers. The letter used in the code is the first letter of the surname. Numbers are assigned to other letters according to an established Soundex guide. Zeros are added to fill out the four characters when necessary. Some consonants (including *w*) and the vowels (a, e, i, o, u) are ignored unless they are the first letter of a surname.

The system is designed to make it easier for researchers to find a surname even if it has been spelled differently over time. Soundex was first applied in 1935 to the 1880 census in connection with the newly created Social Security program, since it was necessary to connect a specific birth date to the right individual to determine eligibility for benefits. You can find more information about the history of Soundex at the National Archives (www.archives.gov/genealogy/census/soundex.html). And there is a surname-to-Soundex calculator available at RootsWeb (searches. rootsweb.com/cgi-bin/Genea/soundex.sh). You can just enter the surname you want converted, and the calculator does the rest. For example, the Soundex code for Robinson is R152.

It's Vital!

Vital records—birth, marriage, and death records—are the bedrock of any genealogy research. Some states and territories conducted their own censuses in certain years. These provide a good resource, because different questions were asked than those found in the federal census. They can also help you confirm information found in a federal census and fill in gaps, such as those created by the loss of the 1890 federal census records.

State Censuses

State censuses were frequently conducted in the years between the federal censuses. State census years usually end in "5," such as 1885, 1895, 1905, and so on. A state conducted its own census for several reasons; for example, to determine its military strength or the financial condition of specific communities. The information in a state census varies with the reason the state performed the count. For example, state census information gathered by Alabama can be found in the Alabama Department of Archives and History for 1820, 1850, 1855, and 1866. Information from the state census of 1820 is available for only eight counties and includes the name of the head of the household, the number of free white males and females in the household and their ages, the number of slaves, and the number of "free persons of color" in various age categories. The 1866 census, however, includes the head-of-the-household's name for African Americans as well as whites, and the number of females and males in different age categories.

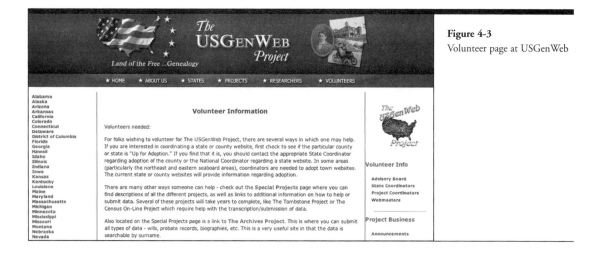

Figure 4-3
Volunteer page at USGenWeb

You can find these records at the Web sites of some state libraries and state archives and through your local LDS Family History Center. You can also search a number of state censuses at Ancestry.com where information is regularly amended. So if you don't find what you need right away, keep checking the site to see if it's been added.

County and State Records via USGenWeb

The county is the place to be when looking for local information about your family tree, and one of the very best county-level genealogy resources is USGenWeb (www.usgenweb.com). USGenWeb was created by volunteers who are passionate about their counties, towns, and neighborhoods (fig. 4-3). Its goal is to provide free Web sites containing genealogical information for every county and state in the United States.

The organization also sponsors other projects at the national level, including USGenWeb Kidz Project, designed to encourage children to find out about their family history; the USGenWeb Family Group Sheet Project, which helps researchers find family lines through family group sheets available online; and the USGenWeb Digital Library (Archives), which is working to provide transcriptions of public domain records on the Internet.

At USGenWeb's site, you can click the name of a state and get a list of available state and county resources. Because each county is "adopted" by an individual, and because there are different types of records available for each county, the design and content of each county site is unique.

For example, the Web site for Cheshire County, New Hampshire, offers a look at penny postcards of the area dating from 1898 to the present (www.rootsweb.com/~usgenweb/special/ppcs/types.html). The site also has the 1790 federal census for the county (http://ftp.rootsweb.com/pub/usgenweb/nh/cheshire/census/1790/pg83.txt), and Cheshire county biographies, arranged alphabetically by surname. Tennessee's USGenWeb site offers links to the Cherokee Genealogical Message Board (www.tngenweb.org/tnfirst/webbbs/cheroqueries/index.cgi), a mailing list for People of Color, South (www.tngenweb.org/tncolor), and early Tennessee detail maps (www.tngenweb.org/maps/tndetail.htm). The Texas GenWeb is one of the best. If you have ancestors who lived in Texas during the war with Mexico and statehood formation, you are very lucky! You're bound to find comprehensive information about these individuals and the times in which they lived.

Excavating Land Records

Deeds are documents that record land ownership and any purchases or sales involving that land. By looking at deeds, you can learn which individuals were allowed to hold land, how land values changed over the years, and what the relationships were between people involved in a land transaction. You can track the history of a piece of land by going from one deed to another, either forward or backward in time. Every deed includes a "chain of title." This lists each owner of a piece of land in succession. A title search allows you to reconstruct a chain of title by looking through deeds. Deeds can be found in county courthouses and are held in deed books, which are generally under the control of a registrar of deeds. Deed books hold records of several different types of land sales. Some property transactions are complicated, but they can yield a gold mine of information for genealogy researchers.

Units of Measure

It can be confusing to read documents without knowing what the terms mean. Here is a quick list of the units of measurement most often found in legal descriptions of land transactions.

Acre = 10 square chains = 43,560 square feet = 160 square rods—
   5,645.376 square varas = 1.1834 square arpent
Arpent = 191.833 feet = 30 toise = 30 compasses
Chain = 66 Feet = 4 Rods = 100 Links
Foot = 12 inches = 0.36 vara
Furlong = 660 feet = 40 rods = 10 chains
Inch = 0.0833 feet
Labor = 177.136 acres = 1,000,000 square varas
League = 4,428.4 acres = 25,000,000 square varas = 25 labors
Link = 7.92 inches
Mile = 8 furlongs = 320 rods = 80 chains = 5,280 feet = 1,760 yards
Rod = 16.5 feet = 1 pole = 5.5 yards = 25 links
Square arpent = 0.84628 acres
Square rod = 272.5 square feet = 30.25 square yards
Vara = 2.778 feet = 33.33 inches

A Map to the Country of Land Records

Start your land record research at the U.S. Bureau of Land Management (BLM) (www.glorecords.blm.gov). Here you will find the General Land Office (GLO) records, which include federal land patents, federal surveys of small pieces of land called plats, and field notes. You can access land conveyance records for the public land states, and for over 3 million federal land title records issued between 1820 and 1908 for eastern public land states. Serial patents, or land titles issued between 1908 and the mid-1960s, are also available.

Survey records include acreage, counties, the office that authorized the survey, dates, and administrative actions pertaining to survey activities noted on a plat or in the field notes. Field note records available at the BLM are images scanned from original field note pages, with each image indexed according to the kind of information in the notes, and the survey or surveys referenced on a page. The BLM's plat records are images scanned in high resolution from original plat documents.

You can search the patent, plat, and field note databases for a number of states, but the information is not yet complete. The BLM is working to put all of these records online, but it is a big job that will take years to complete. Still, there is a lot of information here, and it's worth researching to see if any of it pertains to your ancestors.

Public land states refer to land that the federal government transferred directly to individuals, as compared to land that the British Crown originally sold or granted to individuals. After the American Revolution, the Northwest Ordinance of 1787 placed these lands under government control. Other land was added to the public domain as the country grew. This land was obtained through treaties, purchases from other governments, and the taking of Native American land. States formed from public land are known as public land states. States formed from land not considered to be public land are the original thirteen colonies, and Kentucky, Maine, Tennessee, Texas, Vermont, West Virginia, and Hawaii. These states are called state land states. There are differences in what you'll find in public land state records and state land state records.

🔍 Back to the Land

To illustrate how useful the records at the Bureau of Land Management can be, family researcher Nadine Snider of Lawrence, Kansas, shares her experience:

One of my best finds online was with the Bureau of Land Management's land grants. We were researching my husband's Snider lines and knew from Civil War pension records that one ancestor had been born in Orange County, Indiana. We found records showing that a George Snider had bought land in Crawford County, Indiana, one county away. We also found that a David Snider bought land there. We knew my husband's great-grandfather was George Washington Snider. We did not know for sure that his father's name was George, but thought it could be. We did know from census records that his mother's name was Matilda Ruberson at the time of the census. We eventually made a trip to Indiana to Crawford County and looked up the land records. We found that a George Washington Snider and his wife, Matilda, had sold land there to a Barbara Snider. So, yes, this was the same family. We then looked up probate records and found that George was dead a month after the land sale and about three months after the birth of their youngest child, our ancestor. We also found that David Snider's estate was probated a year or so before George's and that Barbara was his widow. We now think that Barbara and David were George Senior's parents. We are currently working on proving that. But those land records sure did help!

Indeed! Into the Deed Book

One type of land sale recorded in a county deed book is the deed of sale, also known as indenture. This is what you typically think of when you think about the sale of property. The property involved is usually a piece of land, but it might also be household property or livestock.

Another type of sale was called a strawman sale. In such a sale, one individual sold property to another, who functioned as the strawman. The strawman then sold the property to a third person. Such sales frequently occurred on the same day. By using a strawman, sellers avoided certain legal restrictions. For example, suppose a married couple wants to change their ownership status from "tenants by the entirety" to "joint tenancy."

Tenants by the entirety refers to a type of property ownership available only to married couples in which both spouses have rights to a piece of property. When one of them dies, the other receives the title to the property as the survivor. Joint tenancy is a similar method by which two or more people can share property ownership with the same kind of survivor's rights. Tenancy by the entirety is not available as an option in every state. In order to change their tenant status, the couple would sell their property with one type of ownership to a strawman, and then buy it back with the other type. In this way, the couple avoids the legal restriction that dictates you can't sell your own property to yourself. Strawmen might also be used if the law does not allow a simple transfer of partial ownership in a piece of property.

A "lease and release" sale, often found in deeds of sale in early Virginia, is created as a two-part transfer. In the first part, one person leases land to another person, and in the second part, the first person releases the second from his or her lease obligation. This was done for reasons similar to those prompting a strawman sale and was seen as a "cleaner" way to pass legal title to land from one individual to another.

Some deeds are written as gifts of property. They include phrases such as "for $1 and other consideration" or "for love and affection." These gift deeds may also include restrictions, such as requiring a child to care for his or her parents for the duration of their natural lives in exchange for the gift of real property. These deeds are handled in the same way simple sales are.

A trickier type of deed is the mortgage sale, often indicated by the phrase "this deed of mortgage" at the beginning of the record. A mortgage sale may sometimes look like a simple sale, but then include phrases at the end of the document such as "said sale to be null and void" if certain events occur. For example, someone may sell land for a certain price as collateral on a loan, but may get it back if the loan is repaid on time.

Finally, there are deeds involving estate settlements in which a deceased person's property is distributed according to a will, if one exists, or by the probate laws of the state in which they live. An example is a deed of sale by which children sell their interest in a parent's property to other siblings or to someone else. These deeds include phrases such as "the heirs of John Smith, deceased" or "hereby sell their 1/8 interest" in a piece of land. Officers of the law, such as sheriffs, sell land under orders from a court, with the proceeds going into the estate settlement.

The law requires deeds to be recorded in a central location, but that location differs from state to state. Deeds registered in Massachusetts or Maine can be found in the county courthouse where the property transfer occurred. Because county boundaries change over time, information about the deeds to a single piece of land may be found in several locations. In some eastern states, deeds were recorded in towns, but this was not always the case in the western states. Early property deeds might also be located in central state archives. Some good news: deeds, probate records, and court decrees—all of which show property transfers—are typically found in the same location.

Some deed registries have put information, indexes, and some or all of their records online. Some charge fees to access the information. To find a Web site for a particular location, check the official state site first.

🔍 Deed Research Recommendations

An excellent Web site that shows you how to construct a history from the bits and pieces of surviving evidence is DoHistory (dohistory.org/home.html). This site was created by the Film Study Center at Harvard University and hosted by the Center for History and New Media at George Mason University. It uses Martha Ballard's diary as a case study. Martha Ballard lived from 1735 to 1812, and her diary describes her life as a wife, mother of nine, healer, and midwife. You can read the original diary at the site, but what's really interesting is how you can interactively "do history" by exploring the original documents and trying to answer questions about Martha's life and times.

The site offers several recommendations for unearthing relevant information from deeds and includes a downloadable note-taking form (fig. 4-4) to track your deed research. Here are some things that DoHistory suggests you do when excavating deeds:

Write down the names of the buyer and/or seller (the grantee and grantor, respectively) for the land you're researching, and find out whether these deeds or any information related to them is available online.

Check the deed's body for the name of the grantor, the type of covenant (warranty, quit claim, mortgage), name of grantee, description of the property in question, the clause that states the intent of the deed, the volume where the deed is recorded, the price of the transaction, if given, and the chain of title, if given.

Check for a tax stamp, which indicates that a fee was assessed according to the transaction's value. This can help you estimate the selling price.

Check for a release of spousal rights. For example, a release of the right of dower meant a wife agreed to sell the property, while a release of courtesy meant the husband agreed to the sale. A release of homestead rights meant that there was an individual living on the land at the time of sale. You can use this information to establish relationships among family members.

Note the date and time the deed was recorded to establish a timeline for events.

Use the note-taking form to keep track of the information you find. Photocopy the original documents (there may be a fee), and check other sources to verify your findings or to fill in any information gaps. Such sources include tax maps, aerial photographs, insurance maps, town atlases, historical maps, letters, wills, and court records.

Digging for Deed Treasures

Copying the names and dates from your family's deed records is just the beginning. Good researchers try to analyze the information and look for its implications. You can learn to make some educated guesses based on the factual data of the record to expand your research. Always look for clues as you scour dusty records.

For example, check to see if the deed mentions people besides those involved in the actual transaction. Are any of these names familiar from your previous research? If so, and if the persons named are acting in some official capacity, it may be that they were helping out a friend or family member. These additional individuals could be ministers, attorneys, or

Deed Research Notes	
Date:	Location of registry:
Grantor(s)*	Grantee(s)*

* list family relationships to each other if known (e.g., spouse, child)

Residence:	Residence:
Consideration (price):	Date of signature:
Tax stamp amount:	Date of acknowledgment:
Release of: (check one)	Date of recording:
☐ dower ☐ courtesy ☐ homestead	
Town/city, county, state where land is located:	
Description or sketch of property:	

With thanks to Brian Burford, Surveyor and Historian, New Hampshire State Archives

Figure 4-4
Note-taking form for research on deeds

doctors, in which case there may be personal papers or other documentation relating to them in some library or archive. Was the person a justice of the peace or county clerk? If so, your ancestor may have lived near this individual if he or she filled such a local position of authority. If other individuals are listed as the owners of adjacent land, you may find information about your ancestor on their deeds.

If a deed lists more than one individual with the same surname, it could be that these individuals were acting jointly with your ancestor. If you have a legal description of the land, you can plat it and find its exact location on a modern-day map. Look for nearby landmarks such as churches or burial sites. The *type* of deed can tell you a lot about the events surrounding the property transfer. For example, a sheriff's deed indicates that the property was seized for taxes or to satisfy a court judgment against your ancestor. You can look for verification of this in court case records and tax rolls. If you find a quit claim deed, it is likely that someone else had an interest in the property, and you may have to look through many deeds from the specific time period to find an identical legal description of the property to identify another potential ancestor. Deeds of trust are used when a debt is involved. Additional notes may indicate whether the debt was paid, but if these are not available, the tax rolls may provide a solution to the puzzle. Anyone who is listed as guaranteeing the payment of your ancestor's debt is very likely to be a relative.

Additionally, look for an explanation if there is a significant delay between the time a deed was written and the time it was actually filed. You should try to discover how an individual who is selling a piece of property acquired it in the first place. If the property involved is land, it may have been bought from the government, in which case you'll be able to find more information about it at the local, state, or federal level. You may have to look further if the property is not land, searching sheriff's records, tax records, or state or county records to determine the previous owner.

Finally, consider whether slaves were the property involved. The names, ages, occupations, and other data about the slaves are important clues that can help you discover if slaves were passed along to family members as inheritances. Using this information, you may also be able to determine which family members were actually the owners of the stated property. (This can be especially useful in cases where several people in a family have the same name.)

Marching Toward Military Records

Military records are an excellent source of family history information. Even if your direct ancestors were not members of the military, you will find information about collateral relations such as cousins, aunts, and uncles that just might provide that one clue you need to open up an entirely new line of research. Military service records are among the most requested at the National Archives.

Many Web sites providing military records focus on a single war or conflict, particularly the American Revolution, the American Civil War, World War I, World War II, and the Vietnam War. There are also numerous sites devoted to particular aspects of these wars, such as the experience of ambulance drivers in World War I (net.lib.byu.edu/~rdh7/wwi/memoir/Buswell/AAFS1.htm).

℞ The Christmas Truce
One of the most heartwarming stories to come out of the horror that was World War I is that of the Christmas truce. During the Christmas season in

1914, British and German soldiers stood in waterlogged trenches, six to eight feet deep, facing each other across the no-man's-land between their fortifications in Flanders. The British Army was posted along a line running south from Ypres to the La Bassée canal, a distance of 27 miles. Along this front, opposing German soldiers were often only 30 to 70 yards away from the British.

Both sides were hoping for a break in the fighting as Christmas approached. England's King George V had sent greetings to British troops in the form of plum puddings and boxes filled with tobacco, cigarettes, butterscotch, and chocolate. The kaiser had sent the German troops gifts of pipes and cigars. The gifts raised the troops' morale and helped them forget their plight for the moment.

According to a British newspaper, *The Daily Telegraph*, the whole thing started when the Germans and the British successfully swapped cake for tobacco. The two sides promised a ceasefire in honor of the holiday. They also held an impromptu concert and placed candles along the tops of their trenches.

On Christmas Day, the no-man's-land became a place where singing could be heard, gifts were exchanged, and games of soccer were played. The truce lasted all day. In some places, it ended on Christmas night. In other places, the truce held for several more days. Some military officers didn't like the spontaneous truce, but no one was eager to bring disciplinary action against the soldiers who participated. Ultimately, the generals ordered their troops back to the business of war by threatening court-martial. Alan Cleaver and Leslie Park have created a Web site to collect letters from soldiers involved in the Christmas truce. To read some of these letters visit the Operation Plum Puddings Web site (www.christmastruce.co.uk).

The way you research your ancestors' military history depends on what you know about them. The information available varies with the branch of service, the war or conflict, the dates of service, regular or volunteer status, whether your relative was an officer, and whether a pension application exists. The types of records you're likely to find include death and casualty lists, draft records, pension records, registration cards, rosters of individuals in specific military units, and service records.

It helps to know about the historical context of a specific war. State and local histories can help you understand how a war impacted the area in which your ancestor lived. Often, they provide details about the involvement of residents in wartime. State libraries and archives may hold useful nuggets of information for military researchers, and many of these

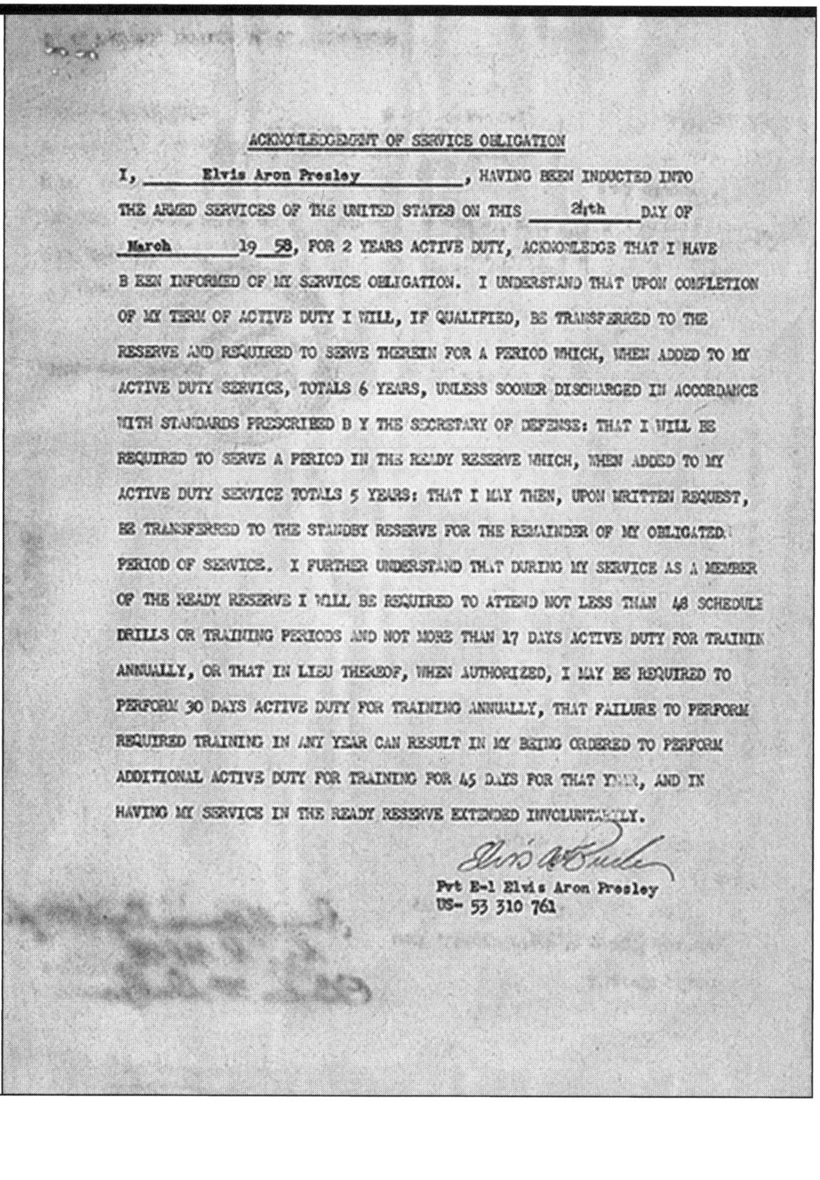

ACKNOWLEDGEMENT OF SERVICE OBLIGATION

I, Elvis Aron Presley, HAVING BEEN INDUCTED INTO THE ARMED SERVICES OF THE UNITED STATES ON THIS 24th DAY OF March 1958, FOR 2 YEARS ACTIVE DUTY, ACKNOWLEDGE THAT I HAVE BEEN INFORMED OF MY SERVICE OBLIGATION. I UNDERSTAND THAT UPON COMPLETION OF MY TERM OF ACTIVE DUTY I WILL, IF QUALIFIED, BE TRANSFERRED TO THE RESERVE AND REQUIRED TO SERVE THEREIN FOR A PERIOD WHICH, WHEN ADDED TO MY ACTIVE DUTY SERVICE, TOTALS 6 YEARS, UNLESS SOONER DISCHARGED IN ACCORDANCE WITH STANDARDS PRESCRIBED BY THE SECRETARY OF DEFENSE; THAT I WILL BE REQUIRED TO SERVE A PERIOD IN THE READY RESERVE WHICH, WHEN ADDED TO MY ACTIVE DUTY SERVICE TOTALS 5 YEARS; THAT I MAY THEN, UPON WRITTEN REQUEST, BE TRANSFERRED TO THE STANDBY RESERVE FOR THE REMAINDER OF MY OBLIGATED PERIOD OF SERVICE. I FURTHER UNDERSTAND THAT DURING MY SERVICE AS A MEMBER OF THE READY RESERVE I WILL BE REQUIRED TO ATTEND NOT LESS THAN 48 SCHEDULE DRILLS OR TRAINING PERIODS AND NOT MORE THAN 17 DAYS ACTIVE DUTY FOR TRAININ ANNUALLY, OR THAT IN LIEU THEREOF, WHEN AUTHORIZED, I MAY BE REQUIRED TO PERFORM 30 DAYS ACTIVE DUTY FOR TRAINING ANNUALLY, THAT FAILURE TO PERFORM REQUIRED TRAINING IN ANY YEAR CAN RESULT IN MY BEING ORDERED TO PERFORM ADDITIONAL ACTIVE DUTY FOR TRAINING FOR 45 DAYS FOR THAT YEAR, AND IN HAVING MY SERVICE IN THE READY RESERVE EXTENDED INVOLUNTARILY.

Pvt E-1 Elvis Aron Presley
US- 53 310 761

Figure 4-5
Acknowledgment of service obligation for Elvis Presley

institutions have Web sites where you can search their collections. You should also examine personal accounts, such as stories told in soldiers' letters and diaries. Much of the most useful information about an individual's military record may be found at the local level, since counties and towns take great pride in the service of their sons and daughters in the military. Counties and local organizations often publish newsletters or magazines devoted to the history of local involvement in the military. For example, the Web site for the Nashville Historical Newsletter (pages.prodigy.net/nhn.slate) has articles such as "Luke Lea in the Great War" and "'With the Sun Behind Him': Captain Edward Buford Jr., Nashville's World War I 'Ace.'"

The National Archives can provide you with military records, but in general, you must request them in writing or visit the National Archives building in Washington, D.C., or the National Military Personnel Records center in St. Louis, Missouri. Individual records are not online. NARA does, however, provide digitized sample records in the Archival Research Catalog (ARC; www.archives.gov/research/arc/topics/personnel-files). Other military documents, including more than ninety documents, digitized from seven personnel files from the army, marine corps, and navy showing the personnel records of Elvis Presley, Audie Murphy, and John F. Kennedy, among others, are also available. You can find a list of the military records NARA has online at www.archives.gov/veterans/research/online.html. Figure 4-5 shows Elvis Presley's Acknowledgement [sic] of Service Obligation.

Death Lists and Casualty Lists

These records provide information about military personnel who were killed in action or who died from injuries received during their military service. You can usually find such lists through state Web sites or sites devoted to particular wars.

Pension Records

Pension records offer information about military officers, disabled veterans, the widows and orphans of veterans, and those who received pensions from the U.S. government. (For more on this topic see Chapter 6.) Debra Warila of Family Tree Growers used pension records to clear up a family mystery. By searching the pension records of Union soldiers in the

American Civil War, she was able to determine that a Confederate hero of family legend had actually been a captain in the Union army.

Draft Registration Cards

These provide information about individuals required to register for a military draft. The World War I draft cards represent an especially rich source of genealogical information for researchers. After the United States declared war on Germany in 1917, the government decided that a draft was necessary to increase its troop levels. Therefore, in 1917 and 1918, about 24 million civilian men who were born between 1872 and 1900 were required to fill out draft registration cards. Over 80 percent of them were exempted from service or got deferrals and were never called to military service.

Genealogists love these cards because they provide information that would otherwise not be available. Many states did not register births in these years, so the draft cards preserve birth information. In some cases, the cards are the only existing proof of birth locations, complete birth dates, or middle names. You may find the following information on an individual's draft card: name, place of residence, date and place of birth, race, country of citizenship, occupation, and employer. The years between 1880 and 1920 saw a significant number of immigrants entering the country, and young men had to register regardless of their citizenship status. Therefore, the cards represent a major source of information about these new residents. Men were required to sign the cards, so you can see your ancestors' actual signatures.

Be sure to check what you find on a draft card against any information you've obtained from your family or other reliable sources. There can be mistakes in birth information provided by the men who were born before 1900, but the cards are generally accurate because the man himself provided the information, which was not always the case in the census. The names and locations on the cards may be spelled incorrectly, and should be checked against other sources for accuracy. You can use maps or gazetteers to verify spellings. The boundaries and names of countries in some areas of the world, such as Eastern Europe, were very different in 1917 from what they are today. Plus, approximately half of all the counties in the United States didn't exist in 1917. Keep these issues in mind when using draft cards as evidence. Figure 4-6 shows the World War I draft card of W.C. Fields at NARA (www.archives.gov/southeast/wwi-draft/fields.html).

Service Records

Service records hold the information that the government collects and keeps about any solider, including enlistment/appointment, duty stations/

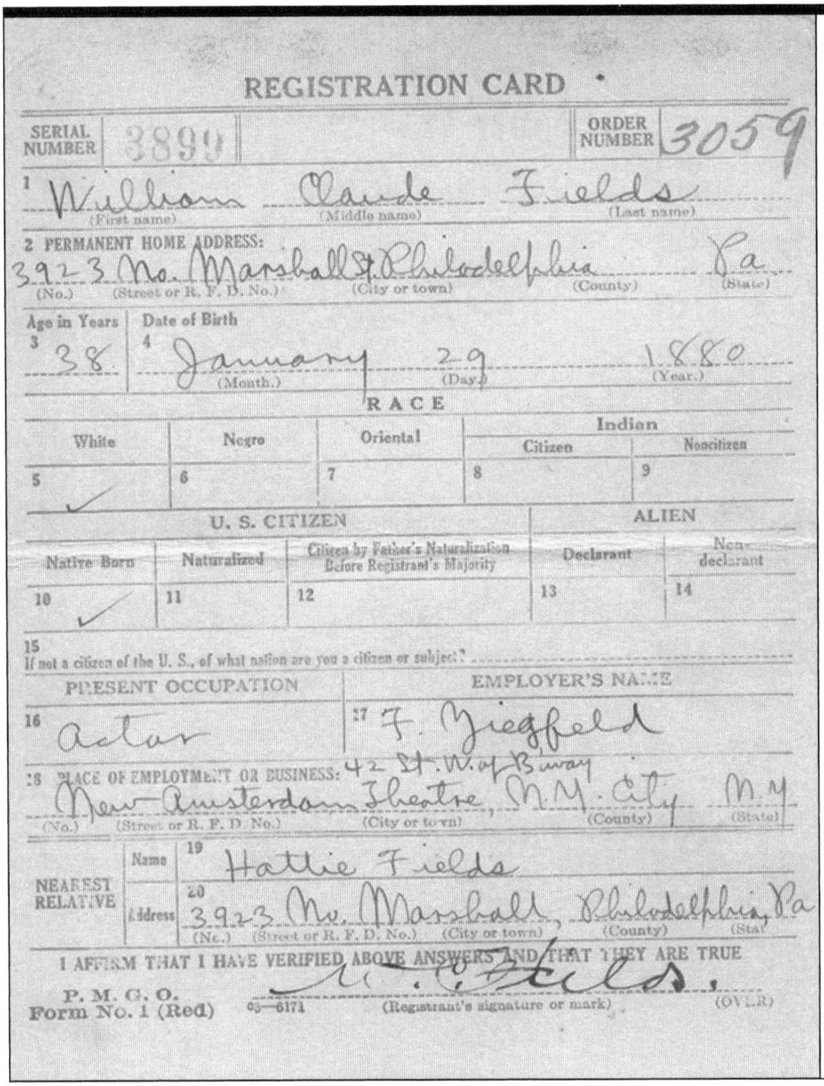

REGISTRATION CARD

SERIAL NUMBER 3899 ORDER NUMBER 3059

1 William Claude Fields
(First name) (Middle name) (Last name)

2 PERMANENT HOME ADDRESS:
3923 No. Marshall St. Philadelphia Pa
(No.) (Street or R. F. D. No.) (City or town) (County) (State)

Age in Years	Date of Birth
3 38	4 January 29 1880 (Month.) (Day.) (Year.)

RACE

White	Negro	Oriental	Indian Citizen	Indian Noncitizen
5 ✓	6	7	8	9

U. S. CITIZEN: Native Born	Naturalized	Citizen by Father's Naturalization Before Registrant's Majority	ALIEN: Declarant	Non-declarant
10 ✓	11	12	13	14

15 If not a citizen of the U. S., of what nation are you a citizen or subject?

PRESENT OCCUPATION	EMPLOYER'S NAME
16 Actor	17 F. Ziegfeld

18 PLACE OF EMPLOYMENT OR BUSINESS: 42 St. W. of B'way
New Amsterdam Theatre, N.Y. City N.Y.
(No.) (Street or R. F. D. No.) (City or town) (County) (State)

NEAREST RELATIVE
Name 19 Hattie Fields
Address 20 3923 No. Marshall, Philadelphia, Pa
(No.) (Street or R. F. D. No.) (City or town) (County) (State)

I AFFIRM THAT I HAVE VERIFIED ABOVE ANSWERS AND THAT THEY ARE TRUE
W. C. Fields
(Registrant's signature or mark)

P. M. G. O.
Form No. 1 (Red) 63—6171 (OVER)

Figure 4-6
W.C. Fields's World War I draft registration card

assignments, training, qualifications, performance, awards and medals, any disciplinary actions taken, emergency information, insurance, separation from the service, discharge, retirement, and other personnel matters.

Where Does the March Begin?

Dare we say it again? The best places to start your search for military records are Ancestry.com and CyndisList.com. While there are many Web sites that provide partial information, specialized information, and local records, Ancestry and Cyndi's List offer the most rewarding results when you're starting out. These sites add links and records every day, so save yourself some time and begin your research here.

Military Records at Ancestry.com

Ancestry's records cover over 300 years of America's wars and military conflicts. There are over 90 million names and 700 titles and databases covering all 50 states. You'll find historical documents relating to every major American war from the Revolution through Vietnam. Records include draft registration cards, veterans' gravesite listings, military pension indexes, enlistment records, muster rolls, and more.

Two of the site's latest offerings are United Newsreel motion pictures from 1942–1946, and issues of *Stars and Stripes,* the U.S. military's newspaper. The newsreels show military operations and events that occurred on the home front. You can read stories the newspaper distributed to members of the American military in Europe, the Mediterranean, and North Africa during World War II.

Ancestry's military collections include several fascinating databases. The Revolutionary War Courts-Martial database allows you to read accounts of over 3,000 individuals brought before a military court, and the database of American Civil War battle summaries contains short histories of some of the most critical battles of the Civil War.

Ancestry provides the World War I draft registration cards of over 24 million men, muster rolls for the U.S. Marines that list over 10 million names of marines who served between 1893 and 1940, and over 8 million names of individuals who enlisted in the U.S. Army between 1938 and 1946. You'll also find a list of U.S. Civil War Union and Confederate soldiers who fought between 1860 and 1865, and burial and gravesite information for nearly 3.5 million U.S. veterans who served between 1775 and 2006.

Military Record Links at CyndisList.com

Cyndi's List has three main categories of links to help you find military records: Military Resources Worldwide; Military, World War I—The Great War; and Military, World War II. The worldwide resources include links to military information sites covering Australia, Canada, the United Kingdom, Ireland, Italy, Eurasia, and Germany, to name a few. The list also includes mailing lists dedicated to the Austro-Hungarian War, the Boer War, French military, German military, Stalag POWs, and the list goes on and on. If you have a specific military interest, you're likely to find a list to suit your purpose.

The World War I list covers battles and battlefields, ships, medals, photographs, regimental rosters and histories, location-specific topics like Australia and New Zealand, and family-specific sites. For example, there's a site devoted to members of the Edgar family from Canada who were killed in World War I (www.geocities.com/canadaww1/ca.html), and a site dedicated to Edith Cavell, "a Norfolk heroine" and nurse during World War I, who was executed by the Germans for harboring enemy soldiers at her nursing school in Brussels (www.edithcavell.org.uk).

Cyndi's World War II list of links includes Web sites that cover the Holocaust, such as the Red Cross Holocaust and War Victims Tracing and Information Center (www.redcross.org/services/intl/holotrace/ index.html), in addition to location-specific sites, mailing lists related to World War II, and sites devoted to particular individuals and families, such as American Aces of World War Two (www.acepilots.com/) and War Brides in Canada (home.istar.ca/~lyster/warbride).

Shipping Out—Ancestors Sailing In

You can find some interesting clues about where your ancestors came from by checking the passenger lists of the ships that brought them to the United States. You need to have as much information about your ancestors as possible before looking at the passenger lists, though, because it is easy to follow the wrong line and end up with people in your family tree who don't belong there!

Most people think of Ellis Island when they think of immigration, but there have been many ports of entry. Ellis Island operated only between 1892 and 1954. Genealogists generally identify two eras associated with passenger lists. One is the period before 1820, and the other is the time between 1820 and the 1950s. An action of the U.S. Congress in 1819 regulated the number of passengers who could travel on a single ship, based on the ship's total tonnage. This law required recording six pieces of information on a passenger list: name, age, sex, occupation, nationality, and the country of intended destination.

Passenger List Pay Dirt!

Rex Bavousett of Austin, Texas, had success in finding information about his French ancestors using passenger lists. And it led to further prizes.

I was using Ancestry.com for searching passenger ship lists. I found my relatives on a list of passengers of the HMS Alliance, *and received a copy of that record from the National Archives. I dove into further online research looking for the ship's captain's name. Lo and behold, I struck pay dirt! I contacted the genealogy assistant and head librarian at the Wiscasset, Maine, Public Library. As it happened, she was the great-granddaughter of the captain of the* Alliance. *This woman was able to give me a photograph she took of a painting of the* Alliance *that she owned. Now I have an image of the ship that brought my relatives Etienne and George Bavouzet to America in July of 1847. When time permits a visit to Maine, I will visit the library to read through the ship's log for further details of the trip..*

The Passenger Act of 1882 required more information, including the name of the passenger's native country. We're sure that genealogists everywhere rejoiced at this, since people frequently traveled long distances from their home countries to reach a port city before they even began an ocean voyage! The U.S. Bureau of Immigration was created in 1891 in response to concerns about the great number of immigrants coming into the country. This agency established consistency and standardization in immigration records and procedures.

When searching passenger lists, use the same methods you worked with when searching census records. Be careful of spellings and handwriting styles that could make your search more difficult. Be sure you have certain information about your ancestor in place to make your passenger-list searches useful. You need to know his or her full, original name; the approximate date of arrival in the United States; and the port of arrival. Other useful information to have on hand is the name of the port of embarkation, the place where your ancestor started the ocean voyage, the U.S. destination, the name of the ship, and the names of traveling companions. Census records and naturalization records can help you find this information. For an excellent guide to searching passenger lists, see the Immigration and Ships Passenger Lists Research Guide (home.att.net/ %7Earnielang/shipgide.html#top). A list of Web sites with passenger lists and relevant information is at members.aol.com/rprost/passenger.html. And Cyndi's List, as always, has very useful links for passenger searching.

The Ellis Island Web site (www.ellisisland.org) lets you search passenger lists for free. The site's information only covers ships arriving in New York, however, so if your ancestors came in through Canada or Galveston, Texas, you're out of luck there. But don't worry. Other Web sites will give you the information you need.

One Stop Professor!

For an efficient search of passenger lists, look no further than Steve Morse's excellent Web site, stevemorse.org. He has created what he calls a "one-stop portal" for online genealogy. Morse feels many genealogy Web sites are difficult to use, or are not as versatile as they might be. He addressed these concerns by creating different ways of accessing some sites and developing his own databases and programs to make genealogy researching easier.

As a professor, author, researcher, and the inventor of the Intel 8086 microprocessor chip, the forerunner of the Pentium chips in modern desktop computers, Morse is well suited to such a project. He's been applying his technological expertise to online genealogy searches since 2001 and has won numerous awards for his work.

Morse designed his first search tool to look through Ellis Island online records without involving the many steps of a conventional search. His Web site includes a detailed account of why his search tool is superior. Using the example of Irving Berlin, the composer who came to the United States in 1893, Morse illustrates the difficulties associated with searching the passenger lists for an individual arriving at Ellis Island.

Get on Board with AncestorsonBoard.com

The National Archives in London and Findmypast.com together offer a database featuring the BT27 outward-bound passenger lists for long-distance trips that departed from the British Isles between 1890 and 1960. BT27 stands for Board of Trade, Series 27, and this information was previously available only in the United Kingdom. The records show arrivals through New York, of course, but also the arrivals at other ports in the United States and Canada coming from the British Isles. The series also includes travels originating in other European countries that passed through a United Kingdom port. The collection even includes the *USS Titanic's* outward-bound passenger lists.

You can search records of individuals or groups who left for destinations such as Canada, India, New Zealand, South Africa, and the United States. The lists include the names of immigrants, of course, but also of diplomats, businesspeople, and tourists. Of particular interest are the names of domestic servants such as maids and valets who traveled with families between 1890 and 1910. You can download, view, save, and print the actual images of the passenger lists. The site offers more than 30 million records. The site is not free, but there are several fee levels to choose from. For more information see www.findmypast.com/paymentOptions/subscriptions/index.jsp.

Stop by the Castle Garden

Another excellent site for searching ship passenger lists is the database maintained by the Battery Conservancy in New York City. Castle Garden, located at the tip of Manhattan, was the first official immigration center in the United States. It is now known as Castle Clinton National Monument. The CastleGarden.org database provides information about some 10 million U.S. immigrants who entered the country between 1830 and 1892.

Mapping Your Way

Maps, atlases, and gazetteers—all of these show where your ancestors came from as well as where they traveled and the routes they took to get there. You can solve many genealogical mysteries by simply looking at the right map. You'll also add to your knowledge about the places your ancestors lived and worked. There are different kinds of maps available to help you flesh out information you've found or to give you clues for further investigations.

Standard Maps and Atlases, Historic and Modern

You can start your geographical research by consulting modern road maps and atlases. These will give you a general sense of the present-day environment. If you can't find the county or town name you are looking for, move on to the maps and atlases in existence during your ancestor's lifetime. You'll find historical maps online at sites such as the Perry-Castenada Library map collection at the University of Texas (www.lib.utexas.edu/maps/historical/index.html) and the David Rumsey map collection (www.davidrumsey.com), which has more than 15,800 maps available for viewing online. For more detail, try county, parish, and province maps. These may show county roads that have not been named, major landmarks in an area, and cemetery locations.

It's Topographic!

Genealogists frequently use topographic maps, which show land contours—hills, valleys, streams, vegetation—to investigate settlement patterns, migration patterns, and structures. Using these and other relief maps, you can often find the location of an ancestor's property according to land descriptions and geological features.

Government authorities carefully maintain survey maps and plat maps that record land transactions. Land maps and plat books can give you details about the location of a specific piece of land and perhaps offer information about neighboring landowners.

Genealogists frequently consult city directories as an alternative to census information. Many directories include a street map with details about major features such as railroads or rivers. You can compare a directory map from your ancestor's time to a present-day map and discover how a town has changed. You'll often find that street names have changed or that certain streets no longer exist.

Where's the Fire Insurance Map?

Insurers use fire insurance maps to weigh risk factors when underwriting a business or home. These maps offer many fascinating details. For example, they show the outline of each building in an area, the function of the buildings, the construction materials, and the locations of doors and windows. These maps also include street names, the width measurements of streets and sidewalks, property boundaries, uses of buildings, and house numbers. The very detailed Sanborn Fire Insurance maps were produced from 1867 to 1969 and show commercial, industrial, and residential areas of certain cities. An online exhibit from the Library of Congress shows examples of Sanborn maps for a number of selected cities (www.loc.gov/exhibits/treasures/trr016.html).

Old Maps Are the Best Maps

One thing that challenges researchers is pinning down the name of a county or town in which an ancestor lived. This seems like a simple task, but towns, counties, cities, and countries may change names over time. In some cases, the boundaries of legal jurisdiction have changed, which means that although your family has lived on the same piece of land for many years, during those years the property may have been under the jurisdiction of several different local authorities or even different counties. Any experienced genealogist can regale you with tales about how county name changes fouled up research. Was great-grandma married in Hardin County, Tennessee, or Hardeman County? Without the help of the right map for the right year, this question may never be answered correctly.

What's That Name Again?

If you run into unfamiliar place names, you can use the Geographic Names Information System (GNIS) (gos2.geodata.gov/wps/portal/gos). This is the official database of place names in the United States maintained by the U.S. Geological Survey (USGS). It includes 2 million entries, even the names of places that no longer exist. The GNIS also includes variations of names. The automated system holds the names of every geographical feature except roads and highways. For genealogists, the fact that it contains information for communities, churches, and cemeteries is very valuable.

Gee, It's GPS

A relatively recent trend among genealogists is the use of global positioning system (GPS) technology to help locate and record the locations of buildings and cemeteries. A GPS receiver uses the signals from twenty four satellites orbiting Earth to determine its locations. As receivers have come down in price, more researchers are using them to record the exact location of graves and buildings. Some genealogy programs support the addition of GPS data. Once you've recorded the position of a grave, for example, you will always be able to find it again, regardless of whether the headstone still stands. If a street name changes, you'll still know the location of that street.

Some professional genealogists believe that recording GPS coordinates is the same as recording any other source material. GPS can be used to find cemeteries, for example, so why shouldn't you add those coordinates to a genealogy database? The exact position of a family farm could be recovered and preserved, regardless of whether it became the site of an apartment building or part of a highway. Professionals are starting to recommend that researchers record the geographic coordinates of any ancestral site into a genealogy database as a way of preserving that information.

Looking Ahead

Now that you've seen some of the records you'll find online, we know you're ready to start your own explorations. In the next chapter, we introduce the most useful—and entertaining—genealogy Web sites available. There are Web sites that you absolutely must visit if you want to call yourself a genealogist. And there are others that you should visit if you want to enlarge your point of view and hone your skills. Other sites are just too much fun to miss!

Chapter 5

Online Stops You Won't Want to Miss

O kay, so now that you know what you're hunting for, let's get going. On the Internet—so many Web sites, so little time!—you will find spread before you a buffet table of genealogy offerings. This chapter provides an opportunity to sample here, sample there, and find some of your favorite resources on the Web. We'll get you started by sharing some of our favorite stops. We've organized this sumptuous buffet table into three categories: Must-Visits, Should-Visits, and Curiosities That Keep You Going. Within those categories are databases, newsletters, blogs, and tools to help you move along.

These Web sites are our favorites for several reasons. Some are just spectacularly useful to a genealogist. Others are interesting for the inspiration they provide. Some will connect you to other researchers, and some are just funny! After all, just like a delicious meal, genealogy should be fun and satisfying. So dive into the offerings, whet your appetite, find your meat and potatoes, and then move on to dessert!

Must-Visit Sites

Many Internet users either visit the same sites over and over, because they are familiar, or compulsively click their way here and there without really stopping long enough to explore. To help you narrow your search for helpful online information, we've provided a list of must-see genealogy sites. These sites are indispensable for beginners, but even if you're experienced in online genealogy you'll return to them again and again. They are just that good! When you're checking them out, be sure you've set aside enough time to explore them thoroughly. There's a lot to learn!

Cyndi's List of Genealogy Sites on the Internet
(www.cyndislist.com)

We know we keep beating this drum, but Cyndi's List should be the first stop on the Internet for every budding genealogist! Cyndi Howells originally created the site in 1996 as a project to help members of her local genealogical society find online resources. Now, her Web site receives over 70,000 page hits each day, has four different indexes, and a site search engine. The category indexes include a Main Index, "No-Frills" Index, Alphabetical Index, and Topical Index. More than 1,500 new links are added each month. There are currently more than 263,150 active links to genealogy-related Web sites. Cyndi's List includes over 120 main subject categories, as well as individual Web pages representing each state within the United States and each Canadian province. Every country in the world has its own Web page with relevant links.

First-time visitors should start by reading the FAQs. These provide an overview of what's on the site and describe the main categories. More adventurous explorers may want to browse the many categories listed in the main index and follow wherever their inclinations may lead them!

Genealogy.com—Genealogical Education
(www.genealogy.com/57_kathy.html)

Kathleen W. Hinckley is a certified genealogical records specialist, owner and operator of Family Detective, executive director of the Association of Professional Genealogists, and trustee for the Board for Certification of Genealogists. She has developed a list of available online and home-study courses in both genealogy and family history. There are free, self-paced courses that cover the basics of genealogical research, and formal tuition based classes, which will give you full professional certification status. Several of the certificate programs award college credits upon successful completion. The free courses at Genealogy.com's Online University are a great way for both genealogy hobbyists and family historians to learn how to hunt down elusive ancestors and document the information they find.

About Genealogy—A Genealogy Research Guide
(genealogy.about.com)

Part of the About.com network, this Web site offers something for every genealogist; both hobbyists and professionals. Here you will find a variety of articles covering a wide range of topics, such as: building family trees, conducting historical research, databases and records, heraldry and arms, DNA and genetics, the origins and meanings of surnames, photographs and scrapbooking, software and tools, writing and publishing your family history, planning family reunions, and connecting with other researchers. You will also find extensive buying guides, tutorials, tips and hints, product reviews, and even a message board! There are free genealogy charts and forms, including U.S. census extraction forms, family tree charts, pedigree charts, family group sheets, and much more. The home page features the latest genealogy news and in-depth interviews with the movers and shakers in the industry.

FamilySearch.org—Family History and Genealogy Records
(www.familysearch.org)

FamilySearch.org, a nonprofit service sponsored by the LDS Church, has the largest collection of free genealogy, family history, and family tree records in the world. The easy-to-use search engine can help you locate your ancestors using the 1880 United States Federal Census, the 1881 British Isles Census, the 1881 Canadian Census, International Genealogical Index, the Pedigree Resource Files, the U.S. Social Security Death Index, and Vital Records Index. The Web site contains extensive research guidance, as well as tips and hints on developing successful search strategies. You can download free genealogy software, including Personal Ancestral File (PAF) and PAF Companion, programs that produce colorful ancestor and descendant charts. Other freebies include downloadable family group sheets, pedigree charts, census worksheets, research logs, request forms, analysis worksheets, and blank timelines. The online store sells databases on CD, including Freedman's Bank Records and the Mormon Immigration Index. You can also buy several U.S., British, and Canadian censuses on CD, as well as vital records for North America, Europe, Middle America, the British Isles, and Australia.

Ancestry.com—Genealogy, Family Trees, and Family History Records Online *(www.ancestry.com)*

How can we even begin to describe Ancestry.com? If you're serious about online genealogy, this Web site is an absolute must! The world's largest genealogy and family history Web site, which is part of the Generations Network, provides members access to historical records and documents, user-submitted family trees, stories, publications, photographs, maps, a learning center and library, member forums, an online store, and much more. The databases are grouped into ten main areas: birth, marriage, and death records; census records; court, land, and probate records; directories and membership lists; family and local histories; family trees; immigration and naturalization records; military records; periodicals and newspapers; and reference and finding aids. There are currently 25,000 databases available, and more are added each day! Two levels of member subscriptions are available: the U.S. Deluxe Membership, at $12.95 per month for an annual subscription, and the World Deluxe Membership, at $24.95 per month for an annual subscription. You should definitely consider the World Deluxe Membership if you want to research ancestors in Canada, Ireland, or the United Kingdom. This membership plan gives you complete access to the entire site. Ancestry.com also makes some areas of its site available for free to nonsubscribers. Using these areas you can build your own personal family tree and access member-submitted trees, the Ancestry World Tree, message boards, and various databases. You really have to see this site to believe it!

Ancestry.com Resources Page *(www.censustools.com/census/ancestry-resources.html)*

Because Ancestry.com has become the most comprehensive source of genealogy information online, the resources page can help you navigate through Ancestry's numerous offerings. This site has all of Ancestry's major links gathered on one page, giving you a one-stop guide for clicking your way through the labyrinths of Ancestry.com. The site also offers spreadsheets designed to make it easy for you to enter and analyze the information you find on census sheets.

National Archives Resources for Genealogists
(www.archives.gov/genealogy)

NARA is the official repository of all federal government records and documents, as well as many state and local records. The Web site, however, does not have many of the actual records or documents available to view online. Instead, it mainly provides research tools, such as finding aids and microfilm indexes. It also provides articles, research guides, and detailed information on how to locate records and how to access them. It does offer some databases of interest to genealogists, however. These include the casualty lists for the Korean and Vietnam Wars; selected Chinese exclusion lists; Dawes Rolls index and Final index (great for looking for your Native American ancestry!); fugitive slave case papers; Spanish-American War compiled military records; prisoner of war lists from World War II, the Korean War, and the Vietnam War; Japanese-American internee file, 1942–1946; and other military-related files. Especially useful are the Web site's research guides, who help genealogists form their search strategies. NARA also offers a great page of Internet links leading to other Web sites of interest to genealogists.

USGenWeb Project *(www.usgenweb.org)*

The USGenWeb Project is a group of volunteers committed to providing free access to genealogical records and information online. Established in 1996, USGenWeb was one of the first Web sites to provide a centralized location for finding genealogical information and connecting with other family researchers. The USGenWeb Project hosts free genealogical Web sites for every county and state within the United States, serving as a gateway to these sites. It also sponsors specialized projects at the national level, including the USGenWeb Archives Project, the Family Group Sheet Project, the African American Griots Project, the Genealogical Events Project, the Kidz Project, the Lineage Project, and the Tombstone Transcription Project. Other projects include the Digital Map Library, the Pension Project, Church and Marriage Records, Census Images, and the Obituary Project. USGenWeb is an invaluable resource for the serious online genealogist and family researcher!

ROOTS-L—The Internet's First Genealogy Mailing List
(www.rootsweb.com/roots-l)

Hosted by RootsWeb.com, ROOTS-L is the oldest Internet mailing list for people worldwide who are interested in any aspect of genealogy. The Web site contains a message archive spanning ten years. It also offers various files and databases, such as the Roots Location List (RLL), a list of locations of special interest to individual researchers and contact information for those researchers; GENSERV, a database comprised of more than 11,000 GEDCOMs; and the U.S. Civil War Units file. You'll also find a "Books We Own" database of genealogical resources owned by Internet genealogists, who, within limits, are willing to do lookups, and United States Resources provides links to U.S. general and military information, as well as links to individual state pages. The ROOTS-L library offers numerous resources, including articles on how to find your way around the LDS Family History Center in Salt Lake City, how to get started on your own genealogical research, and definitions and glossaries. The library includes resources about the American Civil War, historical names and families, and research techniques for specific ethnic, religious, or social groups. Advice about how to most effectively use Internet genealogical resources and Web sites is offered, as well as software reviews and free extraction forms and charts. The home page lists all states alphabetically, and by clicking on the state you're interested in, you will find great links to other sites where you can find free files and databases pertaining to that state. And don't forget to spend time investigating RootsWeb proper (www.rootsweb.com) for advice on starting your research, a list of genealogy search engines, an international database of family trees, message boards and mailing lists, blank forms and charts, and much, much more.

American Memory Project
(memory.loc.gov/ammem/index.html)

The American Memory Project, created by the Library of Congress consists of historical collections documenting the American experience in digital format. Sources include written documents, audio interviews, sheet music, still and moving images, sound recordings, maps, and photographic prints. They chronicle the ideas, people, places, and historical events that have shaped America. The various collections are arranged by topic, including advertising (fig. 5-1); African American history; architecture and landscape; cities and towns; culture and folklife (fig. 5-2); environment and conservation; government and law (fig. 5-3); immigration and American expansion; literature; maps; Native American history; performing arts and music; presidents; religion; sports and recreation; technology and industry; war and military; and women's history. You should run to this Web site! But we have to warn you—you may not be able to drag yourself away from it!

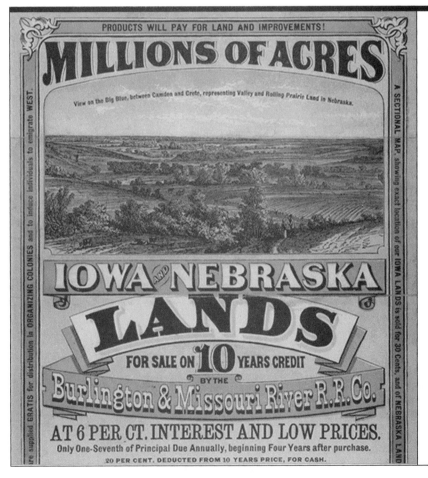

Figure 5-1
Advertisement from the collection of the American Memory Project

Figure 5-2
A classic image that captures the spirit of the times, from the American Memory Project

Figure 5-3
Title page from the special exhibit at the American Memory Project

Social Security Death Index *(ssdi.rootsweb.com)*

The Social Security Death Index (SSDI) is an invaluable tool for researching your family members who have died since 1962 (when the records were computerized). The information found here can provide clues and facts that will help further your genealogical research, such as helping you locate death certificates, track down probate records, find cemetery records, and locate newspaper obituaries. The SSDI Web page, hosted by RootsWeb, contains an SSDI tutorial that includes search tips and definitions. The advanced search engine allows you to input information for a wide variety of fields. The results show name, date of birth, date of death, the legal residence at time of death (city, county, state), the address where the final death benefit (burial benefit) was sent, Social Security number, and the state where the original Social Security card was issued.

Family Tree Magazine (*www.familytreemagazine.com*)

Family Tree Magazine is one of the most popular genealogy and family history consumer magazines available today. Its Web site covers many topics of interest to family history enthusiasts as well as seasoned genealogical researchers. Although articles are geared to beginners, advanced genealogists will also benefit from the site. Topics include genealogy research, family reunions, scrapbooking, oral history, memoirs, ethnic heritage, historical travel, photography, photo preservation, Web sites, genealogy software, and anything else that might help readers discover, preserve, and celebrate their family history. The site provides resources and tools that are not found in the print version, including free research forms and charts, a Soundex generator, writing workshops, tips for exploring your immigrant and ethnic heritage, blogs, and forums. The current magazine issue is available for viewing online, and past issues can be searched for free. Downloadable genealogy forms are available in PDF and plain text formats and include county deed indexes, note-taking forms, a research calendar, a five-generation pedigree chart, and many others.

Genealogy Today (*www.genealogytoday.com*)

Since its creation in 1999, this site has offered a selection of free and subscription-based databases. The people behind it are committed to providing the latest resources and research techniques for genealogists, and offering helpful information for both beginners and experienced researchers. Among its offerings, Genealogy Today includes:

Family Tree Connection—a subscription database with over 700,000 names that provides nontraditional information sources such as school catalogs, telephone directories, Masonic organizations, and club and society member lists.

New England Early Genealogy—a subscription database that includes birth, death, and marriage records, with citations that document original sources and reference materials.

Town Reports Online—a subscription service that provides yearly vital statistics from various towns in New England in a single searchable database.

Military Roots Project—a database of over 100,000 names, which offers a collection of genealogical information from books that contain rosters, muster rolls, and troop histories.

Ancestor Information Reprint Service—AIRS has more than 70,000 names listed and offers a collection of out-of-print books, old photographs, and rare documents.

First Name Basis—a user-contributed service designed to make connections on the basis of "common but unusual" first and middle names.

Missing Persons Register—a user-contributed service that helps people contact those with whom they have lost touch.

Funeral Cards Online—a searchable index of more than 19,000 funeral cards that provide death and birth dates and names of funeral homes.

Online Family Trees—a searchable index of more than 400,000 names from family trees in a file format used by the GenDex project.

Surname Tracker Service—a program that runs 24 hours every day to match information in its databases with the profiles of registered users.

Local Genealogy Directory—a list of links to quality Web sites, transcriptions, cemeteries, historical societies, libraries, and reference materials for more than 30,000 communities in the United States.

Genealogy Calendar—a quick and easy method for finding family reunions for your surname, school and military reunions, regional fairs, local workshops, and national conferences.

Roots Helper—provides assistance in solving various research tasks.

Eastman's Online Genealogy Newsletter *(blog.eogn.com)*

Eastman's Online Genealogy Newsletter is a daily newsletter and blog that is available both online and via e-mail. Dick Eastman, a long-time genealogist, writes the online periodical every day. The newsletter is available in two editions: the standard edition, which is free of charge; and the Plus edition, which costs $19.95 for a one-year subscription and is advertisement-free. There are also thousands of articles available for viewing at the Web site's archives. In addition to announcing any new developments within the field of genealogy, Eastman writes on just about every possible topic of interest to genealogists and family historians. He also reviews computer software and hardware, books, journals, videos, and podcasts.

Genealogy Dictionary
(www.genealogy.com/00000736.html)

This dictionary and glossary is part of the Genealogy How-To Guide at Genealogy.com's Learning Center. By clicking on a type of record, such as "1790 census" or "Directories," you gain access to a page explaining the definition of the term or describing the record in detail. If applicable, such as in the case of a specific census, directions are given on how to access the record. This resource provides a detailed description of the type of information available for each census conducted by the United States since 1790.

Encyclopedia of Genealogy *(www.eogen.com)*

The Encyclopedia of Genealogy, sponsored by Eastman's Online Genealogy Newsletter, is a compendium of genealogical techniques and tools submitted by users. Anyone can search the encyclopedia for free and contribute articles or edit existing ones. The only requirement is that the article pertain to some aspect of genealogy. You can locate subject material or definitions by using either the search function or the alphabetized index.

Genealogy Fast Track — Decision Charts
(www.genealogy-fast-track.com)

Genealogy Fast Track provides tips, resources, and references for conducting basic genealogical research online in the quickest way possible. A series of free decision charts guide you through the specific steps needed to research and document your genealogy. The Web site emphasizes using online family trees, birth and death records, the United States Federal Census, and the Social Security Death Index. It also recommends specific genealogy books and Web sites, as well as computer software and tools.

Census Tools *(www.censustools.com)*

We stumbled across the Census Tools Web site one night by accident, and are we glad we did! Created and maintained by Gary Minder, a family historian who was looking for a way to streamline his genealogy research, the site offers more than forty spreadsheets for handling extracted data from censuses, cemetery listings, passenger manifest records, family group reports, research logs, and various checklists. The downloadable spreadsheets, which are free of charge, require Microsoft Excel 97 (or later) for either PC or Mac. The 160 worksheets contained in the spreadsheets are also available in PDF format for those users who do not have access to Excel. The spreadsheets can be downloaded individually or in one of three collections: U.S. Federal 1790–1930 Collection, International Collection, or the State Collection. You can also download all of the spreadsheets in one file, the CensusTools Collection. The Web site also offers a free newsletter that provides useful hints and tips for dealing with research data.

Louis Kessler's Genealogy Software Links *(www.lkessler.com/gplinks.shtml)*

This extensive list of genealogy software and utility programs includes short descriptions and links to the software manufacturer's or shareware author's Web site. Louis Kessler, lifelong genealogist and one-time beta-tester for the Generations genealogy software program, also provides his own subjective opinion on each software program. Links to formal product reviews, mailing lists, newsgroups, journals, and magazines are included. The Web site's links are organized into lists of the top software programs, the most popular programs, the most comprehensive programs, utilities, programs for mobile handheld devices, and software repositories. The site is up-to-date and well maintained. You can read more about Louis Kessler and his genealogy activities at his personal Web site (www.lkessler.com/index.shtml).

Web Sites You *Should* Visit

Once you've made your way through all of the must-see spots we've just told you about, you'll be ready for the ones that are not necessarily must-sees, but more like should-sees. Although these sites may not make the list of your absolute first stops, they're full of useful information and will expand your online journeys.

Photo Detective *(photodetective.blogspot.com)*

Maureen Taylor has been working with photo identification since 1978 when she "fell in love with" a daguerreotype. Today, she operates the Photo Detective Web site. Maureen is a photo identification and family history expert frequently featured in the *Wall Street Journal* and on television shows, including *The View* and *The Martha Stewart Show,* and on PBS. Maureen is the author of *Uncovering Your Ancestry Through Family Photographs*; *Preserving Your Family Photographs: How to Organize, Present, and Restore Your Precious Family Images*; and *Through the Eyes of Your Ancestors*. With a master's degree in history and years of experience as a photo curator, she is internationally recognized as an expert in her field.

You can send your "mystery photograph" to Maureen via the Web site, and Maureen will apply her sleuthing talents to puzzle out its secrets. Her fees vary according to the project. Her site presents a slideshow of three photographs with audio commentary describing her identification process. For example, Maureen shares how she determined that a photograph (fig. 5-4) of her grandmother was taken on her wedding day in 1912.

Solving Photo Mysteries: A Few Words with Maureen Taylor, the Photo Detective

We had the honor of speaking with Maureen Taylor, a leader in the field of photo research. Since Maureen has been identifying photos for so long, she has personally witnessed the impact that the Internet has had on genealogy research. She believes that today's strong interest in genealogy can be traced to recent DNA discoveries and the ability to have individual DNA tested to learn about ancestral lines.

Figure 5-4
Maureen Taylor's grandmother

Clients ask her to identify every element in a photograph, from the location to the people. She looks at elements such as clothing and jewelry styles, any signs in the picture, and the photographer's name or mark, which is sometimes included on the front or back of a photo. All these clues help her place a picture in its appropriate spot on the historical timeline.

As far as developing a system for organizing your family photos, Maureen suggests filing them according to surname, while also considering the fact that you'll have group portraits. "I'd look at the filing systems used in libraries first and see what's comfortable for you," she suggested. We asked Maureen what the worst thing is that people do when trying to preserve their treasured family photographs. "They laminate them!" she replied emphatically. "It destroys what they are trying to save."

Some of the Web sites Maureen favors include Heritage Quest (www.heritage questonline.com), Ancestry.com, and GenealogyBank (www.genealogy bank.com). These "are three big ones I use all the time. Let's not forget Google.com and Ask.com," she said. "I'm particularly fond of GenealogyBank.com and DeadFred.com (www.deadfred.com). The first because newspapers are an underused resource, and the second because the founder of Dead Fred is on a mission to reunite folks with their photos."

Maureen somehow finds the time to maintain several interesting Web sites in addition to Photo Detective. At the Photo Detective blog (photodetective. blogspot.com), she fills in readers on her latest activities and projects. Maureen's blog, The Last Muster (www.lastmuster.blogspot.com), discusses the very ambitious American Revolutionary War project that she is working on with her partner David Lambert, who is the online genealogist at the New England Historic Genealogical Society (www.newenglandancestors.org).

Maureen and David are trying to find photographs of the last living Revolutionary War veteran and the last living Revolutionary War widow from each state. Many of the men, women, and children who personally experienced the Revolutionary War lived past the arrival of photography in 1839.

To identify Revolutionary War photos, Maureen and David apply specific criteria that give you a good idea of how Maureen approaches her work. First, the pair determines whether the image is a daguerreotype, an ambrotype, a tintype (ferrotype), or a *carte de visite*. Daguerreotypes, the first photographs, were common between 1839 and 1869. They have reflective surfaces, and you have to hold them at an angle to see the image. These were often placed inside cases. Ambrotypes were glass images invented in 1854, which were often backed with a dark material because they were fragile. Tintypes, also called ferrotypes, were invented in 1856. They were made on thin sheets of iron. The *carte de visite* was introduced in 1854. Inspired by nineteenth-century visiting cards, these images typically measure two by four inches.

After determining the type of photograph and its particular time period, Maureen assesses the ages of the people pictured. Are they old enough to be part of the Revolutionary War generation? Anyone who was an adult during the American Revolution had to be at least 80 years old by the time photography was invented. Individuals who were children during the American Revolution would be in their late fifties or older in a photograph. Wives and widows are another story. The last surviving widow of a Revolutionary War soldier, Esther Sumner, died in 1906! (She married Noah Damon when she was 21 and he was 75.) Maureen looks for potential wives and widows in photographs taken between 1840 and the early 1900s. Figure 5-5 illustrates one of Maureen's Revolutionary War finds.

AncientFaces *(www.ancientfaces.com)*

Founded in 1999, AncientFaces was first intended to be a site where people could post pictures of family members who were either unidentified or thought to be lost, so that distant relatives and friends could share their knowledge about these photos. The site has grown from only a few hundred photos to tens of thousands of images from families from around the world. The site offers a free Family Research program, and military and mystery photos, too. Figure 5-6 shows an example of a mystery "grandma." AncientFaces has become a place where families can preserve their histories by creating their own online areas called Family Spaces, which are customized Web sites for individual families.

Ancestors at Rest (*www.ancestorsatrest.com*)

This site is designed to help you find your ancestors using death records. You can search the indexes of several databases, listed by state, for free. You can also search collections of coffin plates, death cards, funeral cards, wills, church records, family Bibles, cenotaphs (monuments to people whose remains rest elsewhere), and tombstone inscriptions. There are links to other death records, including vital statistics, cemeteries, and obituaries. The site offers information, articles, and tutorials about interpreting inscriptions on tombstones, alternative sources for death records, and funeral customs. It even helps you understand some of the stranger

Samuel Curtis (July 30, 1779 –August 25, 1879)
M. Chandler, Marshfield, MA 1879 CDV
Based on the photographer's imprint, date on the back, and research in published vital records, Maureen Taylor determined this was a picture of "Samuel Curtis, died 21 August 1879, aged 100, 22 days." The final piece of identification fell into place with his obituary in the Boston Daily Advertiser, August 25, 1879. It stated, "On his last birthday he had his photograph taken twice, once alone and once in a group." Taylor and Lambert haven't located the group portrait yet. His father Samuel Curtis served as a private with Captain William Turner's band of Minutemen that answered the call for troops during the Battle of Lexington and Concord, April 19, 1775.

If you have information or images to contribute to Maureen's Revolutionary War project, please contact her.

Figure 5-5
Photo of a Revolutionary War veteran identified by the Photo Detective

causes of death that appear on old death certificates and in obituaries. The Ancestors at Rest blog (ancestorsatrest.blogspot.com) provides updates on what's new to the site, along with other timely research information.

Figure 5-6
Example of an uploaded photo at AncientFaces.com

Find a Grave *(www.findagrave.com)*

The Find a Grave Web site was founded by Jim Tipton in 1995, as an extension of his unusual hobby of visiting gravesites. Jim has told us that he didn't plan to become a resource for genealogy researchers, but this is the way his site has evolved. Jim's Web site has become wildly popular, rapidly growing way beyond his expectations. There are over 200,000 individual contributors who submit new burial records, grave and cemetery listings, updates, biographical sketches, virtual flowers, photographs, and editorial corrections. The Web site lists more than 19 million grave records. Besides viewing the cemetery records of ordinary people, you can also view the gravesites of the rich and famous and even the infamous (fig. 5-7). There is a yearly necrology for celebrities going back to the year 1900. You can read the official obituaries of your favorite celebrities and participate in discussion forums and message boards (fig. 5-8).

The National Personnel Records Center *(www.archives.gov/st-louis/military-personnel/index.html)*

This NARA center is making available all of the official military personnel files of military personnel who served in the U.S. Army, Army Air Corps, Army Air Force, Navy, Marine Corps, and Coast Guard before 1946. You can also find the records of all personnel who were discharged, retired, or died while in service before 1946. There are more than six million records. The type of information you can get varies according to whether you have the authorization of a veteran to access it. If you are asking about a veteran who is related to you, or the next of kin if the individual is deceased, you'll need an authorization to gather any information that is not available to the public under the Freedom of Information Act.

GenealogyBank *(www.genealogybank.com)*

This Web site offers over 250 years' worth of U.S. newspapers (from 1690 to 1977), government documents, and historical records (from 1789 to 1980) from all fifty states. The original documents include sermons, novels, maps, and gazetteers. The site also offers millions of American obituaries from 1977 on and millions of marriage and death records. There is a subscription fee of $69.95 per year.

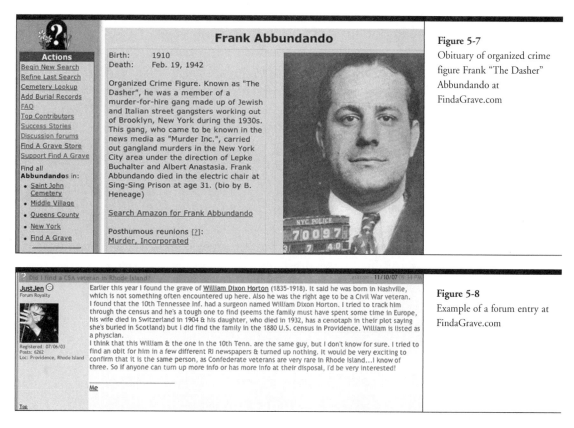

Figure 5-7

Obituary of organized crime figure Frank "The Dasher" Abbundando at FindaGrave.com

Figure 5-8

Example of a forum entry at FindaGrave.com

Census Research for Genealogists
(www.1930census.com/index.php)

When you visit this site, you'll gain a good understanding of how important census information is to genealogists. The Web site address mentions the 1930 census, but the site covers the federal censuses in general and offers many free resources. You'll also find British, Irish, and Canadian census information. And there are some little-known city censuses available. For example, there is the Waterbury, Connecticut, city census of 1876, which was taken to commemorate the centennial of the United States.

1890 Census Substitute at Ancestry.com
(www.ancestry.com/search/rectype/census/1890sub/main.htm)

Fire destroyed many records from the 1890 census and this site is Ancestry's effort to provide researchers with the information that survived. It includes surviving fragments of the original 1890 census, special enumerations of military veterans, Native American tribe censuses, state censuses (1885 or 1895), city and county directories, alumni directories, and voter registration documents.

Census Online *(www.census-online.com)*

The site's owners call Census Online "the Web's largest directory of links to online census transcriptions." Volunteers created census transcriptions by actually copying the information from a census record and putting it into a standard format for Internet researchers. Figure 5-9 shows an example transcription. The directory includes links to federal censuses and indexes, state and territorial censuses, tax lists, voter lists, military pensioner lists, and more.

Ellis Island Foundation *(www.ellisisland.org)*

Here you'll find many free items, including free forms for downloading, free searching of passenger lists, family histories, and a list of famous

Figure 5-9

Example of a transcription from the Arizona Territory 1910 census

```
Year: 1910   Territory: Arizona   County: Coconino   ED: 21   Sheet No: 1B
Reel no: T624-39   SD: 3   Division: Fredonia Precinct   Page No: 1A
Incorporated Place: Fredonia Village
Enumerated on: April-May 30-2, 1910 by: Asa W. Judd
Transcribed by Claudia Breunig for USGenWeb,
http:www.rootweb.com/~census/. Copyright: 2003
```

LINE	Street	House	Dwell	Famil	LastName	FirstName	Relationship	S	C	Age	Ma	Yea	Bo	Li
1			1	1	Haycock	Walter	Head	M	W	31	M	7		
2			1	1	Haycock	Annie C.	Wife	F	W	26	M	7		
3			1	1	Haycock	W. Marinus	Son	M	W	5	S			
4			1	1	Haycock	Elloene	Daughter	F	W	3.	S			
5			1	1	Haycock	Bessie	Daughter	F	W	2	S			
6			1	1	Haycock	Bertha	Daughter	F	W	1/12	S			
7			1	1	Jensen	Bertha A.	Sister-In-Law	F	W	18	S			
8			2	2	Brooksby	William	Head	M	W	31	M	5		
9			2	2	Brooksby	Emma E.	Wife	F	W	20	M	5	2	2
10			2	2	Brooksby	Willaim Oscar	Son	U	W	4	S			
11			2	2	Brooksby	Clarance J.	Son	M	W	3/12	S			
12			3	3	Lewis	Arthur E.	Head	M	W	39	M	7		
13			3	3	Lewis	Mary C.	Wife	F	W	27	M	7	4	4
14			3	3	Lewis	Julia Ann	Daughter	F	W	6	S			
15			3	3	Lewis	Violet	Daughter	F	W	4	S			
16			3	3	Lewis	Arthue E. J	Son	M	W	3	S			
17			3	3	Lewis	Velma	Daughter	F	W	1 1/12				
18			4	4	Nielsen	Hans P.	Head	M	W	31	M	8		
19			4	4	Nielsen	Anne Marie	Wife	F	W	26	M	8	4	4
20			4	4	Nielsen	Thomas J.	Son	M	W	U	S			
21			4	4	Nielsen	Hans Herm*s	Son	M	W	7	S			
22			4	4	Nielsen	Bernice	Daughter	F	W	3	S			
23			4	4	Nielsen	Marie Antonette	Daughter	F	W	9/12	S			
24			5	5	Dobson	Jesse W.	Head	M	W	26	M	1		
25			5	5	Dobson	Euphrasia	Wife	F	W	25	M	1	1	1
26			5	5	Dobson	Zepher	Daughter	F	W	9/12	S			
27			6	6	Dalley	Elastus B.	Head	M	W	38	M	6		
28			6	6	Dalley	Margaret E.	Wife	F	W	31	M	6	3	3
29			6	6	Dalley	Roniola	Daughter	F	W	U	S			
30			6	6	Dalley	Alma E.	Daughter	F	W	U	S			
31			6	6	Dalley	Aution P.	Son	M	W	U	S			
32			7	7	Brown	Abia Wm.	Head	M	W	69	M	46		
33			7	7	Brown	Emma F.	Wife	F	W	57	M	46		
34			7	7	Brown	Rex Rolland	Son	M	W	29	S			

arrivals, including Sigmund Freud, Charlie Chaplin, and Harry Houdini. There are many photos and even a place to tell your family's story. A membership of $45 per year helps maintain the organization and keeps access to the records free, but you don't have to pay the fee to search the records.

Allen County Public Library Genealogy Center
(www.acpl.lib.in.us/genealogy/index.html)
The Allen County Public Library in Fort Wayne, Indiana, has the second largest collection of genealogical materials in the United States. It includes more than 350,000 printed volumes and 513,000 microfilm and microfiche items. Footnote.com plans to digitize the library's genealogical holdings and make them available for a fee.

WorldVitalRecords *(www.worldvitalrecords.com)*
Here's a great deal. For a fee of $49.95 per year, for less than what Ancestry.com charges. this site provides information on more than 500 million surnames. It offers access to Everton's Online Library, the International Parish Register Collection, and the Quintin CD-ROM Library. The price also includes access to Newspaper ARCHIVE, SmallTownPapers, Accessible Archives, Find a Grave, and AllCensus.

Bible Records Online *(www.biblerecords.com)*
Family Bibles often have inscriptions that list the names of family members. Some inscriptions are like family trees and provide birth, marriage, and death dates of individual family members. This Web site is devoted to transcribing the family record information collected from inside family Bibles and digitizing it so it can be accessed on the Internet. The transcriptions included at the site date from the 1500s to the present. You can browse the Bibles by location, look through the surnames mentioned in the Bibles, view photos, and check out links to other Bible records sites.

Bureau of Land Management General Land Office Records
(www.glorecords.blm.gov)
This is the place to go to for access to federal land conveyance records for the so-called public land states, which were created from the public domain. These states are Alabama, Alaska, Arizona, Arkansas, California,

Colorado, Florida, Idaho, Illinois, Indiana, Iowa, Kansas, Louisiana, Michigan, Minnesota, Mississippi, Missouri, Montana, Nebraska, Nevada, New Mexico, North Dakota, Ohio, Oklahoma, Oregon, South Dakota, Utah, Washington, Wisconsin, and Wyoming. You can also see the images of over three million federal land-title records for eastern public land states that were issued between 1820 and 1908. Images of serial patents, or land titles that were issued between 1908 and the mid-1960s, are also available. Images associated with survey plats and field notes that date from 1810 are being added on the site on a state-by-state basis as these documents become ready for viewing. Plats are the official graphic drawings of boundaries created in a survey, and they are used when land titles are transferred from the federal government to individuals. Plats also show the official acreage used in the legal description of public lands.

FootNote.com *(www.footnote.com)*

This relatively new Web site already has many fans. Here you will find images of original source documents—millions of them. Many of these have never been available online until now. You can add annotations to the images, share them with other researchers or family members, and upload your own photos and documents to the site, making them searchable by others. The story pages let you share with other researchers what you know about original sources and invite those interested in the same topic to share their insights with you. A portion of the site is available at no charge, while access to all of the features requires a subscription. The free documents currently include those influencing American history: almost 13,000 government UFO reports, over 100,000 pages of Pennsylvania historical documents from 1664 to 1880, official documents of the original thirteen colonies and the early United States, and copybooks of George Washington's letters in his own handwriting. A free trial membership is available.

Treasure Maps *(www.amberskyline.com/treasuremaps)*

This Web site offers a variety of useful information, including the very popular and recommended tutorial on how to read old handwriting. It also provides information on coats of arms, genealogy search engines, and a series of questions so you can test your genealogy IQ.

American Life Histories—Manuscripts from the Federal Writers' Project *(lcweb2.loc.gov/wpaintro/wpahome.html)*

The Federal Writers' Project compiled and transcribed the life histories of individuals for the U.S. WPA from 1936 to 1940. The collection at the Library of Congress includes 2,900 documents, representing the work of more than three hundred writers in twenty-four states. The collection includes drafts and revisions that vary from 2,000 to 15,000 words. The documents include narratives, dialogues, reports, and case histories. The histories have information about the individual's family education, income, occupation, political views, religion, health, and diet. Often pseudonyms were used for the individuals and places named in the texts. You can search by keyword or by state.

StoryCorps Question Generator *(storycorps.net/participate/question_generator)*

If you're interested in getting oral histories from your family members, this is a great tool. It will help you develop a list of questions for your interviews. The Question Generator was created by StoryCorps, a national oral history project conducted by an independent nonprofit organization whose stated mission is "to honor and celebrate one another's lives through listening." StoryCorps began in 2003, setting up a StoryBooth to record people's stories in Grand Central Station in New York City. The interviews StoryCorps recorded are archived at the American Folklife Center at the Library of Congress. Portions of these stories are broadcast on the National Public Radio show "Morning Edition" every Friday. There are instructions about how you can participate in the national project, and you can get access to selected stories by subscribing to the site's podcasts, via e-mail in the Listen Closely newsletter, or by watching StoryCorps videos on YouTube (www.youtube.com/storycorps). You can keep up with the latest happenings in the StoryCorps world through its blog (www.storycorps.net/blog).

AfriGeneas *(www.afrigeneas.com)*

If you are looking for help in finding clues to your African American genealogy, this is the site for you. It is especially useful for researching African ancestry in the Americas. There is an African ancestry research community available at the site, which features the AfriGeneas mailing list, message boards, and chats on both a daily and weekly basis.

JewishGen *(www.jewishgen.org)*

JewishGen (fig. 5-10), an affiliate of the Museum of Jewish Heritage, is an extensive resource for researching your Jewish ancestry and heritage. Staffed mostly by volunteers, JewishGen provides wide-ranging resources and tools, including discussion groups, mailing lists, link directories, research databases, a learning center, special interest groups, special projects and activities, and fund-raising opportunities. You'll also find a handy calendar conversion tool for translating Hebrew calendar dates. JewishGen hosts various organizations, including the Ellis Island Foundation database, twenty different Jewish genealogical societies, the International Association of Jewish Genealogical Societies International Jewish Cemetery Project, Lithuanian Special Interest Group, and Jewish Records Indexing-Poland. One of the most popular databases on the site is the JewishGen Family Finder, which contains over 400,000 ancestral towns and surnames. Another popular database is the Family Tree of the Jewish People, which consists of user-submitted family tree GEDCOM files. Other databases include JewishGen Communities and JewishGen Holocaust, the JewishGen Online Worldwide Burial Registry, and the JewishGen Holocaust Global Registry. There are also many country-specific databases, catalogs, and files.

Society Hill Directory *(www.daddezio.com/society)*

Historical societies are a treasure trove of genealogy finds, providing information that is not available elsewhere through local records, photographs, and cemetery data. The Society Hill Directory lists U.S. (over 4,500 listings), Canadian (over 770 listings), and Australian (over 600 listings) historical societies.

The Practical Archivist *(practicalarchivist.blogspot.com)*

This is a self-described "geeky" blog for "genealogists, keepers of the family photo album, and anyone who loves a beautiful anachronism." It's jammed with helpful hints and interesting information about organizing and preserving photos, how to decide what to keep, scanning your documents, and numerous other topics. There is also an Ask the Archivist feature where you can post your archiving dilemmas, and links to podcasts created by the blog's author, Sally Jacobs, who lists her occupation as Saver of Memories.

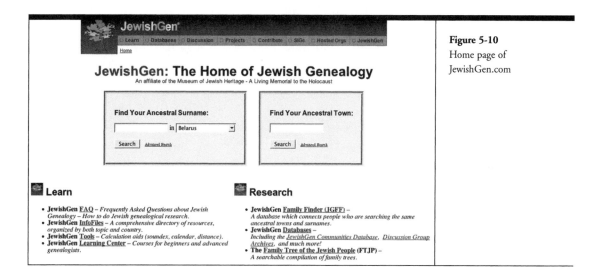

Figure 5-10
Home page of JewishGen.com

Dear Myrtle *(blog.dearmyrtle.com)*

On one of the most popular genealogy blogs, your friend Myrtle offers practical advice for family historians and keeps you current on genealogy topics in the news. She also has links to her podcasts at the site. One recent article announced the donation to the National Archives of two photograph albums that document the art stolen by the Nazis during World War II.

National Genealogical Society *(www.ngsgenealogy.org)*

Here's an excellent site that offers online and CD-based courses (for a fee) covering an introduction to genealogy research, the federal census, special censuses, transcribing information, and extracting and abstracting information records. There are articles on genealogy topics, plus a bookstore, links to other genealogy sites, and information about how to become a member of the society. It includes something for everyone, from beginners to more advanced researchers.

Board for Certification of Genealogists®
(www.bcgcertification.org)
The Board is in the business of assuring quality in genealogy research. Check here for excellent skill-building articles and examples of well-written genealogies and research notes. Look here for information on the steps you must take to become a certified genealogist. This is a good place to visit because it shows you how the pros do it. You'll be able to present your family history in the correct format and with appropriate citations and proofs if you follow the guidelines from certified genealogists.

The Genealogy Home Page *(www.genhomepage.com)*
Many Web sites offer a What's New feature, but this site has a What's Really New list, updated daily, which covers the latest additions to genealogy-related Web sites. The site offers genealogy help and guides; North American genealogy resources; worldwide genealogy resources; religious genealogy resources; family/personal genealogy pages; news-groups and mailing lists; links for searching for related genealogists; information about libraries, maps, geography, deeds, and photography; genealogy software; genealogy societies; upcoming genealogy events; and commercial services. You can also visit its companion file collection, which offers free and shareware genealogy software, the Roots-L file collection, and other text files providing genealogy information and help. There is a link to Genealogy Portal (www.genealogyportal.com), where you can search for surnames listed on Web genealogy sites.

Sites That Keep You Going
Okay, you probably feel totally exhausted from cruising around the Internet. Step away from the computer, do some stretching, massage those fingers, and then come back. We've got some sites for you to visit that will really keep your research going. They may not be your first stops along your online search, but they are fun and interesting, and when you feel completely overwhelmed, you can turn to them for a restorative entertaining diversion, and maybe even a missing clue.

The Genealogue *(www.genealogue.com)*

Ready for another take on genealogy? Author Christopher Dunham says The Genealogue (fig. 5-11) provides "genealogy news you can't possibly use." What a fun and irreverent way to look at genealogy! It's important to remember not to take ourselves too seriously. Dunham's blog profile lists his occupation as "unprofessional genealogist" and his About Me description pretty much sums up the blog's nature. We learn from the description that Dunham is "the descendant of a surprisingly large number of ancestors." His "turn-ons" include "transcribing, cemetery-hopping, and girls with big GEDCOMs." His "turn-offs" are "stingy town clerks, open graves, and girls who don't give sources." Don't miss his list of "genealogy Web sites I don't hate" and his top-ten lists, which include the Top Ten Reasons Santa Is a Genealogist. His Guide to Internet Genealogy Flowchart is a treat, as is the article "Six-Word Biographies."

GenDisasters *(www.gendisasters.com)*

If you're like most people, you're both curious and afraid of things like tornadoes, fires, floods, hurricanes, train wrecks, mine explosions, and tragic accidents. Yet these events became "a part of history and our genealogy." We found a newspaper article on this site about a train accident that listed the name of an ancestor whom we had always suspected had been a railroad engineer! Here we found our proof! Sadly, we also found out that he had died in this accident.

Celebrity Trees *(www.genealogy.com/famousfolks)*

Could you be related to William Shatner? Through this site you can answer that question by checking out the family trees of celebrities. Other celebrity trees available at the site include those of Jimmy Hoffa, Shania Twain, Jesse James, Lizzie Borden, Donald Trump, and Brad Pitt. You can search for common ancestors via a simple search box. The trees are provided in three categories: artists and athletes, royalty and first families, and historical figures. We checked and found that, as of now, we don't have ancestors in common with any of the celebrities here. (We'll keep checking.)

Figure 5-11
Sample blog post at The Genealogue

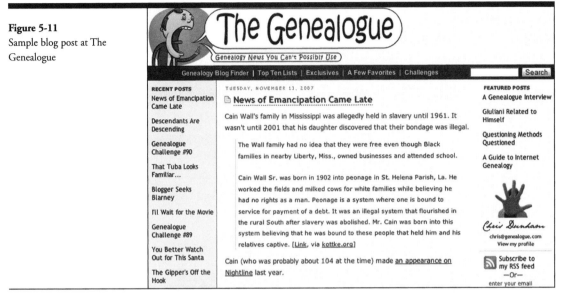

Old Pictures *(www.old-picture.com)*

This site provides a feast for the eyes with its large collection of original, historical photographs dating from 1850 to 1940. The pictures are from many countries around the world and are searchable by topic. You can also browse the collection by theme or title. We admit it: We spent a great deal of quality time here looking at the wonderful old pictures. The picture collections have titles such as American Adventure, African American, Old West, Civil War, Scenes of Rural America, United States History 1900s–1930s, the 1930s and 1940s, and Wright Brothers. What a great source for getting a visual fix on the times in which our ancestors lived. The pictures are provided free of charge, but you must contact the curator of the site (curator@old-picture.com) for permission to use a photo. We asked for and got permission to share figure 5-12 with you. As you can see, this image is fascinating for many reasons. For one, it shows a waffle house in Anchorage, Alaska, at the beginning of the twentieth century. That's not something you see every day. And the business was operated by two women entrepreneurs.

The I Seek Dead People Blog *(deadpeopleblog.blogspot.com)*

The author of this site offers this philosophy: "The dead shall rise, and when they do, I'll have plenty of blank family group sheets and pedigree charts waiting." A recent entry extolled the genealogical potential of regional cookbooks that often include the names of families and other information about their members. It's the sort of out-of-the-way site that offers some real hints and clues that might be missed by less adventurous researchers.

Dead Fred *(www.deadfred.com)*

Dead Fred is a genealogy photo archive that allows you to search a database that has thousands of identified and mystery photographs. If you find a photo of one of your direct ancestors that the site owns, Fred will send you the photo at no charge. You can upload your own photographs too, either for identification or to share. The site offers a newsletter and discussion groups.

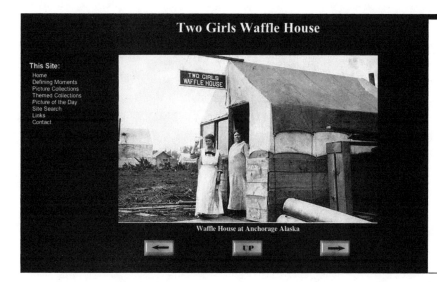

Figure 5-12
Photograph from old-picture.com, obtained with permission

Mayflower History *(www.mayflowerhistory.com)*

Here's the "Internet's most complete and accurate Web site dealing with the *Mayflower,* the Pilgrims, and early Plymouth colony," according to Caleb Johnson, the site's creator and *Mayflower* descendant. Lots of original documents are available here. We're talking full-text primary sources, including letters from Pilgrims! You don't get to read those every day. The *Mayflower*'s passenger list is here, as well as the wills of *Mayflower* passengers and their genealogies. It also includes Pilgrim-related resources.

Daughters of the American Revolution National Society
(www.dar.org/natsociety/default.cfm)
Founded in 1890, the DAR is a nonprofit volunteer women's service organization. Its mission is to promote patriotism, the preservation of American history, and education. It has 168,000 members in 3,000 chapters around the world. Any woman, 18 years of age or older, who can provide lineal descent from a patriot who fought in the American Revolution is eligible for membership. If you're interested in knowing if one of your ancestors was a Revolutionary patriot, you can fill out a form at the site, and a volunteer will look the name up for you in the organization's Patriot Index at no cost. The index includes the names of men and women whose service between 1775 and 1783 has been proven. If other information is available, such as birth and death dates and locations, names of spouses, rank, type of service, or pension papers, these will be included in the report.

Roots Television *(www.rootstelevision.com)*
Videos for genealogists and family historians can be found here. The creators say there is something here for everyone, including "an archives hound, a scrapbooker, a cousin collector, a roots-travel enthusiast, a Civil War reenactor, a DNA fan, a reunion instigator, a sepia-toned photos zealot, an Internet junkie, a history buff, an old country traditions follower, a cemetery devotee, a storyteller, a multicultural food aficionado, a flea market and antiques fanatic, a family documentarian, a nostalgia nut, or a mystery-solver." Currently, the programs can be accessed only through the Web site, but as television and computer technologies continue to merge, it is likely that you'll eventually be able to download them for viewing on your television set or other device. While most of the content is free, there are pay-per-view or download-to-own programs that provide necessary funding to keep the site going. A list of recent programming includes titles such as, "Spanish Parish Records," "Digital Images: Editing and Organizing," "A Psychic Roots Tale," "Lost Tulsa," and "Beneath Los Angeles." There are many programs here, so be sure to visit the site for information and inspiration. What a great idea!

Veterans History Project *(www.loc.gov/vets)*

The focus of this project, created by the Library of Congress, is the collection of personal accounts of U.S. veterans from World War I (1914–1920), World War II (1939–1946), the Korean War (1950–1955), the Vietnam War (1961–1975), the Persian Gulf War (1990–1995), and the Afghanistan and Iraq conflicts (2001–present). Any U.S. civilians who were actively involved in support efforts, including war industry workers, USO workers, medical volunteers, and others, are also invited to share their stories. You can decide to participate in the project by sharing your story, or you can search the stories in a variety of ways through the excellent search boxes.

MapYourAncestors *(mapyourancestors.com)*

Use the maps available through this site to follow the trail of your ancestors as they moved from place to place, look at an ancestor's home from above, create family directory maps to share information, or make chronology maps. Examples included: mapping the trails of George Washington (FamilySearch integration), the Clintons (life chronology map), and the Bushes (family tree map).

Odd Names *(f2.org/humour/language/oddnames.html)*

It may be politically not-so-correct, but we can't help laughing at some of the names that turn up in our research. Maybe that's why we've spent so much time at this site, which presents a list of humorous monikers. Just a sample: Bambina Broccoli, Mrs. Belcher Wack Wack, Preserved Fish, Jr., Primrose Goo, and John Senior, Jr.

Genealogy Blog Finder *(blogfinder.genealogue.com)*

Admit it, blogs done right can be great fun to read. This is a list of links to over seven hundred genealogy blogs. They're grouped into categories such as: genealogy news; tips, resources, and reviews; personal research; single surname; technology; preservation; photography; cemeteries; genetic genealogy; podcasts; libraries; African American; Jewish; international; conferences; queries; obituaries; professional genealogists; and humor.

Honoring Our Ancestors

(honoringourancestors.com/index.html)

This is a Web site created by Megan Smolenyak Smolenyak—yes, this is her real name and not a typo. She is the author of several genealogy books, including *Honoring Our Ancestors: Inspiring Stories of the Quest for Our Roots, In Search of Our Ancestors: 101 Inspiring Stories of Serendipity and Connection in Rediscovering Our Family History*, and *They Came to America: Finding Your Immigrant Ancestors*. She is a cofounder of Roots Television, and since 2000 has been a consultant with the U.S. Army's repatriation project, which traces the families of servicemen killed or missing in Korea, World War II, and Vietnam. She is also the chief family historian and North American spokesperson for Ancestry.com. The site is designed to encourage people to begin a search for their roots. There are grants available through the site for genealogy projects, guidelines for searchers, and the chance to submit your own stories for possible inclusion in future books, articles, or television shows.

Looking Ahead

You've checked out the Web sites, and you're doing fine just tooling down the research buffet, stuffing yourself with as many satisfying tidbits as you can fit on your plate. Suddenly, up ahead, you see a great big boulder in your path. Wait! It's not a boulder—it's a brick wall!

The term *brick wall* is what experienced genealogists call the dead-ends that crop up when researching a family line. It may be that your family members disappear from one census to the next. It may be that you've carefully documented your mother's lineage back five generations only to discover that you've been following the entirely wrong ancestor, and now you're stuck in the Swamp of Unknowing. How do you get back to firmer ground? Read on. In Chapter 6, we show you some alternative approaches that can help you tunnel through that brick wall and get back on track.

Chapter 6

Up Against the Wall

When genealogists come to the end of the line in tracing an ancestor, when they've followed every known avenue in their research and come to nothing, they know they've hit a *brick wall*. According to the *Oxford English Dictionary*, the term has been used since at least 1886, to mean an "impenetrable barrier," but it's taken the genealogical community to use the phrase with that special sense of frustration that comes from spending hours, days, or even years, trying to find the name of Great-grandma's grandma to no avail.

The world of genealogy research is a labyrinth of brick walls, and you can become obsessed with finding one elusive piece of information or looking for a single lost ancestor, only to feel your obsession drift off into hopelessness. Don't despair! In this chapter, we show you some ways to get around the brick walls and dead-ends that every researcher faces. Or, if you find that you can't get around one or go under it, you can at least look at some of the graffiti other researchers have left behind. Their stories will help to keep you hopeful! There's no feeling equal to that of having a solid brick wall suddenly tumble down to reveal an ancestor who seems to have just popped right out of the bricks. It has happened to many of the people we've spoken with, so never give up, it can happen to you too!

Alternatives Abound

While you may grow used to looking for birth, marriage, and death dates in census records and among the documents associated with cemeteries, Social Security, and obituaries, there are also other places to find this information. You can get creative, bypassing the normal paths or the usual suspects. Don't be afraid to look down a dark alley in your research. For example, there are online databases of criminal records, such as those available at Blacksheep Ancestors (www.blacksheepancestors.com). Searching such databases (fig. 6-1) may provide clues you'd otherwise

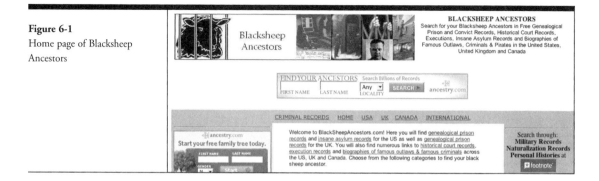

Figure 6-1
Home page of Blacksheep Ancestors

miss, and if you find out something you didn't know, just think of the interesting conversations you'll have at your next family get-together.

While checking a census on Ancestry.com, family researcher Mary Stickney discovered that her great-great-great-grandfather had served time at Sing Sing prison. "That was a shocker," she said. She also found a transcript of his court sentencing in the records of Rockland County, New York. Here's a portion of the record:

It was presented, that Abraham Osborn late of the town of Ramapo in said county of Rockland, laborer, on the fifteenth day of June in the year of our Lord one thousand and eight hundred and forty nine, with force and arms, in the day time, about the hour of eight in the forenoon of the same day, at the said town of Ramapo, in the said county of Rockland, the dwelling house of one Jonas Young, there situate, feloniously and did break and enter, with intent the goods & chattels of the said Jonas Young, in the said dwelling house, then and there being, then and there feloniously, and to steal, take and carry away, five 20 dollar bank notes of the value of one hundred dollars, ten 10 dollar bank notes of the value of one hundred dollars, forty 5 dollar bank notes of the value of one hundred dollars, ten 3 dollar bank notes of the value of thirty dollars, twenty 2 dollar bank notes of the value of forty dollars, thirty 1 dollar bank notes of the value of thirty dollars, and thirty pieces of silver coin of the currency of the United States of America, all of the goods chattels, property of the said Jonas Young . . .

As a result of this little escapade, Mary's ancestor was sentenced to two years in the clinker!

Vital Alternatives

When you start researching your family's genealogy, you begin with yourself and work backward through time, listing the names of your parents, their parents, their parents' parents, and so on, as far back as you can go. The major sources of family names are vital records. But what do you do when these records don't exist for a particular individual?

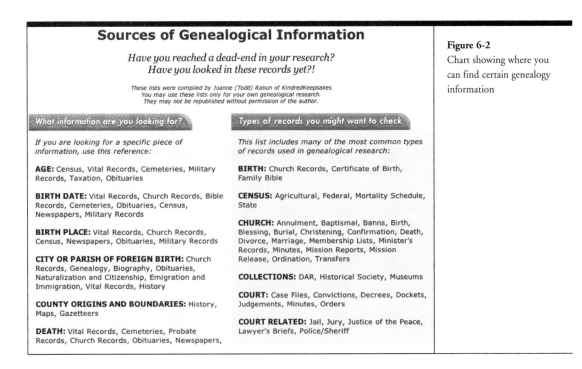

Figure 6-2

Chart showing where you can find certain genealogy information

There are alternatives. To find details about your grandparents, for example, you can check church records, newspapers for obituaries, wedding announcements, or birth announcements. Your family may have Bible records, letters, or diaries that you can check. If not, then you can find Web sites that will allow you to search their collections. For example, Bible Records Online (www.biblerecords.com) has created a database of transcribed family records that were written in family Bibles. As you know, land records such as deeds, mortgages, applications for homesteads, and other property records may also provide the names of relatives or clues about where to find them. Estate records and wills are other sources. The useful Sources of Genealogical Information chart (fig. 6-2) at RootsWeb (www.rootsweb.com/~genepool/sources.htm) is specifically tailored to researchers who feel they've come smack against a brick wall. It details records you may want to check when looking for information about an individual's age, occupation, historical background, immigration date, ethnicity, as well as names of relatives, birth and death dates, and marriage records.

Weaving the Name Pattern

In earlier days, it was the custom for the eldest son to inherit a family's property. To ensure that this occurred, the first-born son's given name was often that of his father. Later on, families wanted all of the children to have inheritance rights, so they frequently gave all of their children the same middle name to indicate their relationship. This shared middle name was often their mother's maiden name. But keep in mind that different countries have different naming patterns.

According to the USGenWeb Project (www.usgenweb.org/research/names. shtml), particular naming patterns were used in England between 1700 and 1875. Many families in the United States continued these customs, so they are worth considering when you're researching hard-to-find ancestors. This is how first names were given according to this tradition:

1st son—father's father's name

2nd son—mother's father

3rd son—father

4th son—father's eldest brother

1st daughter—mother's mother

2nd daughter—father's mother

3rd daughter—mother

4th daughter—mother's eldest sister

Younger children would have the names of earlier ancestors, but those patterns are more varied. It was also common for younger children to be named after local heroes. In the South, you'll find that many children were named Robert E. Lee and Jefferson Davis. Genealogist Jean Lawson offers a list of name variants that can be helpful (www.generations.on.ca/genealogy/naming-pattern.htm). For example, did you know that nicknames for Mary include Marion, Marla, May, Mimi, and Molly? Or that a woman whose formal name is Ellen might be called Eleanor, Elly, Ellyn, Elena, Helen, Nell, or Nellie?

Finding the Females, or, May I Introduce My Maiden Name?

One of the most enduring of all genealogical mysteries is a woman's maiden name. Sometime during the lives of nearly all of your female ancestors, their names were changed. Some of them changed names several times. Once a woman married, she was known by her married name. In many cases, her maiden name is reflected only in a single middle initial. Luckily, there are ways to solve this puzzle. Marriage records are the best source of a woman's maiden name, of course, but sometimes cemetery records will be the only place you can find evidence of a female ancestor. These records may list a woman under her maiden name accompanied by a "wife of ___" notation, or they may list a maiden name as a woman's middle name or initial.

Census records often show young married couples living with the parents of the wife, or having an older relative living with them in their household. The names of these individuals should be considered leads in the maiden name search. And again, land records may provide much critical information about an ancestor. Fathers often left family lands to their daughters, and deeds will include the names of these women. Churches often keep birth or christening records. These generally include both parents' names, so they are a good source for finding a woman's maiden name. Church records are another alternative to civil marriage registration data. If you have some idea about who the parents of your mystery female ancestor were, you can look for their probate record or will. These records include the surnames of spouses and children.

Newspapers published in the area where your ancestor lived, married, or died are another good place to find female names. Local papers frequently have obituaries listing the names of parents, children, and siblings. Plus, a feature story about a family celebration or gathering can offer some clues. It was not uncommon for small papers to include such cheerful stories. A death certificate may also include a woman's maiden name. If a woman's husband or children served in the military, you may be able to find pension applications or military service records that include biographical information. Finally, naming patterns can give you clues about women's maiden names. If you see an unusual middle

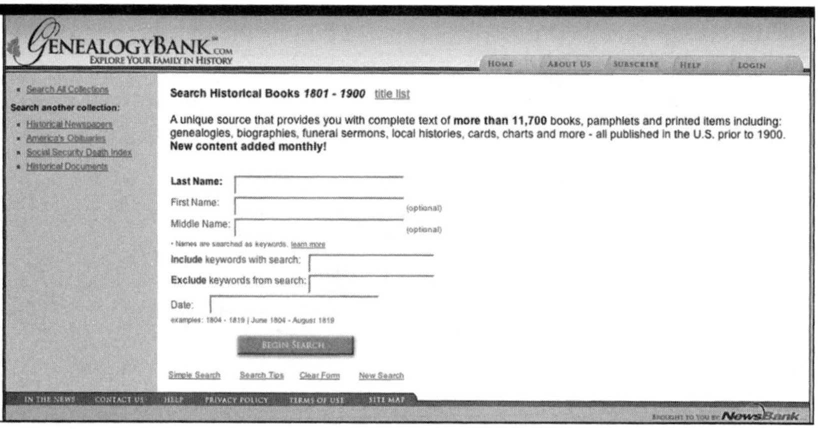

Figure 6-3
Home page and surname search form at GenealogyBank

name, it could be the maiden name of that person's mother or grand-mother. A good source to check is the GenealogyBank (fig. 6-3) Web site (www.genealogybank.com/gbnk/keyword.html), which offers thousands of searchable genealogy books, newspapers, biographies, marriage announcements, local histories, obituaries, and other records. All this information can be searched via a single page—just enter a name, and you're on your way. The searches themselves are free, but accessing the records will require you to sign up for a subscription at $19.95 per month, or $69.95 per year.

Don't Forget the Animals

OK, it's not the first thing you'd consider when trying to find information about a lost ancestor, but records associated with a family's animals can yield important clues. In the past, people depended on their animals for more than companionship. They used horses for transportation and to help them work their land. Cows, chickens, and pigs were critical sources of food. Even cats and dogs had real jobs to do, catching mice or herding sheep, for example. By checking wills and probate records, you can often find mention of horses—often, an individual's most valued possession—given to a spouse, eldest son, or other well-loved relative or friend. Finding these names can open up entirely new lines of research and help you get around a brick wall. When trying to overcome a dead-end in your research, even animal records may be important!

Step by Step, Over the Brick Wall

Experienced genealogists have developed some common procedures for confronting research problems head-on. By following these guidelines, you will be able to handle your brick-wall ancestor confidently, instead of being intimidated and overwhelmed by seemingly insurmountable difficulties. The practical steps will help you to view your challenges with new eyes.

Everything in One Place

Here's why you must keep every scrap of paper and scribbled research note you've ever made (organized and filed so you can find the bits and pieces later, of course). The path over, under, around, or through the brick wall that you'll eventually face often begins with these notes. So start by collecting everything you've found about your ancestor and put all that information in one place.

Write down names and dates and other facts. The answer you've been looking for, or a clue to help you find it, may already be in your hands. You're not the same person you were when you began your research. You've learned more about genealogy, about the places to find relevant information, and about your family lines. In short, you're more knowledgeable, so when you review the material you've gathered, something you previously missed may jump out as a clue. New information appears online every day. There may be new databases available since you last reviewed your collected records. You may find names or place names that seemed meaningless when you started your research, but now that you've put in some time reading the census and other records, these names may have new relevance.

There are even software tools that will help you keep up with new information for your genealogical searches. For example, by registering at the GenealogyAgent Web site (genealogyagent.com) and paying $14.60 per year ($0.04 a day), automated software will monitor five Web sites and conduct 92 genealogy search combinations (things like birth location, death location, parents, siblings, children, spouses) per month to

Figure 6-4

Home page of GenealogyAgent

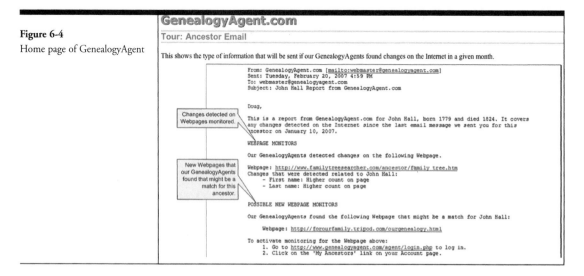

determine if any information has changed for the particular ancestor you specify. This service (fig. 6-4) saves you the trouble of repeatedly checking the same Web sites and performing the same searches over and over, only to find the same old information.

No Room to Assume!

Don't assume that printed records/sources or family stories and legends represent the truth. Yes, family members are some of the best sources for genealogy information, but they may embellish the facts, have spotty memories, or even want to hide things. Published histories and official records can also be wrong for a variety of reasons, so keep your critical eyes peeled when consulting books and other documents. Alta Flynt from the Roots-L mailing list related a great story about how she found the real name of the wife of Elwin Macomber of Dexter, Maine.

I had been given a family tree including the Macombers when I first started genealogy, and she [Macomber's wife] was listed as "Percie" with no surname. I found a book in the Online Genealogy Library at Genealogy.com that said Elwin Macomber married "Persis Chandler." The book was Macomber Genealogy *by Everett S. Stackpole. "Percie" sounded like a nickname for "Persis," so I believed Stackpole had it right—until I started hunting for her parents and found in the 1920 census that Elwin Macomber was married to "Priscilla." My first thought was that Percie had died, and Priscilla was a second wife, but I couldn't find a death record for Percie—and still no parents. Then I remembered that the Abbott Memorial Library in Dexter, Maine, has a number of old obituaries online. I searched for "Chandler" and found two men who were survived by a sister, "Percie Macomber." Their parents were named in the obituaries. I did an online census search, found the family, and learned that their daughter was "Priscilla," and that she was the exact age as "Percie." I still haven't found a marriage record that says either "Persis" or "Priscilla" married Elwin, but in the 1930 census Elwin's son, Linwood, had named his daughter "Priscilla." In every census from 1880 to 1930, both "Percie" and "Priscilla" used the middle initial "C." Looking on Ancestry.com, the Springfield, Massachusetts, city directory says Earl Macomber, a son of Elwin, lived at 134 Magnolia Terrace in 1951, and that Priscilla Macomber, widow of Elwin, roomed at the same address. I think this is pretty good circumstantial evidence that Percie's name was really "Priscilla" and not "Persis."*

And never assume that all primary records (birth and death certificates, marriage records, burial records, etc.) provide accurate information. Someone who didn't know actual dates may have provided the information, or the person recording it may have misheard what was said. When Deb's father was born, for example, his immigrant parents had been in New York less than two years. In 1912, her grandfather completed the birth certificate naming his new son Sam. Of course, he meant Samuel, and Dad happily went all through his life completing forms in the name of Samuel. When he retired and wanted to begin collecting Social Security, Dad had to go to court and provide proof that baby Sam and retiree Samuel were, indeed, the same person. Future descendants who decide to search for us would need to solve this puzzle, except, of course, we've recorded all details accurately! Finally, don't forget that sometimes people lie about their age—there are examples in the census of people aging by only five years between censuses that were taken every ten years. If only staying younger were that easy!

A Timely Use of a Timeline

Be sure to record known information on a timeline. Put life events—birth, marriage, death, and so forth—in chronological order. Then you can easily see where the gaps in your information exist. When you know exactly what you're missing, you can move on to checking the appropriate sources for that information. For example, if you need an immigration or naturalization date, check the federal census records after 1900; if you're looking for a death date, check newspaper obituaries, probate records, or the SSDI. Some researchers find it useful to write down their timeline information in narrative form, like a story. Others discover new clues when they transcribe information into their genealogy software. By concentrating your attention on just a few ancestors or family names at one time, instead of always trying to view the big picture, you can focus more on the details you may have missed in previous reviews.

Brush Up on Your (Local) History

Learn all you can about the history and geography of the place(s) your ancestors lived in or traveled to. You probably didn't expect to become a local history expert, but that's where genealogy research can lead you. Towns, cities, counties, and territories all have their own unique histories. By understanding a town's history, you may discover why court records are not where you expected them to be. For example, you may learn that the information about a person who lived in Shelby County, Texas—information that should have been in the Shelby County courthouse—can now be found in Rusk County, Texas, because the boundary lines were changed at some point.

Put Up Some Collateral

Research an individual's collateral lines—brothers, sisters, aunts, uncles, and other members of his or her extended family. Records that may not exist for the lost ancestor could easily be available for siblings. Check census and other records for every name you have in a family line. It's surprising what turns up when investigating these collateral lines.

Can You Spell?

Try spelling surnames another way. We've seen how census takers often guessed at spellings when filling out the forms, and we noted how different family members may use alternate spellings of the same surname. For example, in searching for the ever-elusive "Mary Ann McKay" of Texas, we've had to expand our thinking to include the surnames McKey and McCoy. And even so-called official information is subject to human error. This is a good place to apply the Soundex tool discussed in Chapter 4, which can help you find surname variations. City directories are another often overlooked source of alternate spellings.

Family researcher Alta Flynt discovered that "Daniel Flint," the name her husband's great-great-grandfather used, was really an alias. According to an old family story, the true family name was "Damon," but the Damon parents had been hanged as horse thieves, or something of the sort, and a family named Flynt had adopted the children. Alta's husband was told that anyone named Flynt was a relative, but that no one named Flint was. Alta eventually found that Daniel Flint had five sons, three of whom spelled the name "Flint," while two spelled it "Flynt."

As Alta tells the tale,

I have the habit of checking the new databases on Ancestry.com every day. One day there was an index of old Maine court records. I searched for "Daniel Flint" and found "Delafayette Damon, alias Daniel Flint." The index gave the volume and page numbers of the record. I sent for a copy and found that Delafayette Damon was married to his cousin Esther Damon in 1805 in Reading, Massachusetts. He went to Maine and changed his name to Daniel Flint—his father's first name and his mother's maiden name. He then went on to marry Lydia Williams in 1812 in Farmington, Maine. Perhaps he overlooked the fact that first wife Esther was still living, and they were not divorced. It seems his brother accused him of bigamy, and Daniel was tried and convicted in 1828. Delafayette, aka Daniel, appealed on the basis that both marriages took place in Massachusetts—the second one was before Maine became a state—and therefore Maine didn't have jurisdiction. The attorney general didn't pursue the matter, and Daniel went free. He and Lydia raised their family in Abbot, Maine.

Ancestral Land

Check land records for mention of additional names, such as those of witnesses to deeds and other land transactions. Often, these witnesses were close friends, neighbors, or members of the extended family. These individuals can open up additional lines of research. Remember, many more families lived in rural areas in the past, so any records dealing with land purchases or sales represent a potential treasure trove of people and place names. When using the census records, be sure to note the county and township borders or the enumeration districts (land divisions made for the purpose of taking the census in more populated areas). This will save you time, because you won't be searching for ancestors in places where they can't be found. Examine old maps to learn the geographical characteristics of your ancestor's home location, which may also spark the discovery of a new clue.

Back to the Beginning

We admit that we're fans of television police dramas such as *Homicide: Life on the Streets,* and we've learned through years of watching that detectives often hit brick walls. Their lieutenants always have the same advice when this happens: start over and recanvass. If you are really at a loss and feeling discouraged, do what those detectives do, and start over! Make a record of your research so you'll know where you've been and what methods you've used to solve the puzzle. You can download a research form at Ancestry.com (www.ancestry.com/trees/charts/ researchcal.aspx?) to help you keep track.

Finally, there is one more thing you can try. Do nothing. Stop looking for a while. Put the lost ancestor aside and come back when your enthusiasm returns. There are other lines to investigate and other stories to find. Some of your new finds might even put a chink in that old brick wall. Even if that doesn't happen, success with other ancestors can topple any old brick wall and keep you going!

Search Down the Street and Around the Corner

You can always learn a lot about someone by asking the neighbors. Your ancestors had neighbors, and by looking for the names and other information about individuals who appear in close proximity to your ancestors in the census records, you can often ferret out additional details and clues that may offer you a door through the brick wall. Families and friends tended to migrate together. As Debra Warila once exclaimed in a discussion of her Texas ancestors, "After looking at the censuses, I get the feeling that these same twenty families have been fooling around with each other for over one hundred years!"

Fellow Travelers

In the days of westward expansion in the United States, people often moved in search of more and better land. Extended families, which tended to live in close proximity, would move together to a new place. Often, their neighbors joined them in the search for a better life. Everyone pulled up stakes and, in the words of Mark Twain's Huckleberry Finn, "lit out for the territory." The same thing happened among immigrants to the U.S.

in the nineteenth century. Sometimes, entire towns were left nearly empty as the inhabitants set out for the golden shores of America.

The study of ancestors in relation to a whole community of extended family members, neighbors, friends, and other associates is called cluster genealogy. Often, individuals who seem to be neighbors are actually relatives. Since you can't rely on a single record or document as proof of a family connection, using cluster genealogy may provide more records to support your theories. And if you recognize the names of other family members in the census, for example, you can sometimes find the individual you're looking for even if that person has been mis-indexed, or if a census taker has misheard or misspelled the name.

Take the Indirect Route

When you begin a genealogy project, you generally search for ancestors in a direct line, moving back in time from one direct relationship to another (from mother to grandmother to great-grandmother, for example). With cluster genealogy, you investigate the family history by researching all the descendants of a given couple. You branch out beyond your family tree to research people connected to your direct-line ancestor.

In actual practice, you do cluster genealogy the same way you do your family genealogy research. Check the censuses, vital records, land records, published books, and all the other sources you've become familiar with. You'll just be expanding your research to include people who are not in the direct family line. Also pay attention to the husbands and wives of the clustered individuals. There may be published histories of these spouses available that include interesting details about their neighbors—your family! The cluster method is especially useful for researching families before 1850. This is the year that the federal census records started to include the names of individual members in a household.

Make Your Society Debut

Local genealogical and historical societies can be extremely helpful when you're looking for elusive ancestors. You should contact the society in the state most closely associated with the particular individual or family. For example, the Ohio Genealogical Society (www.ogs.org) has chapters in different counties that focus on their respective regions. Texas has several genealogical societies because it is so big, including the East Texas Genealogical Society (www.rootsweb.com/~txetgs), the South Texas Genealogical Society (www.beeville.net/STGS/Index.htm), and the Texas State Genealogical Society (www.rootsweb.com/~txsgs).

Many societies publish newsletters or quarterly journals that provide articles of special interest to researchers in their geographical areas. The Georgia Genealogical Society (www.gagensociety.org) for example, offers the *Georgia Genealogical Society Quarterly*. Most of the publications from local genealogical societies are indexed in the *Genealogical Periodical Annual Index*, which you can purchase by the volume at Heritage Books (www.heritagebooks.com), or find in your local genealogical library. Ethnic historical societies such as the Pennsylvania-German Society (www.pgs.org) and the American Jewish Historical Society (www.ajhs.org) also offer excellent information.

National societies have their place in your genealogy toolbox, too. The National Genealogical Society (www.ngsgenealogy.org) offers memberships at $60 per year. In addition to its periodical publications, discounts on research services, and purchases in the society's bookstore, you also get access to the organization's databases and forums. The databases include Bible records and members' ancestry charts, plus abstracts from the *National Intelligencer* of Washington, D.C., for the years 1800 to 1850. The abstracts cover the notices of marriage and death from the newspaper.

The New England Historic Genealogical Society (www.nehgs.org) is the biggest and oldest such society in the United States. For 154 years, it has assisted researchers looking for information about their families in New England and worldwide. The site includes a searchable catalog of the organization's more than 200,000 books, periodicals, and microform materials. You can also search over a million manuscripts dating from the thirteenth century to the present on topics that cover New England and other areas. You can read free articles at the site that cover a wide range of research topics, including genetic genealogy, military research, and ethnic research. And you can sign up for a free e-mail newsletter that will keep you informed about all the latest articles.

A Toolbox for Chipping Away at Those Brick Walls

As you can see, there are many opportunities to get creative and clever in your search for clues that may yield something big enough to smash through your brick wall. As you go through everything you've already gathered, turn a careful eye toward any photographs you have, whether labeled or not, and take a second look around your house for any family heirlooms. These items may offer details about your ancestors that can lead to the discovery of an important name or date. Let's look at some ways to make that happen.

Are You Ready for Your Close-Up?

Most of us have family photographs that include our ancestors. These pictures are chock-full of important clues about our families as they were at a particular moment in time. Sometimes, photos will have names and dates on the back to identify the people and the place they were taken. More often, however, you'll have to apply a little more detective work to discover a useful genealogical nugget. Early photographs were taken by professionals and may include the professional's name on the back. Using the name to find the photographer's place of business, you will be able to prove that your ancestor was in a specific place for at least as long as it took to snap the photo! The clothing people are wearing and the houses or countryside seen in the background may also provide clues. Check the Photo Detective Web site (www.photodetective.com) for more help in discovering the information held in family photos.

Airing the Heirlooms

Heirlooms passed down from generation to generation can provide more than material pleasure. They are historical artifacts that represent the time, society, and culture from where they came. You can study these artifacts for more clues about what your ancestors were like as real, living, breathing people. For example, clothing can provide clues. Did the individual have a lot of clothes suitable for formal occasions? If so, you can use this piece of information to search for their names in newspaper articles about formal or ceremonial events. Are there specific uniforms associated with service groups such as the Masons? If so, you've gained an entirely new clue to follow.

You can date certain events, such as military service, by examining uniforms. Furniture can suggest an ancestor's financial status, while jewelry may be engraved with initials or dates that can help you identify an ancestor. Lockets may even contain pictures of family members or locks of their hair. Letters and diaries are information goldmines, and you're lucky if you have them! In addition to names, dates, and descriptions of important family events, because these documents are written in your ancestors' own words, they can really give you insight into what the authors were like. Women were more likely to keep diaries than men, so you could potentially discover quite a bit about those "hidden" female ancestors by reading a woman's diary. (It's OK to do this when it's for research purposes!)

Swimming in the Gene Pool—DNA

One of the most exciting trends in genealogical research is the use of DNA testing. Using DNA together with traditional research methods can break down brick walls, or can at least make them a little shorter. Genetic genealogy has an increasingly critical role in tracing family lines. The trend was most recently influenced by the descendants of Thomas Jefferson and of a slave on his plantation, Sally Hemings. Their descendants turned to DNA testing to answer questions about their common lineage. According to Ancestry.com, more than 500,000 people worldwide have already taken a DNA genealogy test. There is even an International Society of Genetic Genealogy (www.isogg.org), which was founded in 2005 to encourage the use of DNA in genealogy. The organization has more than three thousand members.

The complexities of DNA and DNA testing are beyond the scope of this book, but essentially the technology has advanced to a point where you can test for your own DNA at home, send your sample to one of the many DNA testing companies, and receive your results within a few weeks. Many researchers have taken the test and been able to confirm whether or not they are following the correct family lines in their genealogical research.

Comparing your DNA test results with the results of other people can show you how closely you are related to them. DNA testing can also show your origins in the dim dark past, 170,000 years ago when humans migrated out of what is now Africa and began to spread out across the continents. As these early ancestors adapted to the areas they settled in, their DNA changed, and each group became distinctly different genetically. These different groups, called haplogroups, can now be traced through a simple test.

The DNA Basics

Every individual has twenty-three pairs of chromosomes that include the sex chromosomes, X and Y. Men have both an X and a Y chromosome, while women have two X chromosomes. Males inherit their Y chromosome from their father and the X from their mother. Females inherit one X chromosome from each parent. There are "heritage markers" on a chromosome that indicate people who are related, or in the same family. These markers are the focus of genetic genealogy.

The Y chromosome inherited by a son from his father is basically unchanged, so it offers genetic genealogists a tool for tracking the paternal line. These researchers examine and compare parts of a Y chromosome with those of other people to determine whether there is any relationship between them. A different kind of DNA is used to trace a maternal line because both parents contribute X chromosomes to female children. All children inherit mitochondrial DNA (mtDNA) from their mothers. Tracking this kind of DNA gives information about the mother's genealogy. You can use mtDNA results to exclude individuals from your maternal line. The mtDNA of the father is destroyed when an egg is fertilized, so a child gets mtDNA only from the mother. Because of this pattern of inheritance, both males and females can send a direct DNA sample—one that comes from them rather than from a relative—and have it tested to determine the maternal line. To test for the paternal lineage, women must send in a DNA sample from a male family member, such as a brother or an uncle.

Q A Genetic Genealogy Glossary

Haplogroup: A group of similar haplotypes that share a common ancestor with a specific mutation. A haplogroup consists of similar haplotypes, so it is possible to predict a haplogroup. There is a test to confirm the existence of a haplogroup. Haplogroups are assigned letters of the alphabet, with further distinctions noted by additional number and letter combinations. Haplogroups pertain to ancestral origins that go back thousands of years.

Haplotype: The term for the set of numbers that represents your Y-chromosome or mitochondrial DNA (mtDNA) results.

Marker: A specific place on a chromosome with two or more forms, called alleles, the inheritance of which can be followed from one generation to the next. In genetic genealogy, this refers to noncoding Y chromosome DNA. Numbers designate the individual DNA segments. For example, 393 = 13 means your allele value is 13 at marker #393.

Mitochondrial DNA: Mitochondrial DNA is passed from mother to child. Only females continue to pass on their maternal mitochondria to their children.

Mutation: A change in the DNA that occurs spontaneously. In genetic genealogy, mutations are used to distinguish different ancestral lines.

Sorensen Molecular Genealogy Foundation (SMGF): Established by philanthropist James Sorensen, the Sorenson database is billed as "the foremost collection of genetic genealogy data in the world." Sorensen project participants submit a DNA sample together with a four-generation pedigree chart. There is no charge to participate, but the organization does not send any test results back to you. However, you may be able to "find yourself" in the results database, which is available online, by matching your pedigree chart with those posted online. At present, the database includes only Y chromosome results. Also, there is a wait of nine months to two years to see the results. If you want to participate, check the Web site (www.smgf.org).

X chromosome: The female sex chromosome. A child who gets one X from the father and one X from the mother is female.

Y chromosome: The male sex chromosome. Only males have a Y chromosome, and they get it from their father, who received it from his father, and so on. Because the Y chromosome is transmitted this way—through the male line—it is used in surname testing to determine if two males have a common ancestor.

Where Do I Sign Up?

There are many companies that will test your DNA for you for genealogical purposes. Ancestry.com (fig. 6-5) offers several types of DNA tests (dna.ancestry.com/welcome.aspx). Ancestry recommends its Paternal Lineage Test (Y-Chromosome 33) test, which helps you find your genetic cousins and ancient paternal ancestors. The cost for this test is $149, and it can be performed only on male DNA samples. A more advanced form of the Paternal Lineage Test provides thirteen additional markers to provide a more accurate comparison with others who have taken this test. It costs $199 and is available only to male participants. A Maternal Lineage Test uses mitochondrial DNA to inform you about your ancestors on your mother's side. Both males and females can participate in this test at a cost of $179.

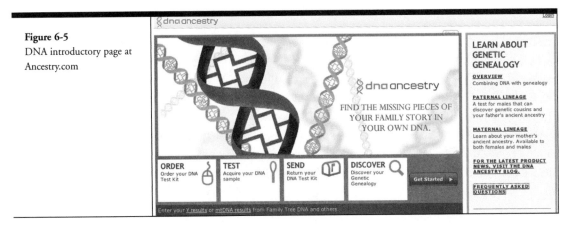

Figure 6-5
DNA introductory page at
Ancestry.com

Several companies that do genetic genealogy testing include Family Tree DNA (www.familytreedna.com), which offers Native American tests, African ancestry tests, Jewish ancestry tests, and a test through which you can discover if you are related to Genghis Khan! The following are some other companies that perform DNA testing:

DNA Heritage (www.dnaheritage.com)

DNA Tribes (www.dnatribes.com)

African Ancestry (www.africanancestry.com)

DNA Print (www.dnaprint.com)

All of these companies will send you a kit with a cheek swab, instructions, and a return mailer. You can see examples of DNA results used in a genealogical context at the Pomeroy Web site (www.dnaprint.com), which is hosted by RootsWeb. In fact, RootsWeb has a mailing list devoted to the subject of genetic genealogy (lists.rootsweb.com/index/other/DNA/GENEALOGY-DNA.html). If you want to keep up with the latest in genetic genealogy, look no further than the Genetic Genealogist blog (www.thegeneticgenealogist.com), which covers news stories, technological advances, and trends in the field.

Second Opinions

Not everyone is sold on the idea that genetic genealogy will provide you with relevant or useful answers to your inheritance questions. The field of DNA and genetics is complex, and too often the companies that encourage DNA testing for genealogical purposes do not educate consumers about what they can really learn from the test. Some consumers are disappointed with the results they receive because they expected more detailed information. Having a DNA test will not tell you the names of your ancestors, and even test results showing that you are related to Genghis Khan become less exciting when you realize that all it means is that you and Genghis Khan belong to the same maternal haplogroup. You won't find out the degree of the relationship, only that both your maternal lines descended from one woman. Additionally, the idea that everyone is from Africa is another example of oversimplifying reality. Many researchers are beginning to say that a certain DNA pattern is "strongly associated" with a location, rather than that "we are all from Africa."

Critics of genetic genealogy point to the fact that most of the commercially available DNA tests are able to trace just a few of your ancestors.

For example, they can't give you the exact place your family line originated. Critics also note that we are all related if you go back far enough in time. Rebecca Skloot, contributing editor at *Popular Science* magazine, is one of many journalists who has expressed reservations about genetic genealogy. In her blog post, The Bogus-ness of DNA Testing for Genealogy Research (rebeccaskloot.blogspot.com/2006/06/bogus-ness-of-dna-testing-for.html), she expresses her serious reservations about the tests, even going so far as to label them "a scam." In an article for *Popular Science,* Skloot investigated whether the technology and the companies offering it were legitimate. She gathered a group of experts in genealogy and DNA testing—one of whom was a scientist who first discovered some of the technology on which many of these companies base their tests—and had her own DNA tested, along with that of six family members. Her purpose was to see "if the tests could uncover something you'd never know from looking at me: My grandfather's great-great-grandmother was black." Her article (www.popsci.com/scitech/article/2003-12/putting-gene-back-genealogy) explains the science of these tests, what they did and didn't find, and expert opinions about the legitimacy of the tests. Skloot concluded that the tests can be fun and have definite uses in medical research, but they cannot provide definitive information about heredity unless two individuals are comparing their DNA samples to see if they are related. As Skloot summarized, "These tests most certainly can't tell you what you're not—as in, you're not African-American. But the general public doesn't know this, and no one seems to be telling them."

Get Educated

If you are thinking about getting a DNA test for genealogy purposes, always read the educational materials available on the Web site of the company you choose to perform the test. Ancestry.com, for example, has an extensive section informing you of how the tests work and what you will and won't get in your results. Be sure to read everything. It can get very technical, but stick with it. You'll be happier with your DNA test if you understand its limitations. Further information is located on Chris Pomery's DNA Portal (freepages.genealogy.rootsweb.com/~allpoms/genetics.html) and the Genographic Project Web site (www3.national geographic.com/genographic/).

Looking Ahead

With all the frustrations and obstacles you face doing genealogy research, it's a good thing you're not alone! Thanks to the Internet you can connect with other people who are researching the same family lines and benefit from what they've discovered on their genealogical expeditions. Family trees grow through sharing information in the form of GEDCOMs, blog commentaries, message board and forum postings, surname-specific Web sites, and mailing lists on just about any genealogy topic you can imagine. In Chapter 7 we explore some of these ways to connect with members of your research family.

Chapter 7

Meet Your Neighbors

I t is so easy to get buried beneath the sheer volume of information that you can find on the Internet. Suddenly, it seems like you're learning more about your family than you ever thought possible. But, just like families themselves, the Internet is, more than anything, a collection of people. So every now and again, lift your head up and away from those plentiful lists and records, and reach out to your neighbors. Not only are you likely to meet interesting people, but your research is also likely to gain depth and perspective that would not be possible if you were to travel this path all by yourself. After all, your distant relatives and long-lost family members may be out there just waiting to meet you!

"How do I find these distant relatives?" you ask. As you might expect, you can start with Cyndi's List for links to sites where you can share what you've learned and discuss your family history with other researchers. But the Internet is full of other interesting options, and many of them are free! So put on your friendliest face, get ready to ask and answer questions, and join your fellow researchers in the social aspects of digging into your history.

Make Family Connections

As you browse the Internet, you're bound to find ways to collaborate with other genealogy researchers. You'll find mailing lists, discussion boards and forums, and Web sites devoted to bringing you together.

Although it's your own family you seek, it's easy to find hundreds, if not thousands, of people looking for the same things that you are.

You'll be delighted to discover the phenomenon of Web rings, which come about when a subject is so popular and complex that indexes are needed for the many Web sites geared to it. All Web sites in a Web ring are focused on a single topic, as you can see in figure 7-1. Each site within a genealogy Web ring, for example, will have a link to the other sites. You can go through the sites one by one, randomly, or browse a list of all the sites included in the ring. Looking at a few Web rings illustrates just how many people are working within the same family lines.

Figure 7-1
An example of a Web site from the Genealogy Web ring

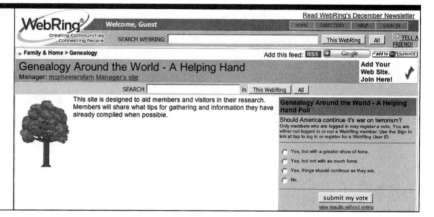

Digging into RootsWeb

As you saw in Chapter 5, RootsWeb is one of the best places to start connecting with your co-researchers. One of the main purposes of RootsWeb (searches.rootsweb.com/share.html) is to make sharing your family history with other people easy. Most of the site's content is contributed by researchers like you.

RootsWeb's Mailing Lists

RootsWeb has over 31,000 mailing lists on topics ranging from the general (how to begin your research) to the specific (lists devoted to a single surname, country, or even county) and the macabre (lists like the one that discusses "mysterious disappearances or appearances, unsolved murders, questionable incarcerations, and other mysterious or unsolved events in an ancestor's life"). You can think of a mailing list as an e-mail party line. When a subscriber sends a message, it goes to every other subscriber. Participating in a mailing list is a great way to connect with like-minded researchers. Lists vary, so you'll need to check each one to see how to subscribe, write messages, and unsubscribe.

Subscribing to a mailing list is one of the best ways to connect to people who share your interests. If you can imagine it, RootsWeb probably has a list discussing it. Does your last name start with *H*? Check out the *H* Surnames mailing list, and you'll probably find a relative. Do your family roots spring from Spain? Consult the Spain mailing list in the international category. Our personal favorite is the Other–Miscellaneous category, where you'll find Gen-Pitfalls (a list for exchanging information and suggestions about the common pitfalls of all genealogy researchers) or Witch-Hunting (a list for discussing and sharing information about the ancestors and descendants of individuals mentioned in original records related to witch hunting). You can browse the list of lists at the site (lists.rootsweb.com/index/index.html), but if you don't find a list on the topic you want, start one!

Message Boards

RootsWeb has hundreds of active message boards. Message boards are similar to mailing lists, but the messages written on a board are not automatically distributed to subscribers. Mailing lists are mostly for in-depth discussions, while message boards are often more public, meaning, anyone can post a message or search through the boards to find information. You can browse or search categories of message boards for topics that interest you (boards.rootsweb.com/topics/mb.ashx). You can see the number of subcategories under a topic as well as the number of boards for each category.

The Surname List

The Surname List at RootsWeb is an invaluable resource. It provides information about surnames submitted by over 194,000 genealogists. Each surname listing includes associated dates, locations, and instructions on how to contact the researcher who submitted the information. If you're investigating the same surname in the same area and time period, you can contact the person who added the name to the database to share and compare notes. The surname database has over a million entries, and it's growing by some 700 entries per day. You can add and edit the surnames you are interested in by filling out an online form (rsl.rootsweb.com/cgi-bin/rslsql.cgi) or you can submit a name via e-mail. The site offers excellent instructions on how to get started with the database. And you get all of this for free, so enter your surname of choice and see what turns up.

We entered the name Olsen and got several pages of results. One submitter had information on an Olsen dating from 1690, and another listed an Olsen who migrated from Norway to Minnesota to North Dakota. All the listings had e-mail addresses for contacting the person with the information.

User-Contributed Databases

Many genealogical records are online, but many are not. Many useful information tidbits remain locked up in printed books, handwritten documents, photographs, and microfilm in churches, organizational and government archives, genealogical societies, attics, and file cabinets. Volunteers continue to submit records from these sources to RootsWeb, making them available online. You can search for databases by country or state, or just browse through the hundreds of databases covering topics such as alumni directories, atlases and gazetteers, birth records, cemeteries, city directories, deeds, Native American records, African American records, newspaper indexes, obituaries, passenger lists, tax lists, state archives, and mortality schedules. If you want to add your own personal database of family history to the RootsWeb collection, you just fill out a form and upload your file (userdb.rootsweb.com/submit). All contributors retain the rights to their databases.

AncientFaces: Another Look in the Mirror

We mentioned AncientFaces in Chapter 5, but here's a look at how you can use this site to meet other genealogists. After registering for free at the AncientFaces Web site (www.ancientfaces.com), you can share your family stories, recipes, and images, including any "mystery" photographs, with other researchers. If you add your stories and pictures to the site, other researchers can view them and tell you about common ancestors. You can search for a family surname or browse the names already listed at the site to find possible connections. The site looks through all the photographs it receives from contributors and categorizes them into groups, including baby pictures, confirmations and baptisms, family homes and reunions, gravesites and obituaries, transportation, American Civil War, and weddings. This can make it easier for you to find what you're looking for. AncientFaces plans to add message boards for researchers. What sets this site apart from the others is the mystery photo feature. We know we'd like to upload some of our unlabeled photos to the site for identification. (And since it's free, who wouldn't?)

CousinConnect

Post your research queries at CousinConnect (www.cousinconnect.com) and get ready for answers. People from all over the world have entered their family research queries into the form at this Web site, and you can too. Here's an example: A query was posted about the surnames Cook, Nazarov, and Zuyeva. The submitter added that the "maternal family was displaced to Germany during WWII from St. Petersburg somewhere around the Siege. The English spelling of the name is Cook. Other names include my grandmother Iraida Zuyeva, and there was a housekeeper (?) named Goya. Does anyone have any information?" (If you do, fill out the form at www.cousinconnect.com/perl/contactform.cgi?id=149544.) You can browse the queries by region or search by surname for relevant questions. It's heartwarming to read the e-mails from individuals who have successfully found long-lost family members.

The site was designed to meet a need among genealogy researchers for a place to ask direct questions about connecting with relatives and missing friends. CousinConnect's creators believe that message boards are meant for conversations, rather than basic queries. You can lose yourself in the discussions on message boards and forums and forget why you went there in the first place. CousinConnect, shown in figure 7-2, lets you ask questions about your family and get answers fast. Its query notification service (www.cousinconnect.com/notify.htm) will send you an e-mail to let you know when a new query matching the surname(s) or regions(s) you are researching has been added to the site. This can save you a lot of time and frustration, and, judging from the success stories, it's well worth a try.

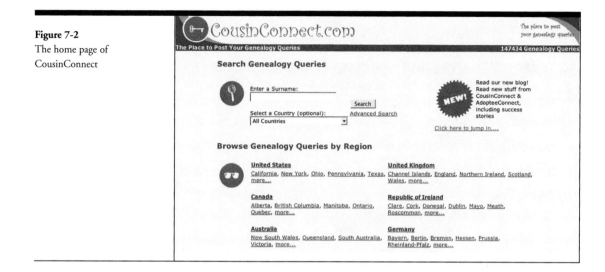

Figure 7-2
The home page of
CousinConnect

OneGreatFamily

While you need to pay a subscription fee to access OneGreatFamily
(www.onegreatfamily.com), it does have several features that make connecting to relatives and other researchers very easy (fig. 7-3). For one
thing, the site will merge two online family trees automatically when it
finds a common ancestor listed in each one. It will also find and elimi-
nate any duplicate information in a tree without any input from you.
The site focuses on collaboration, and you're always working with other
researchers when you add or edit family tree information there. The site's
automatic linking technology makes that possible. The idea behind the
site is that everyone participating there is essentially working on a single
online family tree, although every user keeps his or her own unique view
of how a family line connects to that tree. You can easily view what other
research has already been done on your tree and meet and work together
with other family members. There is a surname index (with alternate
spellings), a newsletter archive, and a genealogy learning center at the site
as well. You can try it out during a free seven-day trial period. After that,
you can pay $14.95 monthly; $29.95 quarterly, or $75.95 annually.

OneWorldTree

Ancestry.com's OneWorldTree (www.ancestry.com/search/rectype/trees/owt)
is a big "community" family tree. Ancestry uses all the trees that are

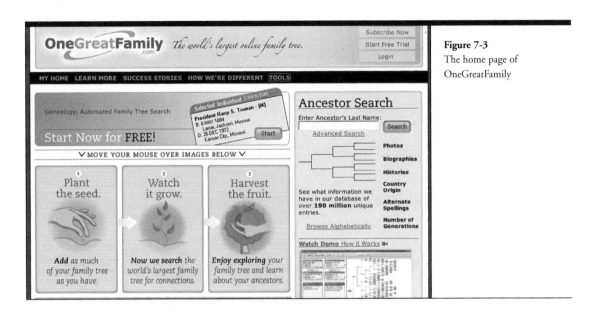

Figure 7-3
The home page of OneGreatFamily

submitted by the site's members and combines them with family trees and records taken from other sources. The Ancestry system can find probable matches in names and then shows the results in a consolidated way in a worldwide family tree. Viewing information like this can provide hints for further research, but you should not rely on the results to be fact. OneWorldTree consolidates so many sources that it's not possible to know if some member-submitted trees contain errors. And the computerized system can sometimes connect the wrong people, even if they have similar names. Ancestry keeps all the original trees and source records, and you can use its connection service to contact the person who submitted the information in the first place. Contact is anonymous. The OneWorldTree system processes millions of names, locations, and dates to find and combine probable matches from multiple sources. It's a great research aid, but as we said, don't rely on what you find here. Always double- and triple-check the information using other sources, too.

Chris Dunham, the Genealogue, Weighs In

Chris Dunham, the creator of the Genealogue blog (www.genealogue.com) is so well versed about the ins and outs of online genealogy that we knew he'd have something to say about Internet collaboration. He also agreed to share

some of his most memorable genealogical discoveries. Chris's blog grew from a longstanding interest in his family history.

I come from a small town in Maine where some branches of my family have lived for 200 years. Half the people on my newspaper route were relatives, though I wasn't always sure how we were related. I came online in the mid-1990s, and one of my first projects was publishing a Web version of the family history my sister had compiled. I spent the next decade improving upon this history online and off, frequenting message boards, and scouring the Web for information on my family. In 2005 I started my blog, The Genealogue, which has evolved into a sort of genealogy tabloid.

Genealogy requires collaboration. It requires asking for information and advice—often from complete strangers. Even professional genealogists ask for help when problems are beyond their expertise, or when the answers lie in places beyond their reach. The Internet allows me to target my questions at the people most likely to know the answers. If I have a question about a family named McGillicuddy, I can post queries to McGillicuddy message boards and be sure that they'll be read by people with knowledge of the surname.

Collaboration can also be long term. The Internet is the perfect venue for cousins from different cities, states, or even continents to swap data and coordinate research. Publishing a family tree online is a sure way to turn up even more cousins, most of whom will want to share information about their branches.

That said, it is a mistake to think that all records will be found online. Local, state, and national archives hold more documents than can possibly be put online. The Internet might help us locate these records, but viewing them will require that we get out of our chairs. The family historian who relies solely on Internet research is missing out on some of the best parts of genealogy. The best moments of my genealogical career have happened in remote grave-yards, at the county courthouse handling documents once handled by my ancestors, and talking about old times with my elderly relatives.

There is no one best way to use the Internet for family history. You can use it strictly for communicating by e-mail; or, at the opposite extreme, you can compile a family history and have it published and made available through online booksellers. In between there are forums, blogs, mailing lists, opportunities to volunteer, and thousands of places to hunt for ancestors. If there is one rule for Internet genealogists, it is this: Help others as you would have others help you. Genealogy depends upon the generosity of everyday folks willing to look up information, snap a picture at a local cemetery, or offer advice to a fellow family historian who has lost her way.

Not all of Chris's finds have been pleasant, however. He says that while some family members may not be happy with what he discovers, as a family historian, he can't overlook these things. "Not every bit of scandalous information needs to be published in the family newsletter, but every significant fact must be recorded for posterity," he says.

When asked to identify the biggest mistake people make when they try to preserve their family history and genealogy, Chris noted that people tend to view all information uncritically. "It's tempting for the beginner to jump in with both feet and fill his database with all the names and dates he can grab. But the Internet is crowded with well-intentioned people peddling bad information. Once this bad info enters a database, it can take years to root out. It's wiser to start slow, use reliable sources, and keep track of these sources. Every piece of information—every name, date, and relationship—must be supported by good evidence, and all evidence must be documented. This may not sound like fun, but neither is spending months or years researching the life of an ancestor who isn't really your ancestor."

Chris's favorite personal genealogy story involves his great-grandfather and the use of the message boards at Ancestry.com.

My great-grandfather, who died shortly before my birth, was a Finnish immigrant. His surname, Tamlander, is uncommon in this country, and only slightly more common in Finland. He and his wife had two daughters—my grandmother and her sister, Helen. With my grandmother's death in 1999, Helen was left the only surviving member of this little family. Five or six years ago, I searched the Ancestry.com message boards for my great-grandfather's surname and found one message. Someone was looking for information on a woman whose maiden name was Tamlander. I immediately recognized the woman as my great-grandfather's long-lost sister in California. I was able to connect my elderly great-aunt with relatives she never knew existed. They've been corresponding by e-mail ever since.

We also asked Chris to share a list of the Web sites he finds especially useful for online research. "FamilySearch.org is indispensable. I use HeritageQuestOnline.com regularly (at-home access is available through many libraries for the price of a membership card). Google is my favorite search engine, and I also use their Book Search and News Archive regularly. I search the indexes at Ancestry.com for clues even when I don't have a subscription to view the document images. Some others sites I recommend are GenForum (genforum.genealogy.com), One-Step Web Pages (stevemorse.org), Online searchable death indexes (www.deathindexes.com), RootsWeb (www.rootsweb.com), LinkPendium (www.linkpendium.com), and Cyndi's List (www.cyndislist.com)."

The Random Acts of Genealogical Kindness™ Web Site

This is another wonderful Web site that can help you connect with other researchers and discover solutions to your genealogical mysteries. This site, commonly called RAOGK (www.raogk.org), runs totally on volunteer energy. Good-hearted people worldwide have volunteered their services to provide complete strangers with research help. The volunteers at RAOGK (fig. 7-4) agree to perform one genealogical research task each month, for free, in their local area. The group currently has more than 4,000 volunteers, spread out in every state and in many international locations. Volunteers will help you document your information by obtaining courthouse records or taking photographs of gravesite markers for you.

To make a research request, you choose a volunteer from a list of people in each state (or from the non-U.S. volunteer list). The list includes a description of the kind of task the volunteer is willing to do. Some volunteers specialize in finding information in a particular county. After you've chosen a volunteer, you fill out a form describing your

Random Acts of Genealogical Kindness™

Our volunteers have agreed to do a free genealogy research task at least once per month in their local area as an act of kindness. While the volunteers of Random Acts of Genealogical Kindness (RAOGK) have agreed to donate their time for free, you MUST PAY the volunteer for his/her expenses in fulfilling your request (copies, printing fees, postage, film or video tape, parking fees, etc.).

RAOGK is a global volunteer organization. With over 4000 volunteers in every U.S. state and many international locations, we have helped thousands of researchers. Our volunteers take time to do everything from looking up courthouse records to taking pictures of tombstones. All they ask in return is reimbursement for their expenses (never their time) and a thank you.

Looking for a volunteer?

Is this your first visit to our site? We want your visit to be a successful one. Our staff has put together a list of Guidelines for making requests for you to view and read before making any requests. A link to the volunteers will be provided after you have read the FAQ's.

Would you like to volunteer?

Please read our Frequently Asked Questions for Volunteers before doing so.

See how our volunteers have helped others

Figure 7-4
The Random Acts
of Genealogical Kindness
Web site

genealogical needs and as much information as you already know about the ancestor in question. You can ask a couple of things about one or two ancestors at a time. If you want to contact the same researcher again for more information, you're asked to wait a month before you do so.

There's no charge for the time that volunteers spend doing research for you, but you are expected to reimburse them for things like film, video, copies or printing, postage, and in some cases, parking fees. Using the services of these kind folks is an excellent way for you to get documentation when you can't get to a source yourself.

Loading Up on GEDCOMs

You are already storing your family information in the form of a GEDCOM, so make the most of it. Most genealogy programs let you upload your GEDCOMs to the Internet to share with relatives and other researchers. And most of the major genealogy Web sites, such as Ancestry.com, encourage you to upload GEDCOMs for sharing.

WorldConnect

The WorldConnect project at RootsWeb (worldconnect.rootsweb.com) began in 1999 with 5.5 million records submitted during a month-long testing period. Today the project has over 312 million records, representing the family trees in the WorldConnect project plus those at Ancestry.com, a sister company of RootsWeb. These records comprise the single biggest collection of family trees available online. The site gives you all the instructions you need to upload your GEDCOM correctly and to tell other people where it is so you can share your research. You can also search the family trees of others and use "sticky notes" in the form of interactive online forms to add information to existing entries.

Making It Social

In addition to uploading GEDCOMs and sharing data with other researchers in traditional ways, there's a new trend in town. It's called social networking. Perhaps you or your kids already live virtual lives on sites such as MySpace or Facebook. These sites allow users to create personal profiles, invite other people to be friends, share photographs, leave messages, and other friendly activities. The genealogy community is also moving into social networking with the appearance of several new sites, such as LivingGenealogy (www.livinggenealogy.com), which lets you create pages for each of your ancestors using a simple template.

At LivingGenealogy, you and your relatives can add comments, photographs, and memories to these pages, to write a collaborative biography of an ancestor. You can also make this information available to other people online. An especially interesting feature at LivingGenealogy is its Place Pages. These are just like Ancestor pages, except they are about the geographic locations—towns, countries, cities—that your ancestors knew. People who have traveled to these places can contribute photos and other information of interest to individuals who haven't been able to visit their ancestral lands. You can also create public or private "user groups," which can connect you with other people to collaborate on family research. Plus, everything on this site is free!

Connecting Through Forums

Genealogist Rex Bavousett recommends connecting with newly discovered relatives through online forums. "E-mail alerts are sent to me each time someone posts a comment or request on a number of family surname forums that I track," Rex explains.

Since my own name was rather rare, I started forums for it as well. On my mother's side of the family, there was one great-great-great-grandfather that I could not move beyond. His name was Nelson Paronto. I followed several forums for French Canadian names, provinces, and regions. One day I was examining the Parenteau family forum and came across a person who was dealing with a Narcisse Parenteau. Could it be that this was the same person as Nelson Paronto? The person in the forum was discussing Narcisse and several other relatives that matched my Nelson Paronto. I replied to the forum asking about Narcisse, and the person provided positive feedback to my concerns. I then ran a search of military files at Ancestry.com for Narcisse and hit pay dirt once again. The U.S. Civil War pension report mentioned that Narcisse Parenteau went by the name Nelson Paronto. I guess when you are in the army, you don't want a name that sounds like you are a "sissy," so he must have changed his name at that point. This gave me seven new generations, and I was able to move farther into the past.

WeRelate (www.werelate.org/wiki/Main_Page) is a collaborative genealogy Web site that operates as what's known as a *wiki*. This free site (fig. 7-5) sponsored by the nonprofit Foundation for On-Line Genealogy, Inc., operates in partnership with the genealogy center at the Allen County Public Library in Indiana. The site's goal is to become the most popular community Web site for genealogy, and it has already become the biggest genealogy wiki online. Okay, so what's a wiki?

The word *wiki* in Hawaiian means quick. (You're probably familiar with Wikipedia, the Internet encyclopedia, which is a great example of the wiki format.) In terms of the genealogy community, it is a kind of Web site that lets many users share information by easily creating new Web pages and editing existing ones without needing any technical computer skills. Members of the WeRelate community just click a button and contribute in any way they choose to any of the wiki's pages.

This means you can share your research, resources, and questions and work with other researchers on a family line. The good news is that all of your information stays in a central location where it can be easily accessed. Because all previously made pages are kept in a permanent archive, nothing is really lost, no matter how many times a page is changed.

The downside is that information can be posted to the wiki that may not be properly checked and vetted. You can find precious gems on a wiki, but you can also find lumps of coal; information that is completely useless or incorrect. Don't take anything you find on any wiki as gospel truth. Unless you know for certain that the source of the information is reliable, accept only what you've learned on a wiki if it can be verified through another reliable source.

Figure 7-5
The WeRelate wiki site

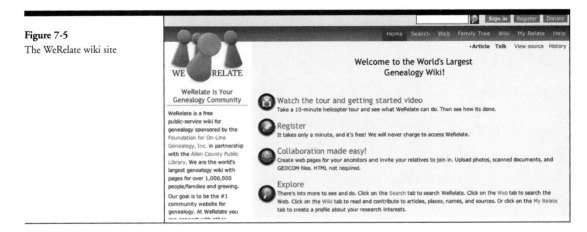

But Is the Information Any Good?

At this point you may think that by connecting with other researchers online, you can simply sit back and relax. Or maybe you think that you can just spend some time posting queries here and there, and kindly volunteers will answer your questions for free then all you have to do is add the information to your genealogy program, check it off your to-do list, and get ready to dazzle them at the next family reunion. Reality check, please! Remember our warning about taking things at face value? If you want to be serious about your genealogy work, you'll have to check and recheck every bit of information and every story someone tells you. That's true even if the good stuff is coming from kindly volunteers!

Evaluation Time

Okay, so not every genealogical record you find should be taken at face value. Names can be misspelled, county lines can change, memories fade. When you find a GEDCOM of one of your ancestors, you should stop and take a breath. We know you're tingling with excitement, but before you add that tidbit to your own research, put on your skeptic's glasses and take another look. You should examine it closely, with a healthy skepticism. All the names and dates in a GEDCOM should be sourced. In other words, the researcher who shared that information should have provided notes indicating where it was found.

It is very easy for errors in a GEDCOM to spread across the genealogical universe and infect many family trees with incorrect information. Debra Warila of Family Tree Growers has been searching for information about her Montgomery ancestors in Texas for some time. When she found an extensive GEDCOM of the family at RootsWeb, she was very excited until she saw that it listed her great-grandmother's name as Hallie, when she has absolute proof from original family documents that the woman's name was Haddie. A small error like this makes an entire source questionable.

Some Montgomery-related GEDCOMs that Debra has found online list the marriage of Mary Ann McKay and William W. Montgomery as taking place in Shelby, Austin County, Texas, in 1841. Other GEDCOMs say the couple was married in Austin, Travis County, Texas. Still others just say Austin. One identifiable problem is that, according to the Texas State Historical Association's *Handbook of Texas Online*, there was no Shelby, Austin County, Texas, on that date! In 1841, the town, settled by Germans, was known by its German name of Rödersmühl (or Röders Mill). It was named for the town's founder, Otto von Röder, who built a grain mill at the site around 1841. Since none of the GEDCOM contributors provided sources for his or her information, it's difficult to find where things went wrong. (Debra suspects that the marriage took place Shelby County, Tennessee, but that's another story!)

So, with sourcing such an important part of your research, we know you'll cruise the Internet questioning everything you find out from other researchers. On the other side of this coin, it is your responsibility to be a good virtual neighbor. Do everyone a favor and source your information before posting it. It takes only a minute to jot down where you found a specific document, and your cyber-neighbors and all posterity will thank you for your effort.

Would You Like Some Source with That?

We know, sourcing is not the most exciting aspect of genealogy, and we can hear you groaning from here, but it is necessary. Many family researchers don't feel the need to cite any sources because they are doing only an informal genealogy for their immediate family. However, even Uncle John and Aunt Patty deserve accurate information, and isn't the history of your family important enough for you to take the time to get it right? We thought so! Most genealogy software programs make entering your source citations simple. And sourcing your information can help you fill gaps and inconsistencies in other material that you may have collected.

The basic idea of sourcing is to cite what you see. If you get a piece of information from a deed book, cite the book. If you receive information in a letter, cite the letter because that is what you've actually seen. If you're getting information from an index or an abstract, cite the index or the abstract. Not so difficult, right? With the right citations, other people can follow your research trail. In fact, citing sources may even save you from frustrating hours of trying to figure out where you discovered the name of great-uncle Jonathan's third wife! If you need help with citation formats or instruction, you can consult the genealogy area of About.com (genealogy.about.com/od/citing/a/sources.htm) or Genealogy.com (www.genealogy.com/19_wylie.html), and, as always, Cyndi's List (www.cyndislist.com/citing.htm).

One if by Land, Two (or More) if by Search Engine

Rex Bavousett has discovered several new relatives and lots of information since he began looking into his family's history. Sometimes he uses a tool no more complex than his favorite search engine. That's how he found information about the long-lost brother of his great-great grandfather.

Shortly after my relatives settled in America, my great-great-grand-uncle moved west, never to be heard from again, as the story goes. I figured that with my family immigrating in 1847, it was possible that my great-great-grand-uncle George went west at the time of the California Gold Rush (1840s).

Sure enough, Google brought up a city directory listing for the Brandy City/Oak Valley area that was posted on a GenWeb site. There he was! Further research showed him to be buried in a Camptonville cemetery. When I then Googled Camptonville, I was able to find the Camptonville Community Courier newsletter and the Camptonville Historical Society. From the publications that were available online, I was able to secure e-mail addresses and phone numbers for a variety of people in Camptonville. This, of course, has led to a wealth of information from other Camptonville Web sites (www.camptonville.com) and from community members. Hence, I now have photographs of George's grandson Herman Edward Ramm, drawings of the area from an 1879 book that describes the region and its settlers (including mine), and photographs of George's home as it stood in the mid-1960s.

Just by using search engines on the Internet to look for possible relatives, Rex has also made connections with two different branches of his family back in France. While he says they have yet to find out just how they are related, he's convinced that, because of their unusual surname, it's only a matter of time before they figure it out. And from these two connections, Rex has been able to communicate with a third branch of the family in France, as well as with six different individuals in that country who are helping him with his research.

Step into Society

If you've never considered yourself a joiner before, now is a good time to become one as you explore your new hobby of genealogy. Genealogical societies generally focus on local history and are great information sources. You can join a society that's in the area where you live now, but don't ignore the benefits of joining a society based in a region where your ancestors once lived. These organizations can introduce you to other people who are working on the same family lines. You might even find a distant relative through a genealogical society. While most groups charge a membership fee, the fees are generally reasonable, with smaller organizations generally having lower fees than larger ones. Most societies publish newsletters chock-full of genealogical and historical details and stories about their local areas. They also offer workshops and meetings where you can get together with other researchers and talk shop. Most important you'll see that you are not alone in your research efforts. And since many societies also have Web sites, you may not even have to travel anywhere to benefit from their work.

You can find genealogical societies by checking the *Genealogical Periodical Annual Index* at your local library. Unfortunately, this resource is not yet available online, but you can buy it from Heritage Books (www.heritagebooks.com). You can also search online for a society at Society Hall (www.familyhistory.com/societyhall/search.asp) and Society Hill (www.daddezio.com/society). You can find a society, along with libraries, archives, and historical societies at The United States Internet Genealogical Society (www.usigs.org/library/gensoc). By searching the Periodical Source Index (PERSI), you will be able to find information that has been published by genealogical societies. Ancestry.com provides access to PERSI to subscribers, or you may be able to access it at your local library.

It's also a good idea to consult Cyndi's List for links to genealogical and historical societies (www.cyndislist.com/society.htm).

The Search for Annie Moore

Chris Dunbar, creator of The Genealogue Web site, helped publicize the 2006 search for Annie Moore (www.ellisisland.org/genealogy/annie_moore.asp), the first person to pass through Ellis Island. "Megan Smolenyak Smolenyak asked for help in finding out what became of the first person to pass through Ellis Island when it opened in 1892," Chris says. "The resulting 'blogswarm' allowed the event to zoom across the Internet as participants devoted their blogs to the topics in hopes of finding the answer. Annie turned up in just over a month. This was a great example of how the Internet can draw together the skills of genealogists—both amateur and professional—to achieve a common goal."

Looking Ahead

You've done your research and collaborated with family. You've got stock-piles of photographs and pounds of documents. You probably want to shout from the rooftops, "I can trace my ancestry back to 1500!" In the next chapter, we'll show you how to choose a place on the Internet to call your own. We'll discuss whether a Web site or a blog is right for you, look at examples of family Web sites, and maybe even figure out ways for you to get a little income from your online presence.

Chapter 8

Take Your Place on the Web

D o you feel like a genealogist yet? Check yourself for the signs. Do you compulsively check your e-mail for communications from other researchers about a long-lost ancestor? Do you feel like celebrating when you recognize a family name on a handwritten census form? Do you want to tell everyone you know that you've discovered the name of your great-great-grandmother's mother? You know you do! Since you've come so far in your genealogy journey by cruising the Web, maybe you're ready to claim a corner of cyberspace as your very own. At your very own place on the Web you can share your discoveries, frustrations, and celebrations with hundreds, or even thousands, of your closest Internet friends. It's easier than you think to create your own family Web site, and easier still to create your own blog. Once you do so, you could even make a little extra money while satisfying your genealogical cravings.

Since every family history is unique, every family Web site or blog will be different. Of course, you'll want to include your family tree. A little history about your family, photographs of some ancestors, and interesting stories and facts will make your site more appealing. You want to reward curious visitors with more than just a list of names and dates. Here's the place to include some family legends. You can also use your Web site or blog to ask for more information about the family and maybe even get clues to help you break down those brick walls.

Set Your Sites

There are so many terms associated with the Internet and the Web, and it seems that more appear all the time. Do you know the difference between a Web site and a blog? What's Web 2.0? And what do you mean I can make money from my family Web site? Don't worry, all this will become clearer as you read on. To get things underway, you'll need to decide what kind of information you want to place on your little piece of cyberspace. Maybe your goal is to share what you know with other family members and encourage them to contribute to the family history. Maybe you have a lot of vintage family photos that you'd like to make available to geographically distant relatives. Maybe you're interested in connecting with distant relatives and want a place where they can easily find you. Or maybe what you really want is just to upload your GEDCOM files to an online database so they are searchable and accessible to the public.

Ask yourself some very specific questions. Do you want to focus on a single ancestor, providing a history of this individual's life and accomplishments? Do you want to trace your ancestors through their geographic history? Or are you thinking about forming an online family community, where family members can contribute their own information and photographs? Maybe you want it all—it *is* possible to include a little of everything!

Web Site or Blog?

What's the difference between a Web site and a blog—a word that started out as a contraction of "Web log?" Just a few years ago, the differences between the two were more pronounced than they are now. Web sites provided pages of information and photos that stayed the same. Many people didn't have the tools or time to update their sites once they created them, so once they were built, the design and information were pretty much set. Web sites were not meant to be interactive. While you could perhaps click on a link to leave the Web site creator an e-mail, you couldn't add comments to the site itself, for example.

Blogs, on the other hand, were more personal and generally less formal. Blogs were written more like dispatches from the front, and visitors were invited and even encouraged to leave comments, add links, or post photographs. Blogs were also much easier to create. A Web site generally had a page or several pages covering a variety of topics, but these pages still remained essentially static over time. You may have tweaked things now and again, but most pages didn't change much. For example, a page that offered the only two photographs of someone's great-grandmother and great-grandfather was unlikely to be altered. (While it is possible that another photo would be found and added to the original two-picture page, a long time would elapse before the third photo was added.) Web sites were time-consuming to create and, depending on the creator's skills, could be challenging to maintain. Special software had to be used to create a site and then put it on the Web. It was necessary to know HTML (hypertext markup language), the software language in which the Web is written, in order to design the site and format articles so they could be read online and appear the way they were intended.

This is why it was once true that Web sites were almost exclusively for businesses. Financial gain was one of the main reasons to venture onto the Web, and businesses were more likely than individuals to gain financially from staking their claim to space on the Internet. This is no longer the case. The Internet has evolved so that special skills are no longer required to create or maintain a site. Through services such as America Online or Google, just to name two examples, you can now create a rudimentary site within minutes. The process has been simplified to the point where families and individuals can create their own sites for any number of reasons, including sharing their genealogy research.

One thing that hasn't changed, however, is that the nature of blogs is more personal than that of Web sites. They have a more conversational tone, and naturally invite interaction between their creators and the people who stop by for a visit. All of the posts (articles and comments) on a blog are presented in chronological order, with the most recent one at the top of the page. The author can update the blog through posts, as long or as short as time and topic dictate. Blogs exist because someone wants to say something and perhaps receive comments on these thoughts from the public. If you want to update your genealogy information frequently or want to have an ongoing conversation with the people who visit your Internet homestead, a blog is a good choice. But if you want to post complete family histories and don't need or want to update your genealogy information often, build a Web site.

Q A Very Short Discussion of Web 2.0

The idea of Web 2.0, and the term itself, arose from a discussion in 2001 between Tim O'Reilly, founder and chief executive officer of O'Reilly Media, Inc., a publisher of computer books, and Dale Dougherty, a Web pioneer and vice president with O'Reilly Media. O'Reilly and Dougherty saw something in common among the Internet companies that had survived the downturn in the dot-com industry in 2000–2001—they emphasized collaboration. The pair also noted that instead of completely crashing, the Web appeared to be more important than ever. O'Reilly felt that the dot-com collapse represented a turning point for the Web, and so he coined the phrase *Web 2.0* to describe its next phase. (The 2.0 comes from the way software creators name consecutive versions of their products as they improve them.)

You can probably find as many definitions of Web 2.0 as there are people to define it. For example, Stephen Fry, an English actor and media personality, believes that the Web 2.0 concept emphasizes the reciprocal exchange of information between a visitor to a Web page and the person who created that page. He stresses the idea of interactivity, since visitors can send information to the Web site (upload) as well as get information from it (download).

Some technology experts, including Tim Berners-Lee, the recognized creator of the World Wide Web, wonder whether the term really means anything at all. He points to the fact that several of the elements used to define Web 2.0 have existed since the early 1990s, when the Web began. And Tim Bray, a software developer and writer who made major contributions to the standards under which the Web currently operates, hates the term and thinks it is just "vacuous marketing hype."

In any case, the most important characteristics of Web 2.0 involve collaboration and the addition of content provided by the users of a Web site rather than just its creators. You don't need to understand the technologies that allow these features to exist to benefit from them. To get a feel for what is possible on today's Web, let's look at some sites that use the concept of Web 2.0. Familypedia, the genealogy wiki (genealogy.wikia.com/wiki/Main_Page), is a place where you can write articles about your family and link these articles to others that discuss where and when an ancestor once lived. You can do all

your work at the wiki site or you can link your articles to the Web. (As mentioned, wiki comes from the Hawaiian word meaning quick, as a wiki is a site
that can quickly be edited by those who visit it.) The wiki format lets you work
together with others to create a network of information about your ancestors.
The creators of the wiki hope that it will eventually provide many details about
the lives of both famous individuals and everyday people who aren't mentioned
in formal histories. The wiki actively encourages participation by contributors
from around the world. Two other genealogy sites that use the Web 2.0 concept
are the MySpace genealogy group (groups.myspace.com/genealogy), which
began in 2004, and GenMates (genmates.net/genmates/index.html), which
calls itself the "MySpace alternative for genealogists."

Spinning a Web (Site)

Since it's never been easier to create and maintain a Web site, you may
decide you want one of your own. To have a family genealogy Web site
you'll need a place on the Web to store your information, a way to get
information to that place, and a method for making that information
presentable to an online audience. As you may recall from our discussion
of genealogy software programs in Chapter 2, most programs will automatically generate Web site content for you. This means you don't have
to have any special computer expertise to build a site.

For example, here's how the genealogy software program Reunion
(the top-selling genealogy program for the Mac) takes the information
you enter and creates a Web site. Almost all the reports you create in
Reunion, including family group sheets, can be output in the format
required to share them on the Web. Reunion saves the standard genealogy
report as HTML. The first step in creating a report in Reunion is to
select a destination for it, or a place on your computer where the information will be saved. When you want to publish on the Web, just select
Web Folder as your destination. Now the report you're creating will be
saved in that folder. As you work, the contents of this folder will be
Internet-ready files, which have been automatically put into the correct
format for the Web. Additionally, the software automatically connects all
these files to one another. You haven't had to do anything special since

you selected the Web folder! For fun, Reunion also lets you choose from among several style options that will change the color of the text and background on your Web pages, so your pages can be unique. When you're finished, you simply upload the Web folder to your Internet service provider (ISP). Support staff at your ISP should be happy to give you information about completing this last step. Here's one word of warning for Mac users. Each Web folder you create contains the specific information that is relevant to the type of report created. You shouldn't rename or move the files in the Web folder, because they are all connected and won't work right if you do. If you look at the names of the items in your Web folder, what you'll see is a bunch of letters, such as IMG, which is the name of the file that contains any images or artwork you've included, and FG_SRC.HTM, which is the name of the file where your sources are stored. These names are used so that people with personal computers (PCs) that use the Windows software (as opposed to Macs) or other operating systems will also be able to see your files on the Web. The Web is what is called a cross-platform entity, meaning it can be used by all types of computers.

Of course, not everyone uses a Mac, but everyone who wants to have a Web site must somehow find Web space to store their site. You can obtain Web space from a number of sources. There are specialized hosting companies that provide storage space for a fee, or, as you've just seen, your ISP most likely offers space for personal Web sites. Many of these ISPs even include a certain amount of storage space as part of the monthly subscription cost, provide links to resources that will help you with your Web page creation, and offer templates that make creating a Web site simple. In addition to the popular genealogy software programs, you'll find other resources available for obtaining Web space for your site.

A good place to start is to check out some examples of Web page templates at Genealogy Web Creations (www.genealogy-web-creations.com/css-layouts), as shown in figure 8-1. Tribal Pages (www.tribalpages.com) and RootsWeb Free Pages (freepages.rootsweb.com) also allow you to develop a family Web site online for free and without any technical expertise or special software on your computer. Some of the sites, including Google's Page Creator (pages.google.com/-/about.html), have design templates specifically for genealogy Web sites.

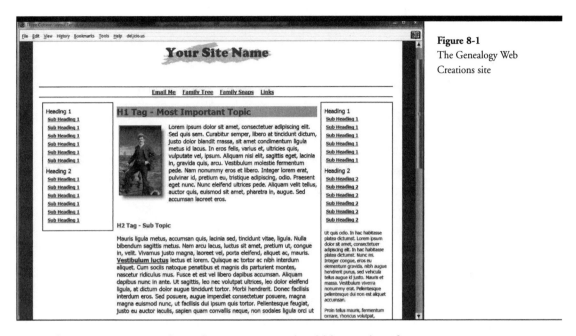

Figure 8-1
The Genealogy Web
Creations site

Before you investigate these alternatives, you should know that if you are adventurous, you can learn how to use HTML. There are many online tutorials to help you. One of the most user-friendly is the HTML course offered by Jennifer Kyrnin at About.com (webdesign.about.com/od/ beginningtutorials/a/bl_htmltutorial.htm). This is a simple, step-by-step basic tutorial that will get you up and running very quickly. Cyndi's List is another place to find help. Cyndi has provided a Web page construction kit that tells you everything you need to know to put your information online (www.cyndislist.com/construc.htm). But if you choose to create your Web site without learning HTML, a description of some genealogy Web sites with hosting services follows.

Tribal Pages *(www.tribalpages.com)*

Tribal Pages offers a free service for documenting and viewing your family history online (fig. 8-2). You upload what you want to include on your Web site—photographs, family stories, timelines, and so on—where it is securely stored on the Tribal Pages servers. Every interaction on the site is password protected, ensuring that only you are able to make additions or changes to your pages. Tribal Pages also gives you an additional password that you can share with your family and friends so they can view your site. You have to register with Tribal Pages to get the free Web space, but its features make registration worthwhile.

Figure 8-2
Overview, TribalPages.com
features

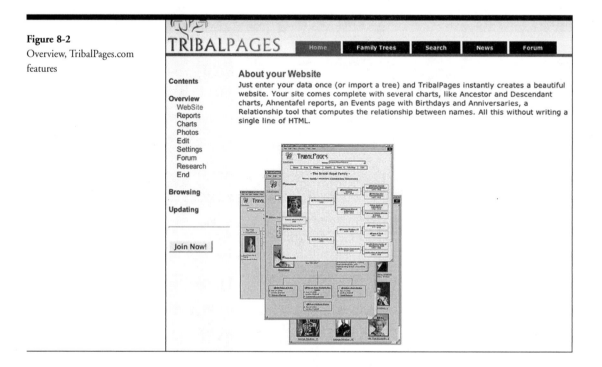

Enter your data once, or import a family tree you've already worked on, and the information is automatically put into a Web site format. The site includes a number of charts, such as ancestor and descendant charts, Ahnentafel reports, and a relationship tool that figures out how various individuals are related. You can also add photographs and organize them into albums in chronological order. Tribal Pages maintains a message board where you can ask questions or discuss Web site topics and get technical support when you're unsure of what do to next. Tribal Pages says its site now has 175,000 members. The site offers a searchable database of more than 200,000 family trees (40 million names) and a Social Security Death Records database that has 65 million names.

Space at RootsWeb *(freepages.rootsweb.com)*

RootsWeb (fig. 8-3) provides free personal Web space for the asking. There are now more than 13,600 personal Web pages on the site. Browse through the listed personal pages, which are stored alphabetically at freepages.rootsweb.com/directory/genealogy.html, to get an idea of the variety of information genealogy researchers like you are putting online. Some users just offer a list of family names, while others have created sites with decorative colors, borders, artwork, and photographs, or sites that include links and photographs.

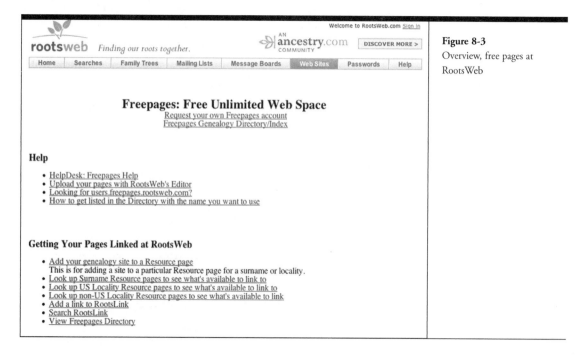

Figure 8-3
Overview, free pages at RootsWeb

Google Page Creator

If you sign up for a free e-mail account with Google, known as Gmail, you'll also gain access to the Page Creator at Google.com (pages.google.com/-/about.html). Page Creator is a free tool that lets you create your Web pages right in your Internet browser and then publish them on the Web with the click of the mouse. You don't have to download any software, and Google takes care of storing your files. Page Creator requires that you use either Internet Explorer or Firefox Web browser.

FamilyCrossings

FamilyCrossings (www.familycrossings.com) is a family social networking site (fig. 8-4). Families use the site to stay in touch, plan family reunions, share information about events such as birthdays or anniversaries, use a common calendar to schedule events, and more. And, of course, it's also good for online genealogy. The site's collaborative features make it useful for sharing family history with relatives and encouraging them to add their own memories and stories. One feature lets you create historical timelines of family events, such as when your ancestors arrived at Ellis Island or when your grandfather was drafted into the army, or even your very own birth! All of the information you add to the site can be searched by keyword or location. You can share photographs, add family news and gift wish lists, participate in secure family chats, and get a real picture of your family history by creating and viewing maps and timelines. One very interesting feature for genealogy buffs is the online family history interview form, with which you can interview relatives about their child-hood memories, work, romance, entertainment, holidays and traditions, and other topics, in addition to birth date and birthplace. The site offers a free version as well as a subscription version. The free version provides 150 megabytes of storage space, which is quite enough to get you started. You also gain access to features such as family news, family photo

Figure 8-4
Home page of
Familycrossings.com

galleries, calendar, address book, live chat, and gift center. For a fee of $9.95 per month, you get all of these features plus others that relate to your family history, a family database, family polls, a wish list, games, special offers, and 250 megabytes of storage.

MyFamily.com *(www.myfamily.com)*

This site is similar to FamilyCrossings in that it is organized as a family networking site (fig. 8-5). It offers features such as family news and e-mail notifications that go out when news is posted, photo-sharing, a "file cabinet" where family members can upload computer files such as legal documents or family records to share with other site visitors, and a chat feature. Family historians will appreciate features like the family tree, where you can upload a GEDCOM file, and all family members can review it without needing any special software. Genealogists may also publish and save family stories and ask other relatives to share personal memories and their own versions of family legends. As we write this, the site is undergoing a major revision. It now offers a free version, but two levels of paid membership were scheduled to be available at the time of this writing.

The free version offers an unlimited amount of storage, and your content will be available for viewing for one year after you upload it to the site. But the free version is also supported by advertising, which

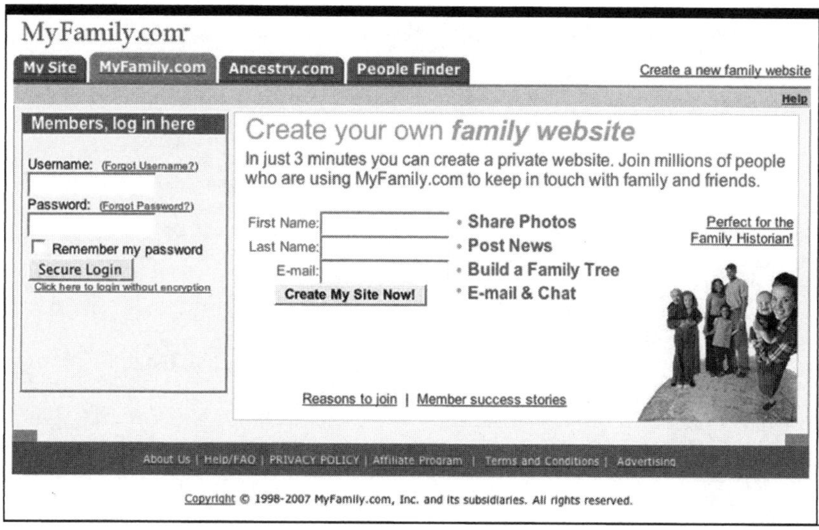

Figure 8-5
Home page of MyFamily.com

means that ads will appear on your pages. If you're serious about putting your family history online, one of the paid versions is definitely the way to go. With the Essentials membership, you get 1 gigabyte of storage, free e-mail accounts for each family member, an ad-free site, and your content will *always* be available for viewing. You also get access to professional designs for your pages. The Essentials membership costs $29.95 per year. For $99.95 per year, you can get the Premium membership, which comes with 5 gigabytes of storage space, a custom domain (jonesfamily.com, for example) hosted at MyFamily.com, a custom public home page, and 100 e-mail addresses at your domain (your_first_name@your_surname.com, for example). If you're going to add a lot of photographs, which are notorious for taking up space, or videos, which are even bigger space-hogs, you should go for the Premium membership. It's also pretty cool to have your own domain!

Figure 8-6
Home page of DrAlex
FamiliaOnline

DrAlex SOFTWARE

Home | FamiliaBuilder | FamiliaOnline | AlbumWizz | About DrAlex | Contacts

FamiliaOnline Home | Features | Questions & Answers | Terms & Conditions | Showcase | Pricing | Join Now!

FamiliaOnline

FamiliaOnline hosts your family tree, pictures, video clips and other related files. Upload a GEDCOM file, add files, and your family site is up and running! Click on any name and view his or her ancestors and descendants. Use our Amazing Rectangle Tool to link pictures to individuals. Use Relationship Finder to find out how are you related to a distant cousin.

Features

Q & A

Showcase

Join *Now*!

FamiliaOnline is a fully online service. No downloads, no installation. Machine-independent. You provide the data, and we generate family trees and other displays on demand, in real time.

Free 30-day trial!

New: Support of all file types, showing where is an individual in video clip and more.

DrAlex FamiliaOnline *(online.dralex.com/home/index.html)*
DrAlex FamiliaOnline (fig. 8-6) will host your family tree, photographs, video clips, GEDCOMs, and other files on its computers. You can click on any name stored at the site and see the ancestors and descendants of that person. There is a Relationship Finder to help you determine how you are related to distant cousins. You can enter your genealogy information either interactively at the site or by uploading your GEDCOM. Then you'll be able to see your family tree in several different formats, including Outline and Roots and Offspring views. An interesting feature of special interest to photography and video buffs—yes, you can upload video to the site—is that you can indicate where a specific person is located in a photo or video clip! This could be very handy for those crowded group shots taken at family reunions. You get 256 megabytes of disk space for your data, and the site offers a 30-day free trial. After the trial period, you can subscribe on an annual basis for $19.95, or you can pay $1.95 per month for a monthly subscription. If you run out of space, you can buy additional storage in blocks of 256 megabytes for $9.95 per year each. You can see an example of how things will look at the creator's own family Web site (online.dralex.com/alexlena).

A Few Words with Paul McWhorter of Old-picture.com

Paul McWhorter, the creator of the old-picture.com Web site, has a background in nanotechnology, science, and entrepreneurship. He was an executive at a high-tech firm in Silicon Valley until recently, when he left the rat race to follow his real interests: history and genealogy. He has been creating historical Web sites ever since.

Paul believes that the Internet has had a major impact on genealogy: "In the past, it could take years and thousands of dollars to answer even a single, simple question about one's ancestry. Today, the same question can be answered in a few minutes with a few clicks. Individuals are able to do family research that in the past could be done only by professional researchers."

Paul has found that building Web sites has made him more organized in his genealogy work. He says, "It sort of forces you to organize the material and also forces you to develop interesting details." Paul's favorite Web site for research is the National Archives (www.archives.gov). Of course, he also believes that history is best told through words *and* pictures!

Paul's family connection to the South prompted his creation of the Son of the South (fig. 8-7) Web site (www.sonofthesouth.net), which he says is the "most extensive source of original Civil War resources with over 7,000 pages of original Civil War content, including photographs, original illustrations, and eyewitness accounts." The site also has all of the *Harper's Weekly* newspapers from the Civil War years available in a searchable format—for free. The quality of the pages you retrieve will vary but it's still worth checking out.

Because his old-picture.com Web site specializes in, well, old pictures, Paul receives many e-mails from people who, for example, see a house in one of the photographs on his site and write to him to say that they live in that house now. He also receives e-mails from people who recognize one of their ancestors in a photograph on his site. "It is interesting how many times people find a personal connection to material on my site."

Blogs Away!

We introduced you to several great blogs in Chapter 5—remember The Genealogue, Eastman's Online Genealogy Newsletter, and the Genetic Genealogist? While these examples cover general and informative issues related to genealogy, you can also use blogs to share your family history on the Internet. If you wander the Internet looking for blog examples, you'll see that they range from the thoughts of would-be novelists (wanderingnovelist blog.blogspot.com) to insightful and useful advice about technical topics written by experts in their field (radar.oreilly.com). However, there are common elements to every blog. If you decide a blog is the way you want to go, yours will include these elements. Each blog has a subject line or title; a body, which contains the creator's actual writings; and a Comments feature that allows visitors to participate in a discussion about what has been

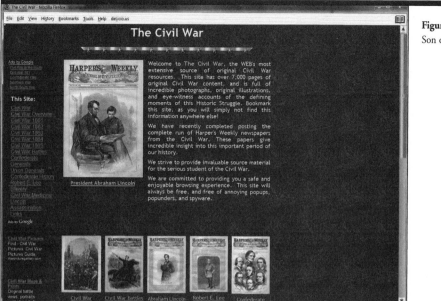

Figure 8-7
Son of the South Web site

written. Since blogs are organized chronologically, each entry also has a time and date stamp, so you can tell which posts are the most current.

There are several blog services that will take care of all the technical aspects of putting a blog online for you and give you space on their host computers where you can store all your information for free. These services will also let you customize the look of your blog, so that it reflects your personality. Many of the family blogs that you'll find online focus on current events and happenings within the family, but there's no reason you can't use the blog format to discuss your interesting genealogical finds, describe your brick-wall problems, and make yourself available to distant relatives. Two of the most popular free blog services are Blogger (fig. 8-8) and WordPress (fig. 8-9).

Blogger *(www.blogger.com)*

With Blogger you can have your blog up and running in three easy steps. First, you have to create a Google account (Google owns Blogger). Next, name your blog. And finally, choose a design template that reflects your blog's personality. Once your blog is created, you will be able to control, through a special page known as the administration area, who can read your blog and who can leave comments on it. The Comments feature lets anyone give feedback on what you've written, but you have the power to delete the comments you don't like. You can set up a blog in which several people have permission to add real posts and not just comments. This is a good choice for families collaborating on a genealogy project, since everyone's ideas will be given the same weight on the blog site, and everyone will be able to see when each entry was written. It's kind of like writing letters, but without the postage and with quicker delivery times. The design templates help you make the site attractive without having to learn HTML. You can post photographs and even send pictures from your digital camera or camera phone directly to your blog. You could blog your next genealogy road trip and add photos to share the experience with other family members. Blogger's services are totally free, and you can have a fully functioning blog in minutes.

Figure 8-8
Home page of Blogger.com

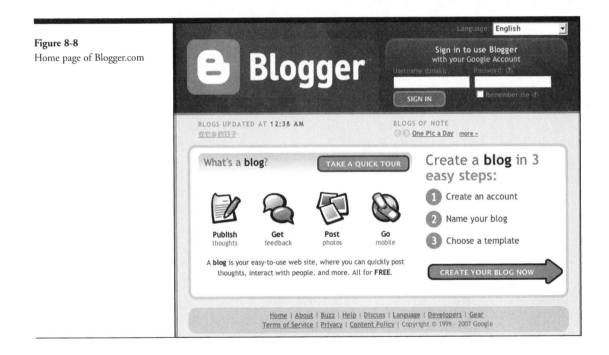

WordPress *(wordpress.com)*

It's also very simple to create a blog using WordPress. You just need to register with an e-mail address and a name, and you can start your blog for free. Your blog can be open to the public, or you can limit it to only family and friends. WordPress offers more than sixty design themes that you can use to customize the look of your pages. There are spell-check and auto-save functions, and you can add images and videos to your blog. WordPress makes an effort to protect your blog from unwanted postings (there are people out there who take pleasure in adding annoying comments to public blogs). You also have several choices for limiting participation in your blog to a select group of users if you choose not to make it available to the general public. A community of volunteers and techies work for WordPress. They can walk you through any difficulties you might have in creating or maintaining your blog. If you decide to go with WordPress, you won't be out there on your own.

Figure 8-9
Home page of WordPress.com

WordPress offers several upgrade options. You can get a domain name and use it at WordPress for $15 per year, and while there is a 35-member limit on the number of users you can have for a private blog, for $30 per year you can have an unlimited number of users. That's helpful if you have a really, really big family!

Get a Little Help from a Friend

A really excellent resource for potential bloggers is Lorelle VanFossen's blog (fig. 8-10) on creating a genealogy blog (www.cameraontheroad.com). Lorelle shares the many reasons to start a genealogy blog, the costs associated with creating and maintaining one, and what to include, among other topics. Her blog also contains a considerable amount of other information for the budding genealogist and blogger, including pages listing research resources, family name resources, location resources, and research tips and techniques. A recent post addressed how to represent an ancestor's religion in a GEDCOM record.

Figure 8-10
Lorelle VanFossen's Blog

VanFossen is a prolific genealogy writer, and her site offers many engrossing articles. For example, "Bringing the Past Alive in Historical Gardens" (www.cameraontheroad.com/family/bringing-the-past-alive-in-historical-gardens) discusses the importance of plants in understanding the geography and natural settings in which our ancestors lived. In the feature "Do You Know These People?" VanFossen presents photographs (and stories about the photographs) of people she doesn't know and asks for help in identifying them. The stories are quite fascinating (see "Nishimura, Sannomiya, Kobe, Japan" for an intriguing example.) The blog, which is hosted by WordPress, is a good example of how the blog format can be used.

Give a Little, Get a Little

In our Web travels, we've all seen those little ads on Web sites, and maybe we've even been interested enough in one of the products or services to click on it to get more information. Did you know that every time you click on an ad, someone might make money? And do you know that you can benefit from the huge market for advertising represented by the Web?

Just by doing some relatively simple things, you can attract more visitors to your site and cash in on the advertisers who want to reach those visitors. Don't worry. It's possible to use these techniques in ways that will not detract from your original purposes or turn your online home into a junky strip mall of advertising!

Optimizing for Dollars

The first thing you need to consider is where your Web site or blog ranks in the list of links that users see when they search for something on Google or Yahoo!, two of the biggest search engines on the Internet. The process of improving these rankings by increasing the number of visitors to a Web site is called Search Engine Optimization, or SEO.

By using effective SEO techniques, you increase the chances that users will find and actually visit your site. Users generally do not go through the many, many pages of results they get when doing a search. When was the last time you visited a Web site that was listed on page fifty of Google's results? So, where a site ranks on the return list is very important for increasing its number of visitors. SEO also increases the chances that a search engine will find a Web site as it looks for specific words on the Internet.

One of the easiest things you can do to optimize your Web site is to find the right keywords to use when creating your content. You should consider words that really describe your site or blog in the best way, and then find similar words that people are actually using when they use a major search engine like Yahoo! or Google. You can find appropriate keywords for free at Digital Point Solutions (www.digitalpoint.com/tools/suggestion), or Google AdWords (adwords.google.com/select/KeywordToolExternal).

The topic of SEO is complicated and far beyond the scope of this book, but you should keep a few things in mind when you design your site, if you want to increase your traffic and take full advantage of online advertising opportunities. For a complete discussion of SEO and how search engines work, go to SearchEngineWatch.com (searchenginewatch.com). You'll find enough information to keep you busy for quite some time.

Google AdSense

Have you ever been on a Web site and moved your cursor over a word only to see an ad pop up? Those ads are likely there as a result of the site owner's participation in a Google advertising program called Google AdSense. Once you're enrolled in the program, Google's computers will crawl around your site and then match ads to your site's content. You get paid when someone clicks on one of those ads. AdSense (www.google.com/adsense/login/en_US) is just one example of this type of advertising program. Participation in these programs makes sense when a site has content that would interest a lot of people, and obviously many genealogy Web sites (or blogs, for that matter) devoted to one family wouldn't fit in that category. But should you get ambitious and add a lot of content to your site, you may want to look into a program such as AdSense.

Affiliating for Money

With affiliate programs, you sign up with businesses that want to sell things and you put a link to their site(s) on your Web page or blog. Each time someone clicks through to the advertiser's site from your Web page and purchases the advertiser's product, you get what is essentially a finder's fee for directing that customer to the business. These fees can range from a few dollars to several hundred dollars, depending on the product and how many visitors you get to your site. There are affiliate programs available for nearly every kind of business, so you can choose to participate in those that reflect your interest. There are many genealogy-related affiliate programs listed at AffiliatesDirectory.com (www.affiliatesdirectory.com/directory/family/genealogy/index.shtml). Among these are The Family History Store (www.thefamilyhistorystore.com), Genealogy Today (www.genealogytoday.com), and OneGreatFamily (www.onegreatfamily.com). Even Ancestry offers an affiliate program (www.ancestry.com/home/partner/default.aspx), as does WorldVitalRecords (www.worldvitalrecords.com/affiliates) and FootNote (www.footnote.com/affiliates).

Doing the Books

Have you ever dreamed of having your own book store, stocked with just the books you find most interesting? It could include books that you found useful and want to recommend to your friends. Genealogists are always looking for books that suggest new approaches for research or that tell them more about the history of a period or location. You can help to meet this need and make a little money for yourself by affiliating yourself with book retailers such as Barnes & Noble. With the Barnes & Noble affiliate program (www.barnesandnoble.com/affiliate), you earn a referral fee of as much as 8.5 percent of the sale of products such as best-selling books, DVDs, and gifts.

Looking Ahead

Isn't it about time you took a trip in the real world to see your ancestral lands? If you can take the time, a world of discoveries awaits you. The Internet is a great tool, and it's made genealogy research easier and more enjoyable for more people than ever before, but sometimes you've got to get away from the computer and explore your family geography. Not that there isn't a place for more computer research when you're planning a genealogy road trip! In the next chapter, we give you some hints about planning for a trip to the old homestead.

Chapter 9

Plan a
Road Trip

The virtual highways of the Internet can be endlessly fascinating, but every now and then even the most devoted online researcher has to leave his or her desk and take to the road. It might be as simple as visiting a local cemetery to see the actual gravesite of an ancestor, or as elaborate as traveling to several countries with experts leading you through the intricacies of languages and cultures. No matter. The real value is in standing in places your ancestors knew. Looking out across the landscape, much may have changed, but some of the scene will still remain. Knowing that your senses are experiencing some of what theirs did is deeply powerful. But, of course, that experience won't happen without a lot of careful planning and hard work.

It's All in the Pre-Planning

We often wonder about the term pre-planning. Isn't the concept of getting ready for something already included in the definition of planning? But then if you think about it, even planning—especially for a trip that involves making arrangements for plane flights and rental cars, or choosing a driving route—requires its own plan! The places you go and the routes you take will depend on what you're looking for and what you expect or hope to find. Of course, some of the most interesting experiences will come from the things you can't plan for, so you'll need to "plan" for those, too!

First Things First

You can't find something until you first know what you are looking for. So your first step is to set a goal. You'll make your best progress if you focus on only one individual or family at a time. Choose the focus of your research, the kind of information you want to find, and the types of documents that could provide that information. Next, determine where the documents might be found and define the steps you need to access them. Now is a good time to create a checklist. Go through the research materials you already have, and, based on those documents and records, develop a list of things you'd like to prove or disprove. Also make a to-do list of the types of records you want to explore. Once you've determined the kinds of records and documents that may exist to help you, you can make a list of the places where those items are likely to be located today.

Getting Familiar

Familiarizing yourself with the kinds of records and sources you may find is especially important if you will be looking for information in a place outside your normal research area. For example, if you have been investigating records in California but need to find information in Texas, you can save yourself some frustration by learning about what records are available in Texas and where they might be. This is a perfect time to return to your computer and use its amazing search powers!

Research Help from FamilySearch

You can obtain research guides through your local Family History Library or visit FamilySearch's Research Helps page online (www.familysearch.org/ Eng/Search/RG/frameset_rhelps.asp). Here you'll find a list of online and downloadable guides for each state and even some countries. You can sort the list by location, subject, title, or document type. For example, if you want to know about what's available for California (fig. 9-1), you can get a research outline describing the major information sources for individuals who live there. The outline includes the names, addresses, phone numbers, and Web site addresses (if available) of libraries, archives, and other repositories of genealogical information in California. It also includes information (addresses, phone numbers, etc.) about where to find Bible records, church records, cemetery records, and a host of other records available on location or in printed materials as well as online. In fact, there's so much information for you to use in planning a research trip that you may never get out the door!

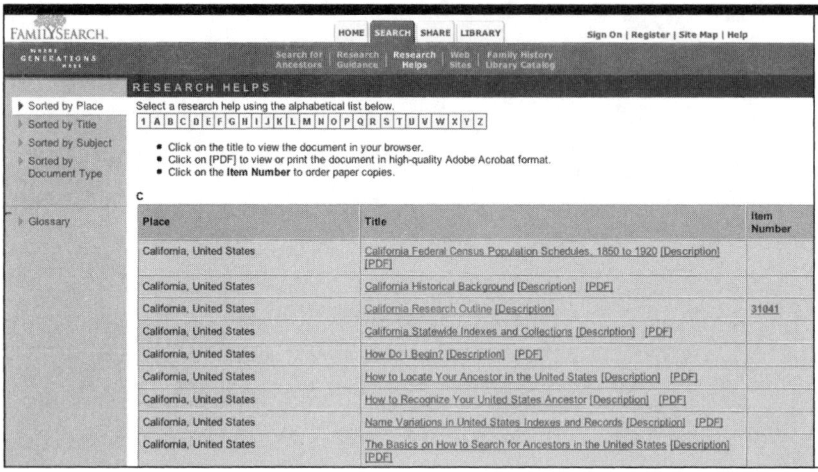

Figure 9-1

FamilySearch's list of research helps for California

Included with many of the entries on the Research Helps table is an item number. (You can find this on the far right-hand side of the table.) Clicking this number will bring you to a page where you can purchase a printed version of the online research help information. Prices vary according to the document, but are very reasonable. The cost of the California research outline is $2.50, while the cost of the Canada research outline is $3.25. Research outlines are not the only documents available for purchase. There are many others as well, including an Icelandic Genealogical Word List, for example, for $1.25.

☌ On the Road: Salt Lake City Family History Library

Many serious family researchers make at least one trip to the Family History Library in Salt Lake City, Utah (fig. 9-2). This library, the largest of its kind in the world, was founded in 1894 to collect genealogy records and to help the members of the Church of Jesus Christ of the Latter-day Saints (Mormons) research their family histories. The library is open to the general public free of charge.

To give you an idea of the scope of its holdings, consider these facts: There are more than 2.4 million rolls of microfilmed genealogy records, 310,000 books and other documents, 4,500 periodicals, 700 electronic resources, and an ancestral file database with more than 36 million names linked to families. There are 202 computers available for use by visiting researchers and seating capacity for 396 at library tables. The library has 125 full-time and part-time professional staff members, and about 400 trained volunteers to help you with your research.

FamilySearch.org offers a Web page devoted to hints and suggestions about how to prepare for your visit to the library (www.familysearch.org/Eng/Library/ FHL/frameset_library.asp?PAGE=library_preparing.asp). Before you visit, FamilySearch recommends that you use the online library catalog via the Internet (www.familysearch.org/Eng/Library/FHLC/frameset_fhlc.asp) to first determine the records you need are at the library. The library cannot house all of its microfilm on-site, so it can take up to three days to retrieve the records you need. Therefore you should phone, e-mail, or fax your record requests to the library before you visit. Also note that many of the records are handwritten and filed in chronological rather than alphabetical order. Be prepared to spend some time at this library!

The Salt Lake Convention and Visitors Bureau has a genealogy page on its Web site (www.visitsaltlake.com/what_to_do/genealogy.html) that offers links to hotel and motel accommodations near the library, as well as contact information for professional genealogy researchers in the area. You can also order a free copy of the Salt Lake Genealogy Planner brochure by filling out a form at the site.

Go Local Online

You'll find a wealth of information on the county and state pages at USGenWeb. The state and county pages can help you locate local volunteers who will do some research for you. You can discover relevant local information about the places you're planning to visit, such as maps of specific counties, addresses of libraries and historical societies, and links

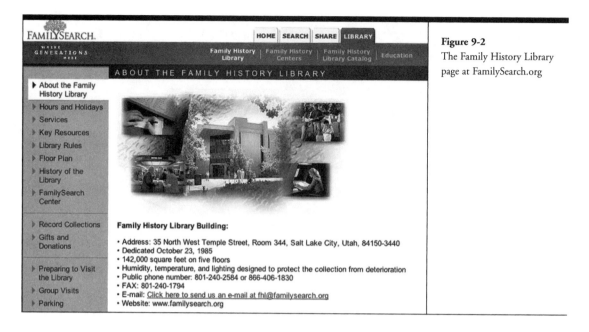

Figure 9-2
The Family History Library
page at FamilySearch.org

to historical events associated with a particular state or county. Historical societies can be very helpful in answering your questions, but make every effort you can to contact a society before you travel. Few historical societies have the funding to be open all day, every day. You can find the names and addresses of many historical societies at Society Hill (www.daddezio.com/society).

Libraries Online

If you know you'll be visiting a library on your road trip, see if that library has a Web site. If so, its catalog may be available online. You can determine if the library holdings include any books or other printed documents that might be of interest to you. Then you can spend your visit using the books rather than searching for them.

A library's Web site will give you its address, telephone number, and e-mail address so you can introduce yourself to the librarians and state your request for research help even before you go. It's a good idea to do this because the information on the Web is not always current. You can find links to the Web sites of all kinds of libraries at Library Spot (libraryspot.com).

Research Facilities: Ask Before You Go

Research facilities such as libraries, state archives, and other document repositories have regular hours of operation, but how will you know what those hours are unless you ask? You may be pleasantly surprised that some libraries or archives are open in the evenings on certain days, or you could discover that a library's local history room has very limited hours. Be sure to ask about special holiday or other closings. Courthouses and archives often close for several weeks during the year to allow staff vacations or to perform housekeeping duties. Individual facilities may be closed for scheduled remodeling or repairs.

Find out whether the records you'll be viewing are in their original form or if they are copies. Ask if you can actually browse through the records collection or whether you'll need to request the specific documents you want to see. Always ask if there is an index you can consult in advance of your visit. An index is a summarized list of original records, usually arranged alphabetically. It will help you find the exact information you're looking for and save you from wasting your time in a random search through thousands of records. Many facilities provide indexes online.

Ask about restrictions on records that could impact your research efforts. There may be limited access to certain records at specific facilities, or your specific document, for example, may be stored at another location. You'll have to arrange to have it sent to the main research area in time for your visit. More recent records are subject to privacy laws, and older records may require the presence of an archivist while you view them because of their value or age. All these circumstances require advance planning.

Be sure to ask about other restrictions for using the documents you find. Will you be allowed to photocopy them? Are there copy machines available on-site and what is the cost of making copies? If you can't make photocopies, you'll have to allow more time to write your own abstracts or transcriptions of the records. Also, make sure you know what you are allowed to bring with you into a research facility. Some archives forbid scanners, cameras, or laptop computers, while others don't allow you to bring in pens or markers.

Finally, ask about the best times to visit your chosen facility, and ask if there is a staff member on site who specializes in your particular area of interest. Such an expert will be able to help you research more efficiently and may also offer suggestions for further investigation.

◙Q On the Road: Orange County, Virginia

When Eldred W. Melton began his family research, he knew only the name of a city—Culpeper, Virginia—and the names of a few family members who might still live there. He decided to write to the postmaster of Culpeper, outlining his problem and enclosing the names of the relatives he was seeking. Shortly afterward, he received a letter from a distant cousin who offered to help him find other long-lost relations. This was the start of Eldred's genealogy journey, which he has been on for the last forty years. He has made many trips to Virginia in that time, and at the age of 80, he says he still has "genealogy fever."

One of the most touching moments in his research occurred in the mid-1970s when he was researching Culpeper, Orange, and Caroline counties in Virginia looking for signs of his great-great-grandparents. Eldred knew they had settled near Brandy Station in Culpeper County and believed that he had found their homestead farm. There were no buildings remaining at the site, just a single American boxwood tree that indicated a home had once stood there. Eldred later discovered that his ancestors' house had probably been destroyed in the Battle of Brandy Station during the American Civil War.

When he expanded his investigation of his great-great-grandfather, he learned that his later years were spent with his daughters and their families. One of these daughters was Mary Skidmore Smith Dunn, who lived in Gordonsville, Orange County, Virginia. He had letters from her to his great-grandfather that were signed "your sister, Skid," and she was known as "Aunt Skid" in the family. Eldred discovered that she had a connection to the Exchange Hotel in Gordonsville, which is currently on the National Register of Historic Places. It seems that her husband's brother may have owned the property at one time.

When visiting the Exchange Hotel, Eldred learned of Maplewood Cemetery, where the Dunn family was most likely buried, and he decided to visit. While walking through the cemetery, reading the stone markers, he noticed a family plot surrounded by an ornate wrought iron fence with a *D* on the gate. He had found his Dunn family relatives! Since the gate wasn't locked, he went in to read the inscriptions on the monuments.

I was stunned to see a beautiful marble stone with the inscription George W. Smith. My great-great-grandfather! I actually had goose bumps. Sadly enough, there was no stone for my great-great-grandmother and, to this day, I do not know her actual burial place. Finally, I accepted that I would probably never find her grave. She died in the winter of 1840 and was most likely buried in an unmarked grave near her home in Brandy Station. So about five years ago, I had a stone designed much like that of my great-great-grandfather's, and, in her memory, I had it inscribed Mariah F. Smith and placed beside that of George W. Smith. It is a ten-hour drive from my home to Gordonsville, but I try to visit the cemetery at least once a year. It has given me a very real sense of knowing my Smith family, now that I have this special place for them.

Mapping All the Way

Once you've defined your research goals and identified places to visit, your next step is to map out your travels. Are you going to try to find several homesteads in the same general area? If so, check a local map to see how far apart these places are. Can you visit them in a single day, or will you need to stay overnight along the way? The more familiar you are with your target location, the more efficient and rewarding your research trip will be. If you can, also try to get maps that were in use at the time your ancestors were living in the area you're exploring.

You've already seen the great value that maps have for genealogists. Use Google's MapYourAncestors feature (fig. 9-3) to map the travels of your ancestors as you create your family tree (www.mapyourancestors.com). Then you can use sites like MapQuest (www.mapquest.com) to get driving distances and print out detailed maps of specific areas. There is a useful chart comparing the features of several online mapping service providers such as Google Maps, MapQuest, and Yahoo! Maps, among others, at TechCrunch (www.techcrunch.com/2006/04/17/comparing-the-mapping-services). Pick the one that's right for you, and remember to double-check all the information you get. The real world may update more frequently than these Web sites.

Figure 9-3

Google's MapYourAncestors feature

It's also a good idea to get an up-to-date printed atlas to consult when planning your genealogy trips. The DeLorme series of atlases and gazetteers for all fifty states (shop.delorme.com/OA_HTML/ DELibeCCtpSctDspRte.jsp?section=10042) offers a combination of detailed maps with lists of historic sites and museums, natural features, scenic drives, and other elements (covered bridges, ferries, lighthouses) relevant to the particular state.

Membership in the American Automobile Association (AAA) gives you access to free printed maps and TripTiks, which are customized, detailed driving instructions. AAA (www.aaa.com) has maps of states, countries, counties, parishes, cities, towns, and villages. AAA membership gives you full access to all of their many services. You can get shaded relief maps, 1-meter aerial photos, and detailed street maps at TopoZone (www.topozone.com), and Multimap (www.multimap.com) provides street-level maps of the United Kingdom, Europe, Australia, New Zealand, Canada, the United States, and several cities around the world, as well as point-to-point travel directions and aerial photographs with map overlays.

Topographic maps, also available at TopoZone, are especially helpful for research. They are prepared by the U.S. Geological Survey (USGS) and created with a scale that requires several maps to cover a single county. They are very detailed and include markings for farm roads, cemeteries located on private land, and churches.

Handheld personal data assistants (PDAs) and global positioning system (GPS) devices are becoming popular with genealogists, particularly for plotting and recording the location of old homesteads and burial sites with their actual latitude–longitude coordinates. GPS devices use satellite signals to track your physical location on Earth. With these devices, you can use the USGS Geographic Name Information System Web site (geonames.usgs.gov/pls/gnispublic) to find specific locations and put the coordinates of the location into your device. For example, you can search Hennepin County, Minnesota, for cemeteries, and you will get a list of all the cemeteries in that county. You also get the latitude and longitude of the particular cemetery you select, so you can view and print out a topographical map to use as a guide to that location for your trip.

Genealogy Tours

You can make your travel arrangements yourself through sites such as Expedia or Orbitz. But if you don't want to make all your own travel arrangements, or if you'd feel more comfortable letting experts guide you on your genealogy journey, there are several professional tour operators specializing in genealogy travel. Many of these companies focus on helping you find your roots in Europe, but as more and more people become interested in tracing their family histories and seeing their home country, tour operators are moving toward providing increased options for individuals who are looking for ancestors in countries outside of Europe.

Spector Travel (www.spectortravel.com/Pages/rc-tours.html) offers genealogy tours of several African countries, including Benin, Gambia, Ghana, Ivory Coast, Senegal, and South Africa. The African Roots and Culture Tours include trips to Dakar, Goree Island, Accra, Cape Coast Slave Castles, Kumasi, Johannesburg, Cape Town, Robben Island, Ganvie, Cotonou, and Ouidah.

European Focus (www.eurofocus.com/html/genealogy_tours.html) does what the name says, and offers genealogy tours through Germany,

Austria, Switzerland, parts of eastern France (Alsace), England, Ireland, and Scotland (fig. 9-4). These are personal and customized tours in which you explore your ancestral towns and villages. The company handles all the advance planning and accommodations, and the tour operators set up meetings with local experts who can help you with your research.

Ancestral Roots Travel (www.ancestralrootstravel.com) offers genealogy tours of the British Isles. The company has partnered with Achievements of Canterbury (www.achievements.co.uk) to offer expert research services.

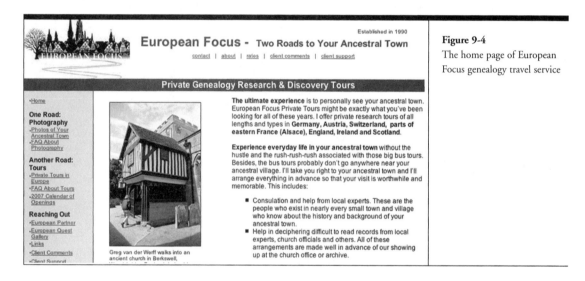

Figure 9-4

The home page of European Focus genealogy travel service

Routes to Roots (www.routestoroots.com) specializes in Jewish genealogy research in Eastern European archives. The firm will arrange customized tours and visits for you and your family, or it will visit your ancestral villages on your behalf and do research for you (fig. 9-5).

On the Road: England, Wales, and Ireland

John Myrick Cherry III, his sister, Jean Brooks, and his wife, Carolyn Butler Cherry, of Macon, Georgia, took a genealogy-centered vacation to England, Wales, and Ireland in 2004. They rented a car and took to the uncharted roads in search of the court records concerning the Cherrys, and to see the ancestral homes of the Myricks and the Butlers. John the Third got much of his information about an ancestor named John Cherry from the Internet. This

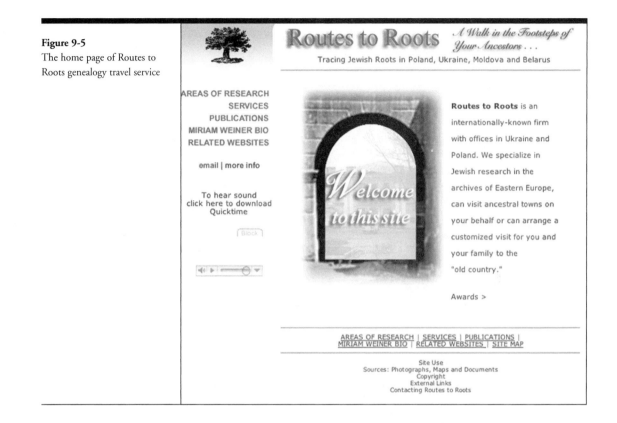

Figure 9-5
The home page of Routes to Roots genealogy travel service

John Cherry was born in Maidenhead/Bray, England, in 1619, and then traveled to the colony of Virginia in the 1630s. John and Carolyn visited Maidenhead looking for a court order mentioned many times online, but were stymied in their search when they were told that a fire during the reign of William III (William of Orange) destroyed most of the relevant Assize Court documents. "All we did in England was have lunch in Maidenhead in a shopping mall that occupies most of the area where the old town was located. Don't you love progress?" John asks.

The major part of their journey involved checking out the old family homesteads. John had read about the Myricks on the Internet and in a book called the *Story of the Myricks*, which he found in the Tennessee State Archives. He discovered a reference to a place called Bodorgan, which had been the ancestral home to the Myricks for a thousand years. Bodorgan is located on the Isle of Anglesey in Wales, just across the Irish Sea from Dublin. John discovered that his family is actually a conglomerate of sorts. The man who occupies the Bodorgan estate must be named Myrick (Mirick, Meyrick, et al.). The resident must legally change his name to inherit the property, and so the current occupants were not John's blood relatives.

John took a chance and wrote to an address he found on the Internet, telling the Myricks that he was traveling to England and Ireland on vacation and asking if he and his family could tour the estate, which is not open to the public. "Lo and behold," John says, "I received a response from the estate manager's office that Sir George planned to be in residence in September and would be glad to show us the estate. And if, for some reason, he was not able to be there, he would have the estate manager show us around."

John's party arrived on September 29, 2004, after following a map supplied by the estate, which showed the back roads on the island of Anglesey that led to the complex. The following is John's description of their tour.

Enter Sir George Davis Eliott Taps Gervis Meyrick, a tall, regal-looking gentleman. He introduced himself and advised us to follow him up the winding drive through the landscaped estate. To the right were woods, to the left was a park—with a herd of albino deer—that stretched down to the Menai Strait, which separates Anglesey from the mainland. Cannons were in place and aimed at the waterway. Sir George stated they were put there in case Napoleon had ideas.

We arrived at the house, which was built in 1780, replacing the Tudor house that was torn down. A wing was added in 1820. We were impressed. Then he opened the door and led us inside. Wow! Filled with antiques, beautiful paintings, and the like. The new wing was basically a gentleman's wing with hunting paraphernalia galore.

When asked, Sir George said he has no plans to open Bodorgan to the public. He could not have been more gracious. His names are a genealogical treasure chest. Wales has a hereditary structure where the Number One son gets all. That is probably why so many came to America to carve out their own niche. The daughters married well, and in the event of no male heirs, estates apparently passed to the Meyrick holdings. This explains the family names tacked on to Sir George. He is a member of Parliament, but I believe he represents Devon in the south of England where there is another estate. A picture of it (I think it is Rosewood) is on the wall at Bodorgan. It was painted by J.E.B. Turner.

Then John and his family went on to Ireland. His wife was born Carolyn Butler, and the Butler family lived in the Kilkenny Castle for some 600 years. The Earl of Ormond gave the family homestead to the state, and it has been restored. There are more than eighty portraits of the Butler family on the wall in the great hall. John noted that the Butler House is a hotel complex across the street from the entrance to the castle grounds, and he noted that the gardens were beautiful, even though it was October. "We did pick up a tidbit of information while touring the castle," John says.

Anne Boleyn was a member of the Butler family. My Myrick ancestor, Meyrick AP Lewellyn, was a cousin of Henry VIII and his bodyguard at the coronation (according to research). Therefore, Carolyn and I are both related to Queen Elizabeth I. No bowing please. We are trying to keep a low profile.

What to Take

Packing for any road trip can be nerve-racking, and when you're packing for a genealogy road trip, there are even more things to think about. You don't want to leave behind anything that will enhance your on-site research, but you don't want to be weighed down with excess paraphernalia.

First, don't even think about bringing any original documents you may have collected. You'd feel terrible if you somehow left that deed from 1860 in a roadside diner! Take your pedigree charts, research logs, and ancestral charts with you, and any copies of documents you think will aid your research. Make sure these charts are filled out as completely as possible so you'll be able to see the blanks easily and know exactly what information you're looking for when you get to your research location. Blank forms should include pedigree charts, family group sheets, and blank census and other forms for abstracting or extracting information from a research source (fig. 9-6).

You should bring along any genealogy and office supplies you may need. If you're going to a research facility that doesn't allow pens, be sure you have enough pencils (and a sharpener). Bring blank charts and forms that you can fill in as you find the information. You might also consider bringing a magnifying glass so you'll be able to actually see the writing or printing on old documents.

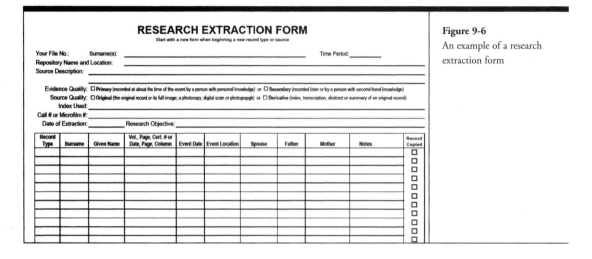

Figure 9-6

An example of a research extraction form

It's important to pack comfortable clothing and shoes, since you could spend a considerable amount of time standing and waiting at research facilities, walking across ancestral properties, or even squatting down to read tombstones. Remember your camera and enough film, batteries, or memory cards (for digital cameras) to last the trip. You may want to bring along a recording device if you expect to meet distant relatives so you can record their stories. You may also want to make two separate checklists: one for clothing and travel necessities, and one for your research needs.

Once You Get There

You can become so focused on preparing for your research that you forget your destination is a place in the real world. In many cases, you'll be walking the streets your ancestors walked, seeing the sights they saw (only without the McDonald's on the corner), or even visiting the houses they lived in. In addition to basic library research, you'll have the opportunity to inject a little of your own energy and interests into the ancestral landscape by visiting a gravesite, talking with old-timers, taking photographs, and using technology to preserve family history for your descendants.

The Cemetery Visit

Many genealogy road trips include visits to cemeteries. Since many of these sites are located in rural areas where the weeds grow high and snakes abound, it's best to wear long pants, long-sleeved shirts, sturdy shoes (even an extra pair in case you stumble upon animal droppings), and gloves to keep off annoying insects and scratchy brush. Bring insect repellant. Consider the season and the weather at the time of your visit. If it's summer, for example, you'll want a hat and some extra drinking water.

When you're at the cemetery, be sure to take photos of the markers and write down the inscriptions on the stones. (A photo may not show the inscription as clearly as you'd like.) If you take a GPS device with you, document the location of the burial site(s). It will prove to be valuable, both to your own records and as part of the overall family history that you're creating.

Many researchers visiting cemeteries take the time to do tombstone rubbings, an activity in which you get a copy of the tombstone's inscription by covering the stone with a piece of paper and then rubbing it with a crayon. (Make sure the stone is stable enough to take the pressure of the rubbing, and it's always a good idea to ask for permission before you do this, as it is illegal in some areas!) For an excellent how-to on rubbings, see Susan Bartolo Carmack's article at *Family Tree Magazine* (www.familytreemagazine.com/articles/oct00/rubbing.html). If you want to do rubbings, practice your technique before you leave on your trip, so you'll know what you're doing. Bring the supplies you'll need for the rubbings: rubbing wax or jumbo crayons, scissors, paper or other material (such as Pellon interfacing), tape to hold it in place, and so on.

You might take some time to spruce up your ancestor's gravesite during your visit. You could include some grass clippers and a brush for clearing away grass and dirt on tombstones. If you know you'll be looking for a cemetery on private land, make sure you contact the landowner before your visit to avoid misunderstandings with neighbors or the law.

Ask Questions!

If you're lucky enough to find relatives on your road trip, you should ask as many questions as you think they can handle. Ask for information about childhood activities, particularly any childhood memories they may have of older family members, as this will extend your knowledge a little further into the past. Ask about marriages, military service, and even neighbors or pets. You never know what question will trigger an interesting memory and provide you with another valuable nugget of information. Try to pin down dates and places if you can. Dates and place names will be very useful once you get home to do more Internet research.

When you're visiting a library or taking a local tour, talk with the people who work there. You could pick up interesting clues from informal conversations with tour guides, library staff, or volunteers at local museums. They could lead you to records or people you might not find on your own. Local old-timers can also be great sources of information. Some may remember where your family lived, or they may have had personal friendships with your ancestors. Old-timers are often very willing to share stories of their town's history, and they are an excellent source for interesting personal facts about your ancestors that might even be classified as gossip! But when you're looking for clues to family history, every detail you find makes the picture more complete.

Be sure to look at local newspapers, read any and all historical plaques located in the area, and pick up any printed information about local historical sites. Check local bulletin boards, local telephone directories, and any other place where you might see family names posted. Check the names on civic monuments. Churches are also a good source of information. You may find more distant relatives or at least more clues that may prompt more questions!

Trust (but Verify) Technology

Many genealogy travelers take their laptop computers with them on research trips. One of the main advantages to this is that you'll have your entire genealogical database with you, so you'll be able to tap into various family lines as facts present themselves. Computers being what they are, take along backups of programs and paper copies of extra forms, just in case your computer malfunctions while you're at the research site.

(Memory cards, known as memory sticks, are very useful to have along for extra storage space.) Dick Eastman of Eastman's Online Genealogy Newsletter (blog.eogn.com) praises the Asus Eee PC 701, a very small laptop. It's about the size of a VHS cassette tape and easily slips into a coat pocket. At only two pounds, Eastman finds it ideal for use while traveling, and its array of features at a relatively low price ($399) is impressive.

On the Road: The Unofficial Historian

Anyone wanting to know about the history of Camptonville, California, has to start by talking with Leland Pauly, the town's unofficial historian. Other than a few years spent in the Army Air Corps during World War II and at the Colorado School of Trades to study gunsmithing, Leland has spent all of his 80-plus years in Camptonville, a town of about 300 residents. Leland grew up at a time when many of the old-time prospectors and miners were still alive, and he spent hours at Meek Mercantile listening to their stories.

Leland still lives in the house his parents bought in 1919, and his home has become the repository of historical photos and artifacts associated with the old-time families who came to the area during the Gold Rush or who lived in town in the 1930s and 1940s. When anyone has a question about Camptonville's history, the advice is always, "You should ask Leland."

In summer, out-of-towners drive the back roads and walk the mountain trails around Camptonville hoping to find traces of their ancestors. Leland often stops while walking to the post office—or while gardening or cleaning up the gravesites in the town cemetery—to help strangers who ask, "Do you know where the Humphrey ranch was?" or "I'm trying to find my relatives who used to live at Weed's Point. Can you help me?" He unfailingly has the information they want. He'll give them directions to a place that was the site of a ranch in the 1930s. He may also provide the names of people who used to live in the area until they lost their jobs, got married, or couldn't take the winters anymore and moved away. At the end of the day, the strangers are no longer strangers, and Leland has shared a little more of his knowledge with the world.

Several months after one of these encounters, Leland is likely to get a packet in the mail that contains photographs and additional information about the families of those strangers he met on the road in the summer. And he adds these to his collection of unofficial Camptonville history. You're bound to find "Lelands" all across the country, and maybe one of them will answer your questions, too.

Be Ready for Surprises

The most important thing to do on your trip is to enjoy it, especially those unexpected happenings that will inevitably occur. With the right mindset, any little glitches in your plan can turn out to be opportunities, or at least good stories to tell when you get home. (If you didn't get that flat tire near that cow pasture, you would never have met the farmer who led you to the local historian who told you where your great-uncle's burial plot was.) Give yourself enough time to talk to actual human beings in your research area. People should come first. Their information may very well die with them. You can always come back to a library.

Upon Returning

Once you get home, don't just collapse on the couch, congratulating yourself on your excellent finds. Your work isn't done. You need to take care of all your new data as soon as possible.

If you didn't bring a laptop computer with you, you will need to enter the new names, dates, and other information you collected on your trip into your genealogy software program. The sooner you do this the better, because you're less likely to make mistakes while the information is still fresh in your mind. Those scribbled notes you made at the cemetery will make more sense right after your return than they will several months later, for example.

If you have a lot of new data, make to-do lists and logs of what you've already taken care of so you'll stay on top of things. If the new information requires revisions to old data, take care of that right away, too. It's less confusing to do these things shortly after your return than to put them off.

Make backup copies of the genealogy files you have on your computer, label them, and put them in a safe place. You don't want to lose everything you collected on your road trip. Store any photocopies and photographs you've gathered in the appropriate places in your filing system.

Use a scanner to make digital copies of important printed documents so you can put them into your genealogy software program. Transcribe any interviews you've recorded. Add new information to your pedigree charts and family group sheets, and analyze all your information to find additional research opportunities or refine new questions to ask.

And be generous with what you've learned. Share your information and experiences with other researchers. Tell others about any helpful tips or hints you discovered from your experiences at research facilities like libraries and archives. Then start planning your next genealogy road trip!

Looking Ahead

After all the work you've done, you'll want to leave your genealogy collection to future generations. In the last chapter, we show you how to give your family—and others—the gift of genealogy. A critical aspect of this is preserving video and photo histories for future use. One of the greatest joys in creating a family history is to recognize your place on a family tree that will continue to grow beyond your current efforts. The work you do now is, after all, your family's own treasure.

Chapter 10

Leave a Living Legacy

Why is genealogy so popular? What drives us to poke through dark archives and dusty library shelves, to scour yard sales and eBay for family Bibles and keepsakes, to Google our family names until we can Google no more? It's because lives matter for more than the moment. It's because someone should take notice of how our ancestors lived. It's because we'd like somebody to remember us, too.

While it's a good thing to have boxes and computer files full of names and dates and documents, it's even better to share all that hard-earned research with other people. Luckily, today's interest in genealogy comes at a time when there are many ways to share what you know and to leave a legacy to future generations.

You could publish a family history book, create a calendar featuring pictures of your ancestors, make a CD of your genealogy including photographs and videos, or build a family Web site. It isn't just your own family that can benefit from your work. There are local history museums and genealogical societies that would be very glad to have a copy of your research. Even the Library of Congress is interested in having copies of your family history book (www.loc.gov/rr/genealogy/gifts.html).

Your Own History Book

Genealogists begin by collecting names and dates, but eventually they focus more on the stories and historical context of their ancestors' lives.

You've probably unearthed a few choice stories that you'd like to pass on to other family members. It's through stories that we really come to know our ancestors as people and gain a sense of where we come from. Imagine the excitement the Harned family (fig. 10-1) felt when they learned that a relative was a very good friend of Walt Whitman, paid for Whitman's tomb, and was one of three literary executors of Whitman's writings (www.harneds.org). Does your family's history include an equally fascinating story?

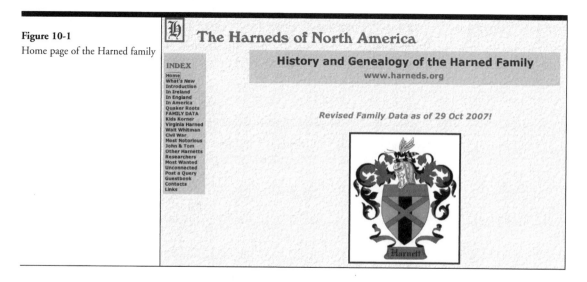

Figure 10-1
Home page of the Harned family

It's easier than ever to research and write your own family history and then publish it in book form. Computers are wonderful, and the Internet is amazing, but there's something about holding a good, solid book in your hand and passing it on for someone else to enjoy. More people are publishing family history books now than at any time since the 1800s, when families wanted to proclaim their social status by finding relationships to royalty or American Revolutionary patriots.

You have many options for getting your family history published. You can work with local printers and other publishing professionals to self-publish, use the services of small-press or on-demand publishers, or work with one of several commercial companies that specialize in making family history books. But before you can publish your book, you have to write it!

Writing a Family History

At first, the idea of writing a family history book can seem like an impossible task, but the steps and processes involved are very similar to what you've already been doing as part of your research. You need to set goals, plan, and organize. You can then create an outline to use as a guide for the actual writing. There are many Web sites that can help you get going, and your genealogy software program may even have an option that will just about write your narrative for you!

Starting Your History

The blank page has frightened many a writer, but this is where you're already ahead of the game. After all, you have all that family information stored in file folders or in a genealogy software program where it's easy to find. In addition to names and birth and death dates, you've probably already collected letters, diaries, photographs, newspaper articles, and other documents that flesh out the personalities of ancestors. So your first task is to review these materials and organize them into categories that make sense for a book.

A family history may involve collecting stories about one ancestor, setting out the genealogical details for a few family generations, or providing a very detailed and scrupulously researched and sourced history that follows several generations of a single family. The choice is yours. You may decide to combine these approaches into something entirely new and appropriate for your own family story.

It is a good idea to look at some published family histories to get an idea of various approaches. You can find some online examples through Google's Book Search (http://books.google.com/). Put "family history" in the search field and explore the results. Most give just a limited preview, but the entire text of some older family history books is available. As you may have guessed by now, you can find a lot of links to Web sites that can help you write your family history on Cyndi's List too (www.cyndislist.com/writing.htm).

Organization

Once you've set your goal and have an idea of the scope of your family history, it's time to get organized. This is the time to decide on the overall structure of the book. Some family histories are organized chronologically, while others are constructed according to life events. If you are focusing on a single individual, you might use general life categories, such as childhood, adolescence, early adulthood, middle adulthood, and later adulthood. There are two basic tools that can help you organize your writing: the outline and a box of file folders.

The outline comes first. While the term *outline* may conjure up some unpleasant associations from your school days, the fact is that outlines are the best way to organize your research if you plan to write. An outline will provide you with a good solid skeleton from which you can then flesh out your history. You could start with something like the following:

Title: The Descendants of Tom Jones

I. Introduction

II. First Generation: Tom Jones and Bessie Smith

    A. Vital statistics

        1. Tom

        2. Bessie

    B. Their children

    C. Details of their lives

    D. Photographs

    E. Miscellaneous documents (e.g., census records, maps, obituaries)

    F. Notes and sources

III. Second Generation: Discuss each of Tom and Bessie's children

    A. Vital statistics

        1. A Child

        2. His or her spouse

    B. Their children

    C. Details of Tom and Bessie's lives

    D. Photographs

    E. Miscellaneous documents

    F. Notes and sources

IV. Appendix

Use the Appendix to include extra items that don't quite fit into any other category/chapter, but that you want to include because they are interesting. Such things might include samples of handwriting, pet photos, favorite recipes, lists of favorite books, and so on.

An outline isn't set in stone; you can make changes along the way, as you get into your subject and perhaps see other organizational possibilities. You might divide your chapters according to individuals, time periods, or events. You can arrange your book any way you want, but making an outline will give you a sense of direction.

When you've finished your outline, it's time to start putting your information into file folders that correspond to the categories you've established. Put all the documents and photos you have that pertain to a specific category into a folder for that category. For example, you might have a chapter on childhood. Good matches for that chapter's folder would be photographs of the individual as a child, school records, or reminiscences of family members about that person. As you review your materials, you can put anything you think is relevant to the person's childhood into that folder, so when you're ready to write the chapter, you've got all your resources in one place.

Once you have some chapters written, ask someone to read them over. It's amazing what another person's review can reveal. Another reader can bring a fresh set of eyes to material you've grown very comfortable with. This is invaluable in identifying places where the story isn't clear or where you've made mistakes. The reader can also make suggestions for additional topics to cover, so don't hesitate to have someone look over your writing. It will only make your book better!

Involve Your Family

Genealogists sometimes wonder how they can get their family members more interested in their projects. One way to spark some interest is to ask your relatives for help. Send e-mails or even old-fashioned letters to explain what you're doing and ask for stories, photographs, or other materials they would like to include. Send self-addressed envelopes to make it as easy as possible for them to mail these things to you. Perhaps your more computer-savvy relatives would be willing to scan and then e-mail photos and documents to you, which would save you a step. You'll be amazed at how much more interested your relatives will be in the family history when they can see their contributions in a printed book.

Publishing Options

You can produce your family history in a book format that will include all the things readers expect from a real book—a table of contents, chapters, photographs and charts, an index—in several ways. For example, you can use a word processing program such as Microsoft Word, which has features that let you create an index and table of contents.

Some genealogy software programs take most of the guesswork out of publishing your story. Family Tree Maker, for one, will take the names and anecdotes you've entered and provide you with a volume of hundreds of pages of charts and records. While the format isn't fancy, it is still an effective way to preserve the information for future generations. Family Origins (formalsoft.com) and The Master Genealogist (www.whollygenes.com) do an excellent job of creating reports in book format.

There is even software available to help you write your family history by breaking your project down into manageable parts. For $29.95, Personal Historian (www.personalhistorian.com) provides a collection of timelines, historical facts, and cultural tidbits you can use to enliven your story (fig. 10-2). You can import documents that you've created with a word processor and photographs you've collected, so you don't have to start from scratch.

Figure 10-2
Home page for Personal Historian

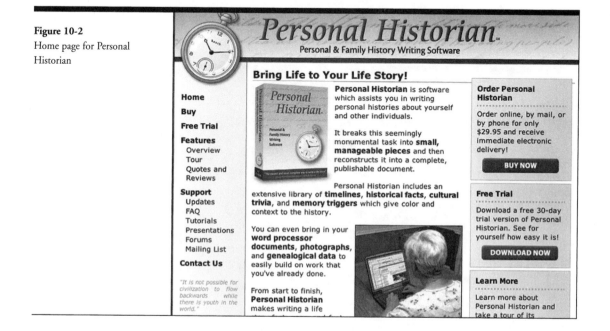

Ancestry.com offers a publishing service (ancestrypress.ancestry.com), which also integrates with Family Tree Maker 2008. It uses information you've already put into your family tree at the Ancestry Web site and transforms it into printed family tree posters ($19.95), or hardcover family history books (introductory rate of $29.95 for 24 pages, additional pages $0.39 each).

Several commercial publishers specialize in printing family histories, such as Family History Publishers, Inc. (www.familyhistorypublisher.com), which offers a range of services, including editing, formatting, printing, binding, and photo processing (fig. 10-3).

Another option is to publish the book yourself, using online on-demand publishing companies, such as iUniverse (www.iuniverse.com). Be aware that on-demand companies are not the same as traditional publishers. There is no one screening manuscripts submitted for publication, and usually your work will not be edited or proofread, although some firms sell packages including these services (fig. 10-4).

On-demand also differs from traditional self-publishing in that you have less control over the publishing process. For example, your book's design and cover style are limited to templates offered by the company. However, if you need just a few copies of a family history or genealogy to give to relatives, using an on-demand service is a good choice. You'll get

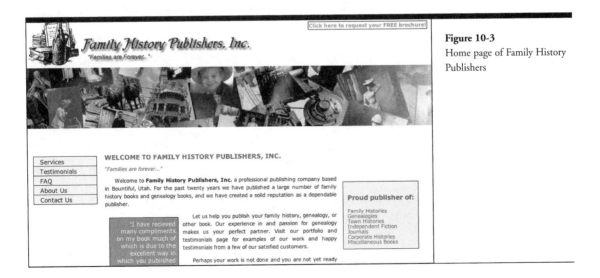

Figure 10-3
Home page of Family History Publishers

an attractive book at an affordable price, and because the company prints only the number of books you order, you won't end up with a huge number of books stored in a spare room!

Think Outside the Family History Book

In Chapter 3, we touched on using CDs and DVDs for storing your genealogy research materials, but you can use the same technology to

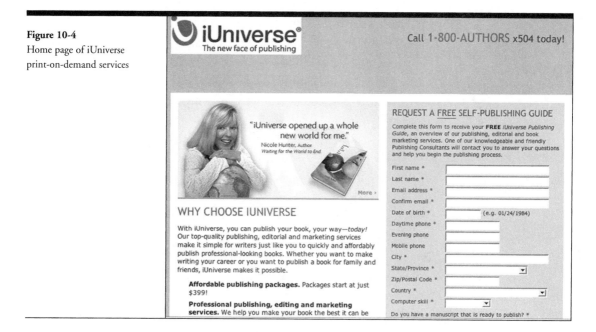

Figure 10-4
Home page of iUniverse print-on-demand services

share your family history with friends and relatives. In addition to the traditional family history, why not put together a family cookbook that includes reminiscences, stories, and photos as well as favorite recipes? Scrapbooking your genealogy finds or creating a family history calendar are other ways to share your legacy.

History on a Disk

You can put a lot of genealogy and family history information on a CD or DVD. These formats also allow you to add video and sound to your family story. As with writing a family history book, deciding what you want to include and what your goal is for your CD or DVD project are the most critical decisions. If you've spent a long time creating a family tree for one family, you'll probably want to put that tree on your CD or DVD. You've probably gathered many original source documents, such as birth certificates and marriage records, so you'll want to include those. (This is where a good flatbed scanner comes in very handy.) If you've branched out into oral history, you'll have recorded interviews and stories to add. You can also include any photographs of ancestral homes, tombstones, or other geographic features that are important to a particular family or individual.

As with Web page creation, you can either go it alone, doing all the formatting yourself, use your genealogy software package, or utilize specialized software or Web-based services. Passage Express software for Windows PCs (www.passageexpress.com) can be used to build sound-and-picture shows and put them on CDs and DVDs (fig. 10-5). You can add and edit pictures, create slideshows complete with visual transition effects between slides, create DVD menus, add sound files, and create labels for your disks. Best of all, if you have genealogy information already entered into the Legacy, RootsMagic, Personal Ancestor File, Ancestral Quest, or Personal Historian software programs, you can import your work into Passage Express without having to re-key it. Additional options allow you to add photographs from other programs while keeping their titles and captions intact. There's a free 21-day trial available, and, if you like it, you can buy the standard version for $34.95, or the deluxe version for $49.95.

Ancestral Author (www.ancestralauthor.com) is a Windows-based software program that creates hyperlinked Adobe Acrobat (PDF) files from your GEDCOMs, pictures, text files, and so on. With this program, you can create high-quality documents that can be printed, e-mailed, posted online, or sent to a printer to be made into a book. The PDF format can be read by any computer, regardless of its operating system, and it retains all the design features you included in your original file. The documents created with Ancestral Author include a title page, table of contents, index of names, source citations, chapter and section headings, and an outline view. View a sample PDF document at Ancestral Author's Web site.

Many genealogy software programs provide a Create CD option. One option for PC users is RootsMagic (www.rootsmagic.com), which

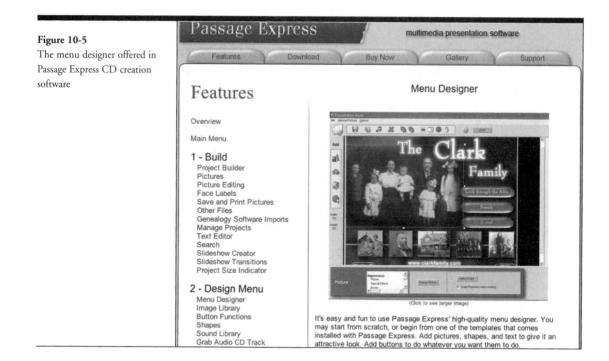

Figure 10-5
The menu designer offered in Passage Express CD creation software

lets you make shareable CDs with custom menus; and for Mac users, Reunion (www.leisterpro.com) offers the same capabilities.

SnapGenie (www.snapgenie.com) is a great tool for sharing genealogy information and photographs on a family Web site. With SnapGenie, you can create slideshows that include audio commentary on the Web. Maureen Taylor, the Photo Detective, used SnapGenie (photodetective. blogspot.com/2007/02/snapgenie-really-is-snap.html) to request information about the unknown individuals pictured along with her relatives in a family photo. And for a blow-by-blow account of how one genealogist created a CD from a 1931 family photo album, don't miss Lula Dawson Bliley's Family Photo Album CD Development story (www.bliley.net/family/Lula_Bliley/Album_CD/Development.htm).

Great-Grandma's Cookbook

Books of recipes have long been handed down from generation to generation. In the past, recipes were even written in the margins, blank pages, and even over the printed text in published cookbooks. Sometimes great-grandmother's cookbook is nothing more than a tattered and yellowing notebook with the pages falling out. But wouldn't it be a good idea to save those recipes along with genealogical information and stories about the woman who created them and the family she fed?

All families have favorite recipes, and all families have stories. Why not combine these into a single presentation? This is another great project that can bring family members together in a genealogical pursuit. Ask your relatives to send you a favorite family recipe and a story they associate with it. Establish a standard format for the recipes to save yourself a lot of work, and then send your request out through e-mail and regular mail. When you get recipes back, you can begin organizing your cookbook by food category, family, holiday, or any other category that seems right to you. Adding family photos and other relevant documents like scans of handwritten recipes will make your family cookbook unique and something that will be treasured by future generations.

Figure 10-6
Family cookbook page at
Heritage Cookbooks

One online publishing option for a family cookbook is the HeritageCookbook Web site (www.heritagecookbook.com). Here's how the site works: you create a trial membership for free, enter your recipes into the site's forms, select a cover design and a format for your book. The company then indexes your recipes and prepares them for printing. You can also invite others to join you in adding recipes, and everyone can work on the book at the same time, watching it come together step by step. When everything is as you like it, with photos, recipes, stories, and any other elements in place, you proceed to the order form and decide on the number of books you want printed. (There is a minimum of four, but you can choose to print hundreds, if you have a large family.) During the free month-long trial period, you can create one cookbook. If you need more time to make your book, you add a month of paid membership at $29.95. There's a two-month membership for $39.95, a four-month membership for $49.95, or a year-long option that allows you to create three different books for $59.95 (fig. 10-6).

Scrapbooking for the Future

Putting together a scrapbook of family history is another way to preserve your genealogy collection and share it with relatives. And making a scrapbook is a particularly good activity for getting children involved with family history. Before you begin, think about who will receive the scrapbook and the purpose of making it. For example, you might want to create a scrapbook of a particular family line for an upcoming family reunion, or to commemorate the anniversary of an ancestor's birth.

Reviewing your family tree is a good way to decide who should be included in the scrapbook, and the order in which you will include information about family members. Remember that going back just a few generations in a family tree gives you 50 to 60 potential people to include—your scrapbook could get very large very quickly!

By now you've been through your family tree many times and probably have a good idea of the kinds of documents and photographs that would make fascinating additions to a scrapbook. So get started!

Copyright Issues for Genealogists

The issue of copyright arises whenever you want to publish information in a book, in a blog, or on a Web site. Copyright is so complicated that if you do a search for the word on Google, you'll get more than 8,800,000,000 hits!

Conflicts over the rights to publish information can really only be resolved in court, but you should be aware of some basic things that may keep you out of trouble.

Stephen J. Danko, in his excellent blog post on ethics and genealogy (stephendanko.com/blog/2007/07/31), notes that facts can't be copyrighted, but wonders about compiled genealogies. What exactly can you include in a published genealogy without infringing on the rights of someone else, and what rights do you have to the information in any published genealogies you produce? You could spend a lifetime studying copyright issues, but a visit to Cyndi's List will provide you with enough links to satisfy your curiosity about the intricacies of copyright as it pertains to genealogy (www.cyndislist.com/copyrite.htm). Another good article about the basics of copyright as it applies to genealogy is the article "Copy Right, Copy Sense" by Mike Goad (www.pddoc.com/copyright).

According to information at genealogy.com (www.genealogy.com/14_cpyrt.html), U.S. copyright laws apply to both your research and the publication of the genealogy. While basic facts may not be subject to copyright, adding narrative (story) elements makes a genealogy a creative work, which is protected by copyright laws. A general guideline is: the more narrative there is in a genealogy, the stronger its copyright status. In such cases, you may want to consider registering the copyright and putting a copy of your work into the Library of Congress. If you find good stories in another source, you must try not to violate the author's rights. The concept of "fair use" allows you to quote short passages of a work, but not to copy large chunks of it and pass it off as your own. Pedigree charts, even computerized charts, are not covered by copyright unless, again, there is a modicum of creative work involved. Family trees submitted to the World Family Tree Project, a GenWeb site, or Ancestral File are subject to the same copyright laws as a printed genealogy. By submitting your family information to one of these compilations, you are agreeing to let your information be published.

What to Do with Your "Stuff"

As difficult as it may be to understand, not everyone is as interested in genealogy as you are. You may sometimes wonder what will happen to all your hard-earned research if you won't be passing it on to anyone in particular. Some genealogists have worked on their research for 25, even 50, years, and have collected boxes and boxes of information, both on their own and donated by other people. Fearing that these boxes could be carted off to the dump one day, many researchers are incorporating the donation of all their genealogy data to local historical or genealogical societies in their wills. Some even include the cost of a new computer to house the data.

Others have decided to post all their genealogy files on the Internet in the hope that some distant relative will one day find it and be overjoyed to have it. Still others have put all their genealogy information onto CDs or DVDs and mailed these out to every family member, hoping that a new interest in the family's history will arise sometime in the future.

You might also consider leaving your research collection to a local genealogy library. You should make sure you provide both printed versions and electronic copies. You should check with the library first, to see if they are interested in accepting your donation! Some libraries only want hardcover materials, while others are interested in information pertaining only to specific geographic areas. Including an index of the people's names mentioned in the materials would be a welcome addition.

Your local library or a library in the area where your ancestors lived would be your best bet, but you can also send your research to any of the following: the Family History Library in Salt Lake City, Utah; the national library in your ancestors' country of origin; or the state libraries in locations where your family lived. Computer files can be uploaded to repositories such as FamilySearch.org, Ancestry.com, WorldVitalRecords.com, or posted to the Internet.

Every state has an archives department or an agency responsible for cataloging and preserving historical information. These facilities are likely to want documented and sourced family history research. They are also likely to welcome any original documents, such as wills, diaries, and letters, which could be saved and made available to future researchers.

Looking Ahead

Now that our work is finished, we'll turn it all over to you. It's your turn to look ahead and decide what comes next. Ultimately this journey was always meant to belong just to you. We'll leave you here with the hope that your future genealogy travels will be endlessly rewarding.

Appendix

Online Ethnic Resources

If, like so many Americans, your ancestors came from western Europe, you are lucky to have an almost embarrassing number of genealogy sites including documentation and historical information. Just a quick Google search for terms like English genealogy or French genealogy will give you hundreds of useful links. However, if your ancestors were African, Native American, Hispanic, or Jewish, your search may be more difficult. Still, as interest in genealogy has blossomed, so have the resources for people of all backgrounds. Many of the major Web sites we've already discussed have areas devoted to different ethnicities. Plus, there are other more specific resources for you to explore.

Multicultural Sites

Cyndi's List *(www.cyndislist.com/topical.htm#Ethnic)*
As with all things genealogical, stopping by Cyndi's List is a good idea. Here you'll find an ethnic topic area listing Web sites on many geographic locations. You'll also find information about some lesser-known ethnic groups, including Doukhobors, Melungeons, Metis, and Wesorts.

GeneaSearch *(www.GeneaSearch.com)*
This site offers a series of pages with links to information about several ethnic and religious groups. The religious groups include Huguenot, Jewish, Moravian, Lutheran, Melungeon, and Quaker. There are also links to history and genealogy pages for Native Americans, Acadians, Hispanics, and African Americans.

The National Archives *(www.archives.gov/genealogy/heritage)*
Here you'll find an annotated list of ethnic heritage links that cover
African American, Asian, Australian and New Zealander, British Isles,
Canadian and French-Canadian, Eastern European and Russian,
Hispanic, Central and South American, Mexican, Caribbean and West
Indian, Jewish, Native American, and Western European. The National
Archives also provides a special exhibit devoted to Native Americans listed
in the censuses between 1860 and 1890 (www.archives.gov/publications/
prologue/2006/summer/indian-census.html).

RootsWeb *(lists.rootsweb.com/index/index.html)*
By now you are well versed in the value of RootsWeb, but the site is also a
good place to find mailing lists (31 at the time of this writing) specifically
targeting individual ethnic groups. These include Ethnic-African, Ethnic-
Alsatian, Ethnic-Austrian, Ethnic-British, Ethnic-Chinese, Ethnic-Czech,
Ethnic-Danish, Ethnic-Dutch, Ethnic-English, Ethnic-European, Ethnic-
Finnish, Ethnic-French, Ethnic-German, Ethnic-Greek, Ethnic-Hispanic,
Ethnic-Hungarian, Ethnic-Irish, Ethnic-Italian, Ethnic-Jewish, Ethnic-
Mixed, Ethnic-Native, Ethnic-Norwegian, Ethnic-Polish, Ethnic-
Portuguese, Ethnic-Romani, Ethnic-Scots, Ethnic-Slovak, Ethnic-Spanish,
Ethnic-Ukranian, Ethnic-Welsh, and Ethnic-Arab.

There are also approximately 174 genealogy mailing lists that discuss
specific countries around the world. Browsing through these archives is
worth your time. The people who participate in these lists are actively
researching, and they are likely to be able to provide you with starting
points, hints, and moral support as you investigate your family tree outside of the United States.

African American Sites

AfriGeneas *(afrigeneas.com)*
This site includes discussion boards, weekly and daily chats, mailing lists,
and much more. Although the focus of the site is African American, you'll
find information about African genealogy here, too.

The African Heritage Project at the University of Florida
(www.africanaheritage.com)
Stop by here for links to genealogy resources that include DNA research. You'll also have the opportunity to participate in building Afriquest (www.afriquest.com), a free, central Internet database of records concerning African and African American history and genealogy. The test version of Afriquest is scheduled for 2008.

Christine's Genealogy Web Site *(ccharity.com)*
This is a great place to start any search into African American genealogy. The site is a powerhouse of historical information and news links, whether you're just beginning or have been pursuing your search for years. You'll find links to genealogy resources that include tombstone transcriptions, a partial list of African Americans who were lynched in the United States, information about free Blacks on the property rolls in Virginia between 1851 and 1863, and several slave censuses, just to name a few.

Slave Genealogy *(www.slavegenealogy.com)*
A relatively new Web site, Slave Genealogy relies on user-generated content that is provided by volunteers. Its creators hope to make the site the "most comprehensive resource for researching your enslaved ancestors." The site has partnered with FamilySearch to offer information about the Atlantic slave trade, a list of slave plantations (some with Web sites), and a number of articles, such as "Six Steps to Tracing Your African American Heritage." You'll also find links to centers for the study of slavery.

Hispanic Sites

CubaGenWeb *(www.cubagenweb.org/index.htm)*
Stop by CubaGenWeb for newspaper lists, passenger information, digitized books, links to the Cuba-L mailing list, and a growing collection of digitized archives from Spain.

The Hispanic Genealogy Center *(www.hispanicgenealogy.com)*
This site, based in New York, is continually developing new Web pages, links, and genealogical resources for numerous Latin American countries

and Spain. The site is particularly good for Puerto Rican genealogy resources, but it is inclusive of other Hispanic cultures as well.

The Society of Hispanic Historical and Ancestral Research (*members.aol.com/shhar*)

This Orange County, California, nonprofit group was founded in 1986. The site offers guidance for Hispanic genealogy research, links and resources that you can consult, and information about early California families. You'll also find articles from the Society's free monthly online publication, *Somos Primos* (www.somosprimos.com).

Jewish Sites

The American Jewish Historical Society *(www.ajhs.org)*

The collections of the Society and several partner organizations are searchable online (in English and Hebrew) through a Web-based search form (aleph.cjh.org:81/F).

Avotaynu *(www.avotaynu.com/jewish_genealogy.htm)*

This Jewish genealogy magazine offers a consolidated Jewish surname index. The index gives you access to information on nearly 700,000 surnames, most of them Jewish. The names appear in 42 different databases, containing over 7.3 million records.

JewishGen *(www.jewishgen.org)*

Here's a good first stop for researching your Jewish ancestors. The site offers a learning center to help you with your research. You'll find an FAQ document that functions as a guide to the field of Jewish genealogy (www.jewishgen.org/infofiles/faq.html).

Louis Kessler's Jewish Genealogy Links (*www.lkessler.com/jglinks.shtml*)

This site offers an annotated list of Jewish genealogy Web sites and resources.

Native American Sites

Access Genealogy *(www.accessgenealogy.com/native)*
Here you'll find a large number of links to Web sites that provide free Native American genealogy information. The links cover tribal histories, treaties and agreements, Native American land patents and census records, and Native American biographies, among others.

All Things Cherokee *(www.allthingscherokee.com)*
This site provides excellent information and links for Cherokee researchers. It also offers query boards where you can ask for help with your genealogical research. In addition, you'll find links to several Native American mailing lists, such as Cherokee-L, which discusses Cherokee history and culture; NA-Cherokee-Freedman-L, a list for those with a genealogical interest in the Cherokee peoples listed as free; Attakullakulla-L, for discussion of the ancestors and descendants of Attakullakulla, Chickamauga Cherokee, also known as the Little Carpenter and White Owl, and related lines, and FiveCivilTribe-L, a list for anyone researching the five so-called civilized tribes (Cherokee, Choctaw, Chickasaw, Creek, Seminole).

The Dawes Rolls *(www.archives.gov/genealogy/tutorial/dawes)*
For information about the Cherokee, Choctaw, Chickasaw, Creek, and Seminole visit the Dawes Rolls, where you'll find a list of the individuals accepted by the government as members of these tribes between the years 1898 through 1914.

The State Historical Society of Missouri
(shs.umsystem.edu/nativeam.shtml)
Stop by here for a research guide for Native American genealogy that describes some available records and the agencies/repositories where you'll find these records. Among those agencies is the Bureau of Indian Affairs (www.doi.gov/bureau-indian-affairs.html).

Useful Genealogy Terms

Ancestor—An individual from whom a person is descended. A common ancestor is a person through whom several people can claim descent.

Ancestral file—Developed by the Family History Department of the Church of Jesus Christ of Latter-day Saints (LDS), this system uses several chart formats—pedigree, family group, and descendant—to link individuals to their ancestors.

Ancestry—Individuals in a line of descent; all of an individual's ancestors as far back as they can be traced.

Application—A computer program that performs a task, such as word processors, spreadsheets, and genealogy programs.

Browser—A computer program used to find and display Web pages; examples include Internet Explorer, Firefox, and Safari.

Collateral line—A line of descent that links individuals who share a common ancestor but who are related through an uncle, aunt, cousin, nephew, etc., rather than through a parent.

Common ancestor—An ancestor shared by any two individuals.

Consanguineous—Descended from the same ancestor.

Consanguinity—Blood relationship.

Cousin—A relative, other than a brother or sister, who is descended from a common ancestor; a term used more extensively in the past to describe relatives.

Deposition—Testimony that is taken, in writing, under an oath of affirmation in the presence of a competent officer in order to replace the oral testimony of a witness.

Descendant—Anyone to whom you are an ancestor; for example, your descendants are your children, grandchildren, and great-grandchildren.

Direct line—The line of descent traced through persons who are related to one another as a child and parent.

District Land Office plat book—A book of maps showing the locations of land patentees (holders).

District Land Office tract book—A book listing individual land entries by range and township.

Double dating—A system of dating used in England and America between 1582 and 1752, since it was unclear in those years as to whether the year began on January 1 or March 25.

Dower—The legal right or share obtained by a wife through marriage in the real estate of her husband; given to the wife for her lifetime after the husband's death.

Download—The process of copying a file via the Internet from one computer to another; for example, copying a song from an online music store.

End user—The ultimate user of a computer program; with regard to genealogy, this is anyone who uses a genealogy software program.

Escheat—A reversion of property to the state when no qualified heirs exist.

Family group sheet—A form that displays the genealogical information of a nuclear family, typically including dates and locations of births, deaths, and marriages.

Family pedigree—Family group sheets linked in a computer system that give access to all database records associated with the individuals listed on the sheet.

FamilySearch computer—A FamilySearch computer contains a number of databases, including the Social Security Death Index, the Military Index, the Ancestral File, and the International Genealogical Index. You can look for information about your family on this computer, and you can even look things up in the Family History Library Catalog. FamilySearch is available at Family History Libraries and online at the Web site of the LDS Church.

Fee—An estate of inheritance in land; an estate in land held on the condition that the holder performs certain services for the owner.

Fee simple—Absolute ownership of property without restrictions imposed.

Fee tail—An estate of inheritance restricted to the direct descendants of the person to whom it was granted.

Franklin, State of—An area in the western portion of North Carolina that was known, but never officially recognized, between 1784 and 1788.

FTP (File Transfer Protocol)—the standard format most often used to get a file from a server via the Internet (download) or to send a file, such as a Web page, to a server (upload).

GEDCOM—The abbreviation for GEnealogy Data COMmunications, a standardized way of formatting family-tree information in a text file so that it can be used by any genealogy software program. The standard was developed in 1985 and is currently owned and managed by the LDS Family History department.

Holographic will—A will that is written entirely in the handwriting of, and signed by the person who is leaving it, and is generally not signed by witnesses.

Home page—The main page of a Web site, which usually acts like a table of contents for other pages or documents that are stored on the site.

Host—(n.) The computer that controls communication within a network or manages a database; (v.) to provide the infrastructure that stores and supports a Web site.

HTML(Hypertext Markup Language)—A system of labels applied to a document that allows it to be viewed on the Web.

Index—In genealogy, this refers to a list of names, arranged alphabetically, taken from a specific set of records. An index of a census record lists the names of people found in a particular set of census records.

Input—Information and electronic materials, such as photographs, that are fed into your computer via a keyboard, mouse, or other electronic device (e.g., digital camera).

ISP(Internet Service Provider)—The company that provides access to the Internet for a fee (for example, EarthLink).

LDS Church—Church of Jesus Christ of the Latter-day Saints.

Link—An electronic connection between two Web sites, also known as a hot link; clicking on a link on a Web page directs you to another page.

Maternal line—A line of descent traced through the mother's family.

Mortality schedule—The count of individuals who died during the year before June 1 in each state of the U.S. in 1850, 1860, 1870, and 1880; the enumeration was conducted by the U.S. Bureau of Census.

Necrology—A list or record of individuals who have recently died.

Orphan—A child whose parents are dead; sometimes used for a child who has lost one parent by death.

Orphan's court—A special court charged with making provisions for orphans recognized as wards of the state.

Output—Anything that comes out of a computer, such as text files.

Patent—A grant of land from a government to an individual.

Paternal line—A line of descent traced through the father's family.

Pedigree chart—A chart that displays an individual's ancestry, also known as a family tree, which shows birth and death dates, marital status, names of parents, grandparents, great-grandparents, and so on, through several generations.

Pre-emotion right—A right given to citizens by the federal government to purchase a quarter section of land or less.

Progenitor—A direct ancestor.

Progeny—The descendants of a common ancestor.

Proved will—A will that has been established as genuine by a probate court.

Server—A computer that is designated to provide services, such as access to shared files or e-mail routing, to other computers in the network.

Sic—A Latin term that means thus, to denote that text was copied exactly as it appears in the original document; it often suggests there was a mistake or surprise in the original document.

Soundex—A phonetic indexing system that places names with similar pronunciations but different spellings into the same group. This system can help you to find ancestors who may have used different spellings of their names over time. For example, a relative of someone named White may have been Wyatt.

Source citation—A note that indicates exactly where a piece of information was found.

Testamentary—Pertaining to a will.

Testate—The person who dies leaving a valid will.

Testator—A person who makes his/her will valid before death.

Transcript—A document that is an exact copy of another, including any mistakes made in the original and using the original punctuation.

Upload—To transfer data from one computer to another.

URL(Universal Resource Locator)—The global address of documents and other types of content on the Internet.

Vital records—Documents that are used by civil authorities to record births, deaths, and marriages of individuals.

Web page—A document that is on the Web; every page a unique address (URL).

Web services—A service provided by a Web site in which Web-based applications are integrated over the Internet using specialized software tools; these services allow the end user to create a Web page without having to learn HTML.

Web site—A location on the Web. Each Web site contains a home page, which is the first document users see when they enter the site. The site might also contain additional documents and files. Each site is owned and managed by an individual, company, or organization.

Web space—The amount of Web storage space that is available for storing text, video, image, and sound files, each of which takes up a certain amount of space on the server; generally measured in megabytes (MB) or gigabytes (GB).

Wiki—Software that allows any Web page visitor to edit the content of the page; also, the output of that software (for example, Wikipedia, www.wikipedia.com).

Witness—A person who is physically present at an event (for example, a marriage or the signing of a document, such as a will), who can verify that the event or signing actually occurred.

WPA Historical Records Survey—A federal government program operating between 1935 and 1936 in which inventories of historical material were compiled.

Index